Studying for an Early Childhood Degree

C000241034

Studying for an Early Childhood Degree, based on the practices of The Pen Green Centre for children and families, exemplifies how student-practitioners can foster strong communities of learners and create student-teacher connections that remain long after studies are complete.

The Pen Green Integrated Centre in Corby, UK, has developed a unique approach to adult education. Highly qualified tutors, with their wide-ranging experiences, have written *Studying for an Early Childhood Degree* in collaboration with current and former students. It illustrates different ways to complete assignments, providing 20 case-studies of work that achieved an excellent grade from students of different professional, geographical, ethnic, educational and socio-economic backgrounds; it also explores the rationale behind *what* contributed to these excellent final grades. Each chapter, linked to the key themes of the Quality Assurance Agency (QAA) Early Childhood Studies degree, includes discussions, reflections, commentary and extracts from students' works through Levels 4–7, as well as suggestions for further reading.

Studying for an Early Childhood Degree is an essential read for learners as well as educators and practitioners. It will be a key resource for students having varied learning needs, professional heritages, writing styles and interests. Further, it will also support other educators to consider the unique and often competing demands of being an adult in higher education.

Tracy Gallagher holds overall strategic responsibilities for the effective running of Pen Green Centre, working with the multi-professional team. She is particularly interested in leadership within the Early Years.

Joanne Benford has worked in different roles at Pen Green since 2000, having developed a suite of courses including bespoke training, the Level 3 Early Years Educator, apprenticeships and undergraduate programmes.

Sandra Clare first visited Pen Green as a parent. She has always felt strongly towards the rights of children and the communities they inhabit, possessing a passion for critiquing educational inequalities and learning.

Dr Christine Parker has worked as an educator in many settings in the UK and abroad. She feels strongly towards children's unique learning patterns based on their social contexts and believes that it is important for Early Years staff to focus on these aspects of education.

Pen Green Books for Early Years Educators

Titles in this series include:

Improving Your Reflective Practice through Stories of Practitioner Research
Edited by Cath Arnold

Young Children Learning Through Schemas
Deepening the dialogue about learning in the home and in the nursery
Katey Mairs and the Pen Green Team, edited by Cath Arnold

Using Evidence for Advocacy and Resistance in Early Years Services
Exploring the Pen Green Research Approach
Edited by Eddie McKinnon

Working with Children aged 0-3 and their Families
The Pen Green Approach
Edited by Tracy Gallagher and Cath Arnold

Democratising Leadership in the Early Years
A Systemic Approach
Margy Whalley, Karen John, Patrick Whitaker, Elizabeth Klavins, Dr Christine Parker, Julie Vaggers

For more information about this series, please visit: https://www.routledge.com/Pen-Green-Books-for-Early-Years-Educators/book-series/PENGREEN

Studying for an Early Childhood Degree

Using Inspirations from the Pen Green
Students to Achieve Outstanding Results

**Edited by Tracy Gallagher,
with Joanne Benford, Sandra Clare
and Dr Christine Parker**

Routledge
Taylor & Francis Group

LONDON AND NEW YORK

Cover image credit: Nicole Prentice at Iselia Photography

First published 2023
by Routledge
4 Park Square, Milton Park, Abingdon, Oxon OX14 4RN

and by Routledge
605 Third Avenue, New York, NY 10158

Routledge is an imprint of the Taylor & Francis Group, an informa business

© 2023 selection and editorial matter, Tracy Gallagher; individual chapters, the contributors

The right of Tracy Gallagher to be identified as the author of the editorial material, and of the authors for their individual chapters, has been asserted in accordance with sections 77 and 78 of the Copyright, Designs and Patents Act 1988.

All rights reserved. No part of this book may be reprinted or reproduced or utilised in any form or by any electronic, mechanical, or other means, now known or hereafter invented, including photocopying and recording, or in any information storage or retrieval system, without permission in writing from the publishers.

Trademark notice: Product or corporate names may be trademarks or registered trademarks, and are used only for identification and explanation without intent to infringe.

British Library Cataloguing-in-Publication Data
A catalogue record for this book is available from the British Library

Library of Congress Cataloging-in-Publication Data
Names: Gallagher, Tracy, editor.
Title: Studying for an early childhood degree : using inspirations from the
    Pen Green students to achieve outstanding results / edited by Tracy
    Gallagher.
Description: First Edition. | New York : Routledge, 2023. |
    Series: Pen Green books for early years educators series |
    Includes bibliographical references and index.
Identifiers: LCCN 2022046693 (print) | LCCN 2022046694 (ebook) |
    ISBN 9781032222394 (Hardback) | ISBN 9781032222387
    (Paperback) | ISBN 9781003271727 (eBook)
Subjects: LCSH: Early childhood education—Study and teaching
    (Higher)—Great Britain. | Early childhood educators—Training of—
    Great Britain. | Community and college—Great Britain. |
    Pen Green Centre (Corby, England)—Influence.
Classification: LCC LB1139.23 .S777 2023 (print) |
    LCC LB1139.23 (ebook) | DDC 370.71/1—dc23/eng/20230104
LC record available at https://lccn.loc.gov/2022046693
LC ebook record available at https://lccn.loc.gov/2022046694

ISBN: 978-1-032-22239-4 (hbk)
ISBN: 978-1-032-22238-7 (pbk)
ISBN: 978-1-003-27172-7 (ebk)

DOI: 10.4324/9781003271727

Typeset in Bembo
by Apex CoVantage, LLC

Access the companion website: www.pengreen.org

Contents

Figures

Tables

Boxes

About the contributors

Tracy Gallagher
Joint Head of Centre
Tracy started her career working with children and families in 1986, she has worked in various settings and has always been deeply passionate about her work. In 1994 Tracy took on a full-time role as a lecturer and taught at a local college of Further and Higher Education and at a centre for unemployed adults. Tracy relished the opportunity to teach adult learners and taught a wide variety of Early Years courses.

Tracy joined the Pen Green Team in 2000 and has been one of the Joint Heads of Pen Green Centre, with her colleague Angela Prodger since 2016. Tracy has a very wide and varied role which includes overall strategic responsibilities for the Pen Green Integrated Centre. The Pen Green Centre comprises a large Maintained Nursery School, Early Years provision, Children's Centre services across four sites, Adult Education and an offsite nursery. Tracy sets high standards for herself and believes that leading by example influences the behaviour and attitudes of her colleagues and parents, and helps her to guide and motivate others. As one of the Joint Heads of Pen Green, Tracy has responsibility for offering training and professional development opportunities to parents and staff. Tracy works with the parents and the staff to think deeply about their role in supporting children's learning and development. She strives to ensure that all staff feel suitably knowledgeable and skilled to offer the highest quality experiences for children and their families. It is critical to Tracy that she works collaboratively with parents to gather their views and feedback, which in turn assists the Centre staff in shaping the services they have on offer. Tracy is also deeply interested in leadership within the Early Years and enjoys working with the staff team to understand the complex role of a leader.

Joanne Benford
Assistant Head of Pen Green Centre
Joanne has worked at Pen Green since 2000. Initially her role was the crèche co-ordinator, in this role she had the opportunity to lead the team working in the crèche. She was responsible for developing practice and setting up systems to ensure the children were being cared for appropriately, and their

achievements were being documented accurately. She introduced the team to the legislative requirements of their role and was able to write and develop qualifications to support this development.

Joanne has been working in the Research, Training and Development Base since 2008; initially as a co-leader on various short courses. She has used her experiences of working in the crèche to support her in the learning environment. At present, she has responsibility for Level 3 and apprenticeships, and leads the undergraduate programmes offered at Pen Green. Her role extends to being the programme lead for the Early Years Initial Teacher Training course.

Becoming a member of the Pen Green Centre Leadership Team supported Joanne to develop her leadership skills. She has been part of the Centre Leadership Team since 2010. During this time she has taken on full responsibility for adult learning in the Centre.

Dr Christine Parker
Pen Green Tutor and Consultant
Christine has taught in nursery, infant, first and primary schools for over 35 years in Sheffield, Leeds, Bradford and Peterborough (UK). She has also benefitted from a period of working abroad in Karachi, Pakistan, in the role of advisory teacher. This experience, of several years, enriched her as a person and as a professional, and will forever inform her in all that she does.

Christine believes in a positive view of the multilingual child, which all children have the potential to be when we view children as capable, curious and leaderful learners. Over her extensive career she has become increasingly of the mind that a co-constructive approach to children's learning is of benefit not only to the children themselves but also to their families.

Now, at the more mature phase of her career, she explains she has to pinch herself that she is now working at the Pen Green Centre and supporting nursery and primary teachers of the future as well as teaching on the MA Course. It is her belief that what is of most value to the Early Years' practitioner is to continually develop their understanding of how children learn within each child's unique social context. What we are expected to teach in schools will change, and she anticipates will change radically, so the more we enrich our theoretical knowledge within the context of practice, the better we will be equipped for the challenges of the future.

Sandra Clare
Pen Green Consultant
Sandra first came to Pen Green as a recent law graduate and young parent with three babies in tow, going on to have a fourth quite soon thereafter. She has always been a curious and avid reader, fascinated by small and big people and how they all interact with each other. The rights of children and the communities they inhabit are something she cares deeply about. The social policies and political constructs that dictate how life is for marginalised fellow humans is a consistent area of interest.

After a number of years as a service user and volunteer, she worked in Pen Green's Family Room, completed her Master's degree and subsequently became a senior researcher and tutor teaching across the degree programmes. She was heavily involved in several Department for Education projects considering how visible and valued children with special educational needs and disabilities are. This involved revisiting her love of law, writing and teaching about the importance of understanding the legislation to ensure young children are receiving the education they are legally entitled to. Other participatory research projects focused on the experiences of families with babies born early and how they transition from the Special Care Baby Unit to their home and community services. And the lived experiences of young parents, setting up a bespoke drop-in space and researching what difference such unique spaces can make to children and their families.

A lifelong love of learning, and passion for problematising educational inequalities, led to becoming a doctoral candidate at the University of Manchester. She is keen to consider the historical legacies of women's place within education and the home, developing the novel approach of critical-activist research to unpick experiences of mothers within education, and lobby for change.

Foreword

"Most learning is not the result of instruction. It is rather the result of unhampered participation in a meaningful setting."

—Ivan Illich, 1971, 'De-Schooling Society'

When Pen Green opened in 1983, early childhood educators working with children and families were often minimally qualified and almost always poorly paid. At the same time as developing a high quality, locally responsive integrated service, we had to build up a strong workforce of reflective practitioners. We had to ensure all staff, parents, and volunteers had access to stimulating and challenging professional development, which brought together rich academic theory and powerful practice wisdom. To continue the Illich analogy, what we wanted to provide for children we also wanted to offer staff and all the other important adults in the children's lives – "self-directed education, supported by intentional social relations, in fluid informal arrangements."

It's now more than 26 years since the first Pen Green MA in Integrated Services was established at Pen Green. This higher level degree course, and the undergraduate degree courses (Foundation Degree and BA Hons) that were subsequently set up were all designed and delivered by Pen Green practitioners in conjunction with deeply knowledgeable collaborators. In early childhood education and care, we truly stand on the shoulders of giants whose theoretical constructs have enabled us to reflect deeply on our own practice, and at Pen Green we were lucky enough to engage directly with many of them. Over the last three decades, Tina Bruce, Chris Athey, Patrick Whitaker, Colin Fletcher, Karen John, Robert Orr, Pam Cubey, Wendy Lee, Chris Pascal, Julia and Joao Formosinho, Colwyn Trevarthen and many others have made rich contributions to our courses. In addition, several hundred participating adult learners on these courses have regularly reviewed and helped to co-construct the underpinning knowledge, the programmes of study and the pedagogical approach to course delivery. This book demonstrates this creative partnership between academics and practitioners from the UK and overseas. Each participant has left a mark on both the curriculum and the delivery, and in this way the courses continue to be both rich and relevant.

The adult learners, then and now, who have chosen to study at Pen Green have often had spectacularly diverse learning journeys prior to enrolling; and the current student co-authors in this publication are no exception. Their powerful engagement with their course of study is matched by an equally powerful commitment to the children and families that they currently work with in their diverse settings.

> The practitioner research contributions in this publication are deeply reflexive and challenging and celebrate practitioner enquiry. The student participants who have worked with their tutors to co-produce these chapters are well-informed rigorous thinkers, prepared to critically investigate their own practice. They are clearly deeply concerned with their own learning whilst equally concerned with the learning of the children and parents that they work with. The result is a "democratic dialogue" (Malaguzzi, 1995), where contradictions can be tolerated, important problems can be posed and important questions can be answered.
>
> — Dr Margy Whalley CBE

Former Director of Pen Green Centre for Children and Families and the Pen Green Research, Development and Training Base (1983–2016)

Acknowledgements

Tracy Gallagher, Editor

Along with the authors, I would like to begin by thanking all the adult learners and the Pen Green tutors who have willingly contributed to this book.

The adult learners readily collaborated with the tutors and authors to provide their assignments and agree to extracts being included. There are 20 examples of excellent assignments and the contributions have significantly influenced the development of each chapter. Without their readiness to take part, we would not have the comprehensive range of material to share with you. I would also like to acknowledge the children and families who allowed the learners to work with them every day and for willingly contributing to the studies.

The Pen Green tutors generously gave their time and thoughtfully made recommendations for a selection of work to be included. The tutors then helpfully and sensitively liaised and brokered between learners and the chapter authors to assist with obtaining permissions and gathering the necessary material to form the text.

Over many years Patrick Whitaker supported staff at Pen Green and inspired us to develop our adult learning work. The authors, tutors and I would like to express our gratitude to all he taught us and the legacy he left that has significantly informed our thinking and the development of our work with adults at Pen Green. There is considerable reference to Patrick's work in chapter 1.

I personally would like to thank the authors; Joanne Benford, Sandra Clare and Dr Christine Parker who have worked with dedication and enthusiasm to write the chapters. They kindly gave their time and joined me in regular meetings to ensure the chapters reflected a breadth of work and achieved the timeframe for publication. It has been a joy to work with such considerate and knowledgeable people. I have huge respect for the time they unselfishly gave to planning the chapters, contemplating the content to be included, writing the material and liaising with the tutors and learners. We all agreed we wanted to include assignment material from learners representing the courses from Level 4 through Level 7, and this is evident throughout the book.

Thanks go to the staff at Pen Green for supporting their colleagues and providing magnificent administration support in preparing the manuscript.

Immense thanks go to the family and friends of the authors who have supported and enabled them to dedicate time to writing for this publication.

Finally, our immeasurable thanks go to Dr Margy Whalley for her vision, her inspiration and her words of wisdom that continue to guide us all.

Introduction

Tracy Gallagher

I initially visited Pen Green in the 1980s as a student, and the visit inspired my career working with children, families and adult learners. I came to work at Pen Green in 2000 and valued the ethos, values and principles of the Centre. I respected the work of the staff who worked directly with children and families. I also had a deep admiration for the commitment the team had to facilitating adult learning opportunities and supporting and developing the Early Years workforce. Dr Margy Whalley was the founder of the Centre, and she had a vision that there would be a service for children aged under five and their families, a service which would honour the needs of young children and celebrate their existence.

Margy was committed to ensuring staff were highly trained and had access to meaningful professional development, regular supervision and opportunities to engage in reflection and professional dialogue about their work. Margy set up the Pen Green Research, Training and Development Base in the late 1990s. Margy and the team wanted the courses on offer to be rooted in practice. The team worked with parents and practitioners to conceptualise adult learning opportunities and developed a suite of training possibilities including formal education qualifications. The team have continued to facilitate learning for many practitioners from education, health and social care backgrounds and joyously celebrated as they have gained Foundation, Bachelor's, Master's and PhD degrees.

Margy retired in 2016 and I took on the Joint Headship with my colleague Angela Prodger. At the Centre we offer a breadth of services including a Maintained Nursery School and the Research, Development and Training Base. Angela and I have the privilege of working with staff across all domains of work within the Centre. Felicity Dewsbery has the role of Deputy Head within Pen Green and has lead responsibility for the Research, Training and Development Base. Felicity has been influential in conceptualising and further building on the work with adult learners and supporting the Early Years workforce locally, nationally and internationally. The staff within Pen Green facilitate adult learning opportunities by offering Further Education and Higher Education courses, bespoke training events and courses, school to school support and facilitating ongoing professional development for schools, PVIs, nurseries and childminders.

At Pen Green we recognise and value what a significant role it is to facilitate the learning and development of young children whether that is as an Early Years Educator, a teacher, a health professional or Family Support Worker. We have developed our course material to enable students to deepen their understanding of theory and also reflect on their practice working with children and their families. The tutors at Pen Green also recognise what a meaningful role they have in facilitating the learning for adult learners who have chosen to study at Pen Green.

Over the years we have developed a respectful approach to adult learning and higher education studies, working with experienced practitioners in ways that honour the practice wisdom and life experiences they bring with them. Study sessions are timetabled to ensure that busy practitioners can immerse themselves in the learning environment, taking a break from the daily challenges of practice, and often home life. We know that working in such an intense way builds a strong community of learners, optimising learning and offering social connections that remain long after studies are complete.

Pen Green tutors, themselves highly qualified, deeply reflective, with wide experiences in practice, have written this book. This has been done in collaboration with current and former students. The book will be useful for learners new to study, learners progressing with their course of study, as well as for tutors, educators, and practitioners. The hope is that materials support adult learners to access their own degree course with as much additional knowledge as possible. Additionally, the materials have the potential to support other educators to consider the unique, and often competing, demands of being an adult in higher education.

In this book we have worked together to detail what it is like to study at Pen Green and outline the different modules that learners cover in their courses of study. Currently our degree courses are validated by the University of Hertfordshire. Adult learners often ask for examples of the work of others, with an emphasis on the personal and unique. What we have aimed to do, throughout this book, is include extracts that have been selected from a range of assignments across different levels of study to illustrate how differently, yet successfully, assignments can be completed. The adult learners involved have kindly revisited and edited past assignments, as well as spent time reflecting on how their studies have impacted their practice with children and families. Ensuring work remained ethical and principled was of critical concern for all involved. Whilst consents would have been sought for individual assignments prior to submission, adult learners needed to seek explicit permission from those featured within their writing before commencing work on their chapter.

Across the degree programmes there are five common threads or themes. The authors have taken each thread to write their individual chapters. The chapters introduce the theme and explain the relevance and importance of the theme in the Early Years sector. The authors then go on to explain how, at Pen Green, we approach each theme in the courses of study. Within each chapter, the authors have also included extracts from adult learners' work. The extracts are from Level 4 assignments through to Level 7, together with reflections from the adult learner and commentary from the tutor team.

When reading this book, you will gain an understanding of the Pen Green approach to working with adult learners and an overview of the study skills we offer to support them on their course of study. The authors acknowledge their responsibilities when working with practitioner students, which may include adults returning to education and those experiencing higher education for the first time. Throughout the book the authors communicate the Pen Green approach to research and developing best practice – demonstrating practitioners researching their own practice and using research to inform the development of their practice during higher education.

The book concludes with a glossary of the common terms used throughout the book.

I hope you enjoy embarking on this journey of discovery with the authors, tutors and adult learners as much as I have enjoyed assisting in its production.

1   Principles of working with adult learners

Joanne Benford

In this chapter you will find:

*   An overview of the Pen Green approach to working with adult learners.
*   An opportunity to understand how the Pen Green degree programmes have been designed and developed.
*   A summary of the author's own research.
*   Information to help you to consider the range of skills needed to write an assignment.
*   How to identify with the skills required to bring together your thoughts, practice and reading so that it meets the requirements of both ethical and methodological processes.
*   A summary of the key points you need to understand with university guidelines regarding ethics, plagiarism and how to present an academic assignment.

The historical context of adult learning at Pen Green

Pen Green is an Integrated Centre for Children and their Families (for further information you can read other books in this series or visit the website at www. pengreen.org). At Pen Green the staff have always been committed to supporting adult learning and providing meaningful learning opportunities to Early Years practitioners.

One aspect of the Centre's work is the Research, Training and Development Base. The team in the Research, Training and Development Base offer continuous professional development courses for the Early Years sector. The training opportunities and courses are offered locally, nationally and internationally.

In the 1990s Margy Whalley was the Head of Pen Green. At that time Margy worked with adult learners from across the country and heard from them the need to be able to attend courses of study near to their home. Margy worked with Tina Bruce, Chris Athey and Cath Arnold to develop a Master's course. Tina, Chris and Cath all played significant roles in developing the Master's course alongside Patrick Whitaker and Colin Fletcher. The team helped to conceptualise a range of courses for Early Years practitioners – courses that

DOI: 10.4324/9781003271727-1

would be easy for adult learners to access. The expert team also generously offered training to the nursery staff at Pen Green.

In 2007 staff working within the Research, Training and Development Base decided to embark on writing and validating a Foundation Degree in Early Years. At that time, we partnered with a university to support us through this process. Over 3,000 Early Years practitioners have graduated with us to date. We have revalidated the original programme and added a BA (hons) Top-up to our portfolio of courses. In recent years we have rewritten and validated our Master's programme. I am the programme lead for the undergraduate courses. Alongside my colleague Felicity Dewsbery and the tutor team, we designed and developed the current courses at Pen Green. The tutors have been informed and influenced by the thoughtful work of Patrick Whitaker, an external consultant, who played a significant role in helping staff to conceptualise the suite of Further and Higher Education courses on offer.

This opening chapter will give you insight to what studying at Pen Green is like for adult learners. I will start by introducing the premise of the Pen Green programmes.

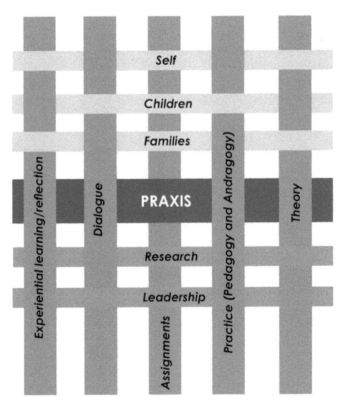

Figure 1.1 Diagram to illustrate the connectivity between the themes studied at Pen Green

There are some common themes that run through all of the courses we have developed (see Figure 1.1). The practice that then emerges throughout each module includes Reflection, Dialogue, Pedagogy[1] and Andragogy,[2] and Theory. Central to these themes and practices is the notion of praxis, that is, how the practitioner's knowledge and understanding of theory informs their embedded practice and capacity to self-reflect (Freire, 1970; Formosinho and Oliveira-Formosinho, 2012a).

So, what does the Pen Green Learning experience look like? The adult learners are central to everything we do, in the way Early Years practitioners hold children and families at the heart of their thoughts, ideas and actions, the tutor team hold the adult learners in the same way.

The process starts with the information sessions we offer for potential learners through to graduation and sometimes beyond! During the information sessions we ensure that we answer any questions and address the fear individuals may be experiencing. Often questions arise in these sessions about capability, highlighting the fear some potential learners have. We frequently hear how potential learners have spent years considering doing a degree but never had the confidence to apply, and hear questions such as "Am I too old?," "What will I have to offer?", "Will everyone else know more than me?" and even "I think I might look stupid." Encouraging words, acknowledging the fear being felt and explaining in a clear but coherent way what the potential learners can expect seems to help. In this way the enquiries from the information sessions subsequently turn into applications.

What is a study block

Clare and Clark (2021) identify that all degree programmes at Pen Green are delivered in a unique way whereby students attend for study blocks, these take place two or three times per academic year, depending on the course. The tutor team recognise that rather than expecting tired and hungry practitioners to race from a day working with children to an evening lecture, or juggle a weekly study day, the study weeks support a deep understanding of their needs as adults and as learners. Our study blocks are planned in a way that allows for the adult learners to immerse themselves in their study, and to cause minimal disruption to the children and families that they work with. Employers report that this approach is far less disruptive than losing a member of their team once a week or expecting busy practitioners to study in the evenings. In addition, those learners with families express how the block weeks allow them dedicated time for their studies whilst their families support them.

What to expect during a study block

Our planning sessions include us allocating time to consider how the learners might be feeling and with this in mind, each day starts with a "check in" session – this involves everyone having the opportunity to say how they are feeling and what is "on top" for them that day. The tutors participate in this too. Our intention is to identify any potential concerns, worries or anxieties that might be emerging. For the tutors it is an opportunity to "contain" (Bion, 1961) and to "hold" the learners in mind (Winnicott, 1964). At the end of the day, we round off with a "check out," again this time is for everyone in the group, including tutors, to share how their day has been and if anything from the morning "check in" is still unresolved. There are times when these sessions are celebratory, times when there are tears and times when there is laughter. Whilst most learners will say it feels strange at first, I have had experiences when learners have said it is the most important part of their study week, claiming it starts them off and "gets them into the room."

During the study week, tutors see themselves as facilitators of learning. Most of the sessions involve tutors offering a starting point, for example, we may set off small groups of learners to research theories, concepts or ideas. During these sessions we ask them to identify what are the key messages, who are the main theorists and what does it looks like for them in their practice. We avoid the use of scenarios and focus on real life experiences that the learners have within their practice. By participating in these small research groups, the learners can grapple with tricky theories and ideas and make sense of them. Adult learners' feedback consistently tells us that this is preferred to long lectures, seminars and extended periods of listening to others. Studying in such a way helps to build a strong learning community, optimising academic potential and offering social connections that remain long after studies are complete. I will share my understanding of experiential learning later in this chapter (Kolb, 1984).

At the end of the course of study, we hold a graduation ceremony. The graduation is a time to celebrate, having taken the learners through their studies we recognise it is important to acknowledge each of them individually. Our ceremonies are deeply personal with time given to each learner to acknowledge and sum up their time with us. The tutors write a personalised comment for each learner which is read out during the ceremony. Families, learners and employers all share with us how special these days are for them. We understand it is an opportunity to celebrate everyone, and to show just how important each learner is to us.

Our view of andragogy

There are a number of definitions of andragogy, but the one that best summarises my own views are those of John (2019:4) who states: "Andragogy is an approach to learning that places the needs, feelings, thoughts and experiences of participants at the heart of any educational programme." Whalley and colleagues remind us that "It is important to recognise that adult and professional learners do not usually respond well to a continuation of pedagogic practices that they were likely to have encountered during their schooling experiences" (NCSL, 2004:23). Returning to learning can be one of the most daunting decisions an Early Years practitioner makes. If experiences of education have not been particularly positive or have left us with a sense of inadequacy, then taking the plunge to step back into a learning environment takes courage. The questions asked during the information sessions demonstrate the prevalence of this even when individuals are considering dipping their toes back into the learning environment.

In the 1950s Knowles was trying to establish a theory of adult learning; he describes how learning could be "formal" or "informal." Formal learning can take place in educational establishments; informal learning can take place in groups and clubs (Knowles, 1950:23). In his work on andragogy, Knowles (1970) defines the process as the art and science of helping adults to learn. He argues that an adult with barriers to learning needs to be treated with respect, and that their experience should be an integral part of their learning process. Knowles identified that for adults, learning is more than just one person trans-mitting knowledge to another and is in fact "a lifelong process of discovering what is not known" (1970:54).

Knowles identified the six principles of adult learning as:

1   Adults are internally motivated and self-directed.
2   Adults bring life experiences and knowledge to learning experiences.
3   Adults are goal oriented.
4   Adults are relevancy oriented.
5   Adults are practical.
6   Adult learners like to be respected.

Experiences an individual has had in school or in previous learning environ-ments will, according to Knowles (1970), always impact on how they feel about entering a new learning environment. If the adult learning space leads the learner to feel they are likely to be treated like a child, they are less likely to engage in the process of learning. If, however, the conditions are congru-ent with their self-concept as autonomous individuals they are more likely to embrace the opportunity and open their minds to learning. Knowles (1970) goes on to explain that for an adult learner, there are two elements that are required for the individual to feel motivated to learn:

1   a sense of dissatisfaction about where their current knowledge base is and a desire to learn and understand more
2   a sense of direction for self-improvement.

According to Rogers and Tough (1996:5–6) there are two characteristics that set adult learners apart from others: firstly, they are voluntary learners, and sec-ondly, they come with the intention to learn. Rogers and Tough (1996:62) go on to remind us, "Each learner brings a range of experience and knowledge."

Knowles (1970:59) reminds us of the importance of "the learning climate." He is referring to more than just the physical climate; the psychological climate should be one that promotes acceptance, respect and support.

As I consider how the programmes of study have developed at Pen Green, and how in particular we have developed ways to support adult learners to re-engage, I am drawn to the ideas of Pascal and Bertram (2012:480) who use the phrase praxeology as "a developing paradigm for early childhood research." They describe praxeology as a mix of "phronesis, (reflection), praxis, (action), power, (politics) and a sharpened focus on values (ethics)." Formosinho & Oliveira-Formosinho (2012b:600), use slightly different terminology. They describe the aspects of praxeological research to be "the work (practices), the worker (self), and the workplace (context power relations)." During a praxeology research project undertaken by tutors at Pen Green, each member of our research team focused on different elements of studying at the centre. The small focus group discussions I was part of gave me the opportunity to deeply reflect on what has worked for me and why. It was also an opportunity for me to understand my role in developing other people's experience. Formosinho & Oliveira-Formosinho (2012a:7) describe the notion of praxis as "action impregnated in theory and supported by a belief system." This way of thinking about how theory and practice are interlinked was one of the main theoretical frameworks for the praxeology project. When our thoughts as a team turned to developing higher level qualifications, this idea of praxeology was at the forefront of our minds. The Pen Green team wanted to develop programmes of study which embedded pedagogical practice (pedagogy), self-reflection and theory within our own andragogical practice.

In my experience with adult learners, it is during their first study week at Pen Green where this starts to emerge. During the study block, we encourage learners to consider their own journey of learning; thinking about who and what has influenced them alongside what some of the barriers have been. I recall with detail how one learner had a realisation that her school experiences were at the root of her fears about returning to study, and subsequently her belief that she was not actually good enough to be a degree level student. We introduce learners during this process to the work of Clance and Imes (1978) who describe how high achieving women often carry their "imposter" with them during their working life, just waiting to be caught out as an imposter. Many learners recognise this feeling and refer to it throughout their studies. As each chapter within this book includes students' work and reflections, this will become evident throughout.

It seems now it is appropriate to share a little bit of my context and experiences. As a pupil in a secondary school, I held the view that academic subjects were for those who could show how clever they were. I am not saying these were the views of my teachers, however, it was how I felt at the time. Aligned with the views of Dweck (2006) "clever" is a term that I struggle with. In my experience it leads us to labelling; if you are not clever, does that automatically mean you are not academic? This was certainly a view I held in school. Patrick Whitaker once said to me that being academic is about being a specialist in a particular subject, the subject could be anything! All of us have the capability to be "clever" or to be "academic," we just have to find our specialisms. I keep these words at the forefront of my mind as I continue to learn and as I engage with others in their journey of learning.

As an adult learner I have achieved qualifications that far exceeded my own teenage expectations. Many of our learners express the same. The reason I believe I have been able to achieve the levels that I have is in part due to my life experiences, the jobs I have had, the people I have met and the opportunities that have been afforded to me. Kolb et al (1971) use the term "experiential learning" to describe the learning process an individual will go through when they take their experiences and learn from them. This has what I recognise has worked for me. My motivation came from wanting to learn more, being interested in the area of work I was studying, and having a supportive network around me to encourage, motivate and challenge me when I needed them to. Marshall (1999:157) identifies how "we draw on our lives and their themes in the topics we choose to study." I certainly believe my life experiences have influenced my decisions and ultimately my studies. Allman (1983) suggests that development in adults is inextricably linked to the degree and quality individuals are in touch with their social and historical contexts. As tutors this is something we are mindful of, getting to know each person's context, understanding their past experiences, including their learning experiences, and then building up their confidence as an adult learner.

Allman's (1983) account of adult learning reminds us that until the 1970s it was believed that adults would not have the capacity to continue to learn. However, she highlights how in the 1960s it was becoming clear that this was not the case, and the adult brain could continue to grow and develop. According to Allman (1983:107), psychologists in the 1960s had started to realise that development, or lack of it, was "inextricably linked to the degree and quality of individual's interactions with their social and historical contexts." She describes the fluctuating nature of social interactions, and the consequent brain development as a "plasticity" model. When describing adult education, Allman believes that its function is to enable development; for this to be true, she identifies how we should see potential in all learners, regardless of age and academic capability. When examining the views of adult learners, it became clear that during our interview processes, our tutorials and when giving feedback on submitted assignments, tutors recognise potential and adapt their approaches according to each individual's needs.

When discussing adult learners, Weil (1993:159) poses the question, "are students being helped to learn how to learn?" She studied adult learners who had returned to either further or higher education, she explored their perspectives on their learning, five years after their return to study. Her findings led her to define the process of learning as one that will include *disjunction, integration, equilibrium* and *self-validation*.

Disjunction (confusion): Weil concluded that with careful planning, educators would be able to support learners to make sense of and manage the disjunction they feel as they return to study.

Integration (getting it together): Educators should encourage conditions that are conducive to an individual being able and willing to learn, much in the way a pedagogue will provide environments for children where learning becomes an intrinsic process. Without this, Weil believes "mis-education" is likely.

Equilibrium (on an even keel): Studying in conditions that promote integration enabled the participants of Weil's study to have a sense of equilibrium. They knew what to expect, they understood what was expected of themselves and the learning opportunities were tailored to suit individual needs.

Self-validation (taking ownership): Her ideas are based on the supposition that adults have the capacity to learn from their primary experiences. They can draw on their previous and current experiences to influence their thoughts and ideas. Weil (1993) claims the learner needs to use and draw from a variety of knowledge and situations. These include experiential, tacit, practical and propositional. For the students in her study, Weil (1993:164) states: "to experience learning situations characterised by such conditions and an overall sense of integration often served to repair severely damaged confidence and self-esteem, and to compensate for prior experiences of education." Aldridge and Lavender (2000:12–15) claim that improved self-esteem, together with improved confidence, are two of the main benefits of learning for adults.

Freire and Macedo (1995:67–70) describe three teaching approaches that foster transformative learning. The centrality of **critical reflection**, an approach to teaching that supports **"acts of cognition** not the transferal of information"** which involves dialogue and problem posing, and finally **students and teachers being on an equal footing** (ibid.). A key approach to this for us is the use of journaling. Journaling offers the learners the opportunity to revisit their thoughts and feelings from the study week, or from their time in practice. Taylor (2008:11) claims how important it is to engage learners in classroom practices that "assist in the development of critical reflection through use of reflective journaling, classroom dialogue and critical questioning." This gives opportunity to reflect on real experiences, a function Kolb (1971) reminds us is crucial to "experiential learning."

Later in this book you will have the opportunity to see how and when learners have used their journals to enable them to reflect critically with the sensitive support from their tutor. In most cases this leads to changes in practice and transformation of ideas and knowledge.

My own study

In 2013 I carried out a small-scale research project as part of my Master's studies, which identified our main andragogic strategies being used with the students on our courses. To understand the experiences of our adult learners I asked questions, I carried out case studies to explore in-depth what took place during studies at Pen Green. The participants of the study identified some key elements of their experiences prior to starting their studies and then in the early days of their adult learning experiences that were key to our principles for working with them. They were:

Capability, the reluctance to return to learning was rooted in the fear of not being good enough, not feeling academic.

For nearly all respondents their **past learning experiences** were also an influencing factor. School was not particularly easy for many of the participants; often they had failed at maths, and many entered childcare as they were deemed not to be good enough for anything else. They felt a distinct lack of confidence in their own abilities.

The thought of **having to share what they were learning** with their colleagues was very daunting, and not something the majority felt confident in doing. This seemed to be problematic from the start. Many respondents felt their voices would not be heard, and as nursery nurses they were not seen as being important, and therefore worried their ideas would not be supported by their colleagues. In particular they were worried that managers would not take them seriously and would disregard their ideas.

I recognise here that the experiences of students can often be likened to Mezirow's (1981:125) concept of "perspective transformation." Mezirow (p. 126) describes 10 stages a person goes through when experiencing a change in perspective (see Table 1.1). Mezirow believed that in order for a transformation to take place, each of these stages needed to be explored.

The participants recalled situations that arose during their studies (similar to those you will read about later in this book), whereby their perspectives transformed. Referencing Mezirow (1997), Taylor (2008:6) wrote, "A perspective transformation often occurs as a result of an acute personal or social crisis." Mezirow (1981:126) describes this as a "disorienting dilemma." Mezirow

Table 1.1 Ten stages of perspective transformation (from Mezirow, 1981)

1.	A disorientating dilemma.
2.	Self-examination.
3.	A critical assessment of personally internalised role assumptions and a sense of alienation from traditional social expectations.
4.	Relating one's discontent to similar experiences of others or to public issues – recognising that one's problem is shared and not exclusively a private matter.
5.	Exploring options for new ways of acting.
6.	Building competence and self-confidence in new roles.
7.	Planning a course of action.
8.	Acquiring knowledge and skills for implementing one's plans.
9.	Provisional efforts to try new roles and to assess feedback.
10.	A reintegration into society on the basis of conditions dictated by the new perspective.

(2000:25) goes on to claim that at times perspectives are changed through intentional critical reflection, and at other times individuals are catapulted into situations that trigger the process. When approaching us to study, adult learners are intentionally opening themselves up to critical reflection or a "disorientating dilemma" (Mezirow, 1981:126).

Each time a learner has a powerful learning moment, or their perspective on a situation has changed, it seems to follow an emotional response or reaction to something. I often hear during tutorials, "I can't do this," "I don't know what to write about" or "I don't know what you want from me?" I often wonder if the students are avoiding taking a risk, or are these students finding my approach as a tutor too difficult to manage? I wonder if my expectations of them are too high. Are they experiencing a "disorientating dilemma" (Mezirow, 1981:126), and if so, what is the outcome of it? Do they allow their perspective to transform, or do they remain in their current state of equilibrium? My study identified that our role as tutors is to recognise this avoidance, celebrate when taking a risk turns into the recognition that an individual can embrace their "disorientating dilemma" and their perspective on a situation, practice issue or area of learning transforms. Each of our assignment briefs have been written with this in mind. Students are actively encouraged to think beyond their current experiences and consider new ways of approaching their practice.

During my study, participants could give very clear examples of how tutors on their courses had supported them as they experienced their own disorientating dilemmas. Often these times would involve the tutor offering "containment" Bion (1959), offering a space whereby anxiety can be felt, experienced and re-framed in a way that makes it manageable for individuals in an intellectually challenging environment. Freire (2006:71) claims authentic dialogue is required if an individual is to find belief in him or herself, and Kirkwood (1991:184) explains:

> people are subjects, able to analyse their reality, to become aware of the constraints on their lives, and to take action to transform their situation. The educator's job is to design approaches which will encourage the process of what he *(Freire)* calls conscientisation.

Another way to describe this is critical consciousness or becoming aware that critical reflection can result in a change in perspective.

Formosinho and Formosinho (2005) developed their concept of "pedagogical isomorphism," which we have found useful at Pen Green and to share with adult learners. Formosinho and Formosinho (2005) describe how certain conditions will encourage growth and change in an individual. They are the opportunity for **dialogue, challenge, containment** and **reflection.** My study demonstrated how the participants all described times when these four aspects have either been or not been present during their learning experiences. For one participant it was during their first tutorial, for another it was during a study block. The isomorphic aspect of this thinking is that if you can give these opportunities to a person, they are likely to be able to offer them to someone

Table 1.2 What learners need and what tutors can provide

Learner needs	Tutor can provide
Trust	Sensitivity and empathy
Resilience	Containment
Persistence	Belief in the learner
Motivation	Dialogue
Previous experiences to draw on	Acceptance of what the learner brings to the learning environment
A place to feel they belong	Holding in mind
Someone to show an interest	Faith

else. Whilst participants were experiencing disorientating dilemmas (Mezirow, 1981:126), tutors were on hand to provide them with the opportunities to reflect, feel contained, talk things through and be challenged.

As my study came together, the key themes became clear; trust, resilience, persistence, motivation, previous experiences, a place to feel they belong and someone to show an interest. These were all things that the learners identified as being important during their studies. From this I was able to identify what we were able to provide as tutors (see Table 1.2).

In his early work, Knowles (1970) asserts that pedagogy and andragogy are fundamentally different. However Pen Green's practice with adult learners has highlighted distinct similarities in the way we support adults in a learning environment and how we support young children.

At Pen Green we also draw on the work of Podmore et al (2001). Whilst considering how to assess children's learning experiences in New Zealand, Podmore et al developed a set of "children's questions." They are:

> **Do you know me?** (Do you appreciate and understand my interests and abilities and those of my family?)
>
> **Can I trust you?** (Do you meet my daily needs with care and sensitive consideration?)
>
> **Do you let me fly?** (Do you engage my mind, offer challenges and extend my world?)
>
> **Do you hear me?** (Do you invite me to communicate and respond to my own particular efforts?)
>
> **Is this place fair for me?** (Do you encourage and facilitate my endeavours to be part of the wider groups?)

These questions seem to me to have some relevance to the experiences of adult learners on Pen Green courses. I have taken the themes I identified earlier in the study and linked them to Podmore et al's (2001) questions (see Table 1.3).

Table 1.3 Themes identified in Table 1.2, linked with Podmore et al's (2001) child's questions

Learner needs	Child's questions	Tutor can provide
Trust	**Can I trust you?**	Sensitivity and empathy
Resilience	**Do you hear me?**	Containment
Persistence	**Is this place fair for me?**	Belief in the learner
Motivation	**Do you hear me?**	Dialogue
Previous experiences to draw on	**Do you know me?**	Acceptance of what the learner brings to the learning environment
A place to feel they belong	**Is this place fair for me?**	Holding in mind
Someone to show an interest	**Do you let me fly?**	Faith

This demonstrates how, as tutors, we appreciate the learners as individuals in the same way as we appreciate each child is an individual and has unique experiences to bring to the learning environment. Having recognised these similarities, I began to see how these points could be re-written into a set of strategies that could be considered when working with adults in a similar way to those developed by the nursery team at Pen Green for children. They called these "Pedagogic Strategies, (Whalley & Arnold, 2001; Lawrence & Gallagher, 2015). I, therefore, felt the term "Andragogic Strategies" was appropriate.

1   To always try to do what you say you will, and if you are not able to do this, say so.
2   To be sensitive to individual students' needs and circumstances.
3   To be available for students as they experience challenge, dis-equilibration, and success.
4   To provide an environment where students can feel valued and respected.
5   To provide opportunities for equal dialogue.
6   To understand and appreciate each student's context.
7   To see the potential in students.

I recognise that the content of our programmes changes with each cohort of learners. Even though the learning outcomes for each module stay the same, the way each study block is planned and presented has evolved. As tutors we discuss and reflect on our experiences at the end of every taught session, this enables us to be guided by the needs of the learners and the events of each day. Learners may not be aware that we meet to discuss what has taken place during the study sessions, but their experiences and responses demonstrate they were aware that we would be guided by their thoughts and ideas and would present things in a way that met their needs and made sense to them. This I believe could be another strategy:

8   To be flexible during teaching and be prepared to change direction or level of challenge depending on the discussions and responses from the students.

So far in this chapter I have contextualised Pen Green, shared my own study and summarised the Pen Green Andragogic Strategies. I will now share with you some study skills that will support you in your course of study. This following section of the chapter has been conceptualised and produced taking into account the wisdom and significant writing of Patrick Whitaker.

Developing your skills to undertake academic writing

Developing academic capabilities is extremely important to the tutor team at Pen Green. In the following chapters, you will have the opportunity to read the modules and assignments that learners embark on when studying at Pen Green. For many of the adult learners, writing academically is daunting and not something they feel confident doing. Over many years the tutor team have developed a range of techniques and strategies that help learners develop the skills they need. We had the privilege to work with esteemed colleagues such as Patrick Whitaker to write material to support adult learners at Pen Green. In more recent years our colleague, Eddie McKinnon, reviewed and updated some of this material.

The following information is taken from Patrick's material that the tutors use at Pen Green and that we have been sharing with adult learners for the past ten years.

Becoming academic – Approaches to academic learning

Becoming an effective and successful academic learner is largely a matter of practice – the more you do it, and the more familiar you become with its conventions, the more capability you develop. Like most specialist fields, the academic world has its own concepts and conventions, and these need to be understood as we become more familiar with academic practices. There are many ways we can demonstrate that we are being academic. Here are a few:

- Being academic means engaging in the scholarship of the theory and practice of a field. Fields can be categories of knowledge such as history or mathematics, for example, or professional fields such as physiotherapy or early childhood education and care.
- The main impetus for academic enquiry is curiosity, a habit we were heavily endowed with when we were born, but which may have become dimmed as a result of early experiences.

- Being academic means delving into what is known in the field of our interest and trying to understand it. Much of this knowledge is contained in literature and can be examined in books and journal articles. This knowledge provides the basis for professional training in the field.
- Beyond initial training and education, being academic means looking into what is not known, pursuing new lines of enquiry or devising new approaches.

The academic approach goes beyond personal preference and opinion and tries to get at the heart of things. It is concerned with intellectual rigour and safety, of establishing on what basis an assertion is made. Consider the following statement: "I think play is a waste of time." The speaker is quite entitled to this point of view and may have good reasons for holding it.

Now consider an alternative statement: "A number of recent studies have questioned the value of play." This is the sort of statement you might hear in a lecture about young children's development. You might also encounter such a statement in a professional journal. It is the sort of statement academics may make. Academics are interested in an approach that operates on the satisfying of curiosity through study and research. The purpose of research is to find out, to establish propositions and to test them in the field. When academics present the outcomes of their research, they usually refer to other research in the field. They outline how their own programme is similar or different, explain the methods they used to generate information and the results those methods produced. They then analyse those results, considering them alongside other research, trying to establish what they mean. The final section of most research reports is a conclusion where the academic researcher states how the present state of knowledge and understanding is affected by this particular study.

Our courses are constructed to provide practice in this approach and provide us with opportunities to consider:

- knowledge and understanding which has already been established
- areas where knowledge and understanding are "thin"
- areas where knowledge and understanding are contested and where further research and enquiry is required.

Academic reading

The literature of our profession

Most professions have literature containing thoughts, reflections and ideas of practitioners, campaigners, policy makers and scholars. The Early Years have a history of drawing on comprehensive literature, reflecting the broad nature of the field and the diversity of interest groups who are involved in it.

The catalogue of texts available is a daunting one and expanding all the time. It would be impossible to have a detailed knowledge of the whole field, but it is useful to acquire a grasp of the sub-divisions to specialise and locate the particular information we need.

Types of text

It is useful to distinguish two levels of text: journalism and scholarship. Journalism is mainly concerned with current issues, enabling those engaged in the field to keep up to date, to understand the range of perspectives present, to keep abreast of policy developments and to gain knowledge of the significant participants in the professional community. These texts are found in the press, professional magazines and newsletters and the documents of professional associations.

Scholarly texts are produced by those whose concern is to study the field and to investigate and research its various dimensions. Scholars will include, for example, historians, philosophers, sociologists, and educationalists. Some will be employed in academic institutions, undertaking and supervising research, while others will be practitioners in the field but with a specialist interest. Texts in this category are found in books, specialist journals and research reports. Many specialist journals have a system of peer review, where texts submitted for publication are assessed by other specialists in the field to ensure that they satisfy the academic standards and conventions of the journal concerned.

Engaging with academic texts

Studying at all of our degree levels requires that we engage more fully with this scholarly level of professional writing. This can be a daunting experience initially. Scholarly texts are concerned with detailed technicalities, theories, and principles of specialist areas, each of which has its own technical language or jargon which tends to be familiar within the specialist community, but not so well known outside it.

Given the broad and complex nature of the Early Years, it is not surprising that most of us will find some texts difficult and seemingly inaccessible. Academic writing is essentially a process of synthesising, in which new ideas, insights and understandings are built on to what is already known. It takes time to become familiar with a specialist discourse and its history. Difficulty in understanding is almost always a case of unfamiliarity rather than inadequacy on the part of the reader. Consideration for the reader should always be among the highest concerns of academic writers, yet understanding can sometimes be made difficult using complex terminology and awkward sentence structures.

Experience of academic reading

One of the consequences of schooling is the inculcation of the belief that if we are clever enough, we would be able to understand a text on the first reading. In a field rich with theories and complex practice, this is not always possible.

Many students have commented that they know the meaning of the individual words in a text, but comprehension eludes them when they are arranged in a particular sequence.

The purpose of study is to increase understanding, and in academic reading this involves the journey from what we know and understand to what we come to know and understand.

One of the advantages of undertaking a qualification in a learning community is engaging in dialogue with each other, sharing insights and teasing out meanings. While for much of schooling, collaboration in learning was discouraged (often described as copying), it is a vital part of courses at Pen Green. If the ultimate purpose of our work is improved services for children and families, then a learning process of mutual support and encouragement is more likely to prove effective.

Academic writers

A joy of academic study is discovering texts which tell us more about ourselves. This can happen when we read writers who have travelled similar journeys, developed similar values and beliefs, struggled with similar experiences and who share similar hopes and visions. Their texts can affirm us and give us the courage to press forward and recognise the nature of our own contribution. But there are other writers who have different experiences, perspectives and cherished ideas. These will challenge us and make us question our assumptions, beliefs and sometimes our professional practice.

When we read we engage in a discourse with the writer. If we understand their argument, we can agree or disagree. We can be helped to think about something, perhaps for the first time, or reconsider a long-held belief.

The process of reading invariably changes us – it can significantly alter the way we view the world. Not all our reading will be comfortable. Although our prejudices may be confirmed by a writer, we can also be challenged. From the privacy of the page, we can be offered the opportunity to correct a misconception, modify a belief or change an aspect of practice.

Objectivity and subjectivity

Academic credentials are important. We need to know why we should take what a writer says seriously, considering the experience they bring to their writing. Are they speaking personally or attempting to establish a more general truth? What evidence for their assertions are provided? What support have they gathered from the field? These are the sorts of questions we need to ask when engaging with authors and their texts.

It is not the case that academic work is concerned only with the outer objective world. Perhaps our greatest insights into Early Years growth and development have come from children themselves, speaking with authority about their own unique experience. Writers working from a subjective stance can claim a personal truth: "This is what it was like for me." When authors make claims about the outer world of objective reality, we must ask what their evidence is. If they are drawing on evidence provided by earlier research, we need to ask if they are representing the research correctly. Critical thinking in our academic reading is vital if we are to serve the interests of children, families and communities well.

Searching before reading

Most academic texts contain information and ideas which have the potential to help us understand more deeply the field, and to satisfy the enquiry we are currently engaged in. The view that books or articles should be read from the beginning to the end is still common among those coming to academic study later in life. There is also a belief that the text will not be understandable unless read in that way.

A useful aspect of being academic is to learn to deal with texts efficiently and effectively, making a distinction between two academic purposes:

1   reading to gain familiarity with a field or subject
2   reading to locate a specific idea or concept.

However committed we are, very few academic books are likely to sustain a high level of interest from beginning to end. Like the proverbial "curate's egg," many academic books are likely to be helpful only in parts. Since most of us are engaged in academic study in a part time capacity, getting to those parts quickly and efficiently is important. Abandoning fixed habits and beliefs about how books should be treated is necessary for learning ambitions to be realised. What is worth remembering is that reading should not begin until the information we are searching for has been located. Locating information is a large part of what academics spend their time doing. The first thing we notice about well-constructed academic books is that they have several components that are rarely found in works of fiction.

1   Cover information − the clue to what an academic book contains is usually summarised on the cover, telling you what the book is about and the nature of the contents. Here you should also find information about the authors, identifying which discipline or field they are placed in, whether they are a full-time academic, or a professional practitioner, and what other texts they have written.
2   Title page: this states the full title of the book, the name of the author and the name and location of the publisher.
3   Imprint page − this contains the copyright notice, printing history, the ISBN number, Library of Congress Catalogue number, the publisher's

name and address, and any additional copyright information. The printing history tells you when the book was first published and the dates of subsequent editions. This is the date you need to use in citations if you refer to the book in assignments.

4   Table of contents – this lists the chapters or sections of the books and gives a useful indication of where particular subject matter is located.

5   Foreword – these brief sections are usually written by someone other than the author, a series editor for example, or another leading specialist in the field. They are commendations to the reader and contain comments on the timeliness of the text, its unique contribution to the literature and often something about the wider work of the author.

6   Dedication page – usually a short statement thanking those who may have supported the author in the preparation of the book.

7   Acknowledgements – this is a list of those who have assisted in the production of the book, often giving interesting insights about the author's perspective on the subject matter.

8   End notes – additional information about a statement made in the text, usually referenced by a number. Sometimes this appears in the main text as footnotes. Different academic disciplines have different traditions.

9   Appendix – a collection of relevant information and resources, which support or expand on material in the main text.

10 Glossary – definitions of terms in the book.

11 References – a list of books, articles, and other resources the author used in writing the book, providing a valuable insight into the interests of the author.

12 Index – a list of key words with their associated page numbers, designed to help the reader find information inside the book. A detailed index is a boon to the academic student and is usually the sign of an author and publisher committed to helping the reader access information readily.

These various pages and sections can prove invaluable in locating passages of text to read in detail. Becoming skilful at this is an academic skill well worth developing, it can save you valuable time and ensures that you do not waste time with texts unlikely to be helpful. This is sometimes known as "raiding the text."

Organising notes and documents

Whatever approach to organising assignment documentation you have used previously, it is worth reviewing procedures with the requirements of your degree course in mind. Raising awareness of our own habits is important, particularly in the identification of which habits tend to consistently cause problems, for example, not knowing where a particular idea has been recorded, or forgetting to put the page number or reference against a quotation copied into a notebook. The following checklist is offered to support a useful review.

1   Notetaking

- Decide on location: phone, tablet, laptop, Dictaphone, journal, notebook, ring files, index cards, post-its.
- Use key words as headings. Record source title, author, date, and page number.

2   Marking up texts

- Unless the book is yours, photocopy pages for marking up and storing. Ensure the full reference of the document is written on the front of the photocopy or take a photo of it.
- Use highlighter pens to mark up the text.

3   Storage and filing

- Magazine and document boxes can be obtained from most stationers.
- Lever-arch files are good for storing articles and longer documents.

4   Assignment preparation

- It is useful to set up a file or folder for each assignment. Planning notes, references and quotations can be added.

5   Planning and review

- A study stint of one hour, with 10 minutes of planning at the beginning and 5 minutes of reviewing at the end, can develop effectiveness and efficiency. The 45 minutes in the middle is likely to be more productive than a whole hour without a planning and review component.

Academic writing

The academic assignments associated with degree courses are the training exercises of scholarship. Preparing and writing assignments enables us to develop a range of academic skills and capabilities such as:

- thinking out lines of enquiry
- constructing an investigation
- selecting what we already know and understand
- seeking out new information and ideas
- surveying the literature.

Academic writing serves several important functions:

- It enables us to document the knowledge of our specialist field.
- It enables us to note and record the discourse of those who have engaged in research and debate about the nature of this specialist field.
- It helps to stimulate and formalise enquiry and the management of professional curiosity.
- It provides support for the development of those entering the field.

The main challenge for academic writers is to present their ideas in a form that is understandable and interesting to those in the field. Do not think of your purpose as pleasing the tutors who will mark your assignments. At this stage of your academic development, they are representing the general reader and are considering how well you convey your ideas, present your arguments, handle your evidence, and draw your conclusions.

Good academic writing draws on a range of literary modes:

- Narrative – this is a writing mode that tells stories and is used in assignments to describe incidents and events. It is also used to describe the sequence of events in a research enquiry. The skill involves knowing how much of the story to tell. In most cases it will be just enough to enable the reader to understand how the incident or event relates to the wider purposes of the report you are writing.
- Descriptive – this mode is used to help the reader to get a clear picture of an object, place, person or incident. Fiction writers depend heavily on their descriptive powers to generate images which are vivid, atmospheric and evocative. This is not quite so vital in academic writing, but it is important that descriptions contain all the details that are significant in determining a course of events or a particular outcome.
- Explanatory – in this mode, complex ideas need to be conveyed as simply and clearly as possible. The ability to summarise key concepts and theories succinctly is a vital skill in academic writing, and it is worth making a deliberate effort to notice how the writers you are drawing on achieve it. Which writers do you find it easy to understand, however complex the ideas they are trying to convey? Who are the ones whose explanations seem confusing and almost impossible to grasp? Compare the way these different writers handle the challenge of explanation. What are the features of explanations that are clear and accessible? What is it that seems to obscure understanding in those writers you find difficult?
- Reflective – reflection is a major feature of the learning approach used in our degree courses and a method where we can use our own experiences to illuminate our understanding. Good reflective writing gives us access to the inner world of the writer, helping us to understand what it is like to "be" them. Some of the keys to powerful reflective writing are openness – getting to the heart of things, honesty – admitting to difficult

and uncomfortable feelings and emotions and pondering – giving the reader access to the indecisions, confusions, uncertainties, and yearnings that feature so strongly in our thinking about our work and its demanding challenges. Your learning journal is the key place where you can experiment with this mode of writing. Many of our previous students tell us that sharing in other participants' deep, and sometimes painful, reflections about their practice was one of their major sources of learning and understanding about their own practice and that of their colleagues'.

- Analytical – in this mode ideas are taken apart, concepts deconstructed, and theories challenged. One of the key purposes of academic work is to push at the boundaries of understanding, to test out ideas and to make sense of the data that is accumulated in a research study. The key question that analysis addresses is – what does this mean? Our capacity to answer that question is at the heart of what we do in an assignment. It is not enough to give our opinions or to describe what we have come to believe through experience, we must draw from a range of perspectives and collect a variety of views or experiences. Analysis is a process of weighing and balancing, comparing and contrasting and then seeing what patterns and configurations emerge. It can be tricky and painstaking work but work that enables new insights and understandings to be achieved and new knowledge to be created.

- Critical – this is the mode we use when ideas, concepts, assertions and assumptions are being challenged. Its purpose is not concerned with what is "right" and "wrong" but with what seems to work and what can be supported with evidence. Before a theory can become a law or a principle, it must be submitted to relentless testing and rigorous examination. A theory, after all, is a supposition offering an explanation. Theories are provisional knowledge, useful until they can be proved or disproved. In the complex interpersonal world of Early Years work theories are useful tools for investigation, for stimulating courses of enquiry. The purpose of the critical mode is to see how far a theory might take us in attempting to establish new insights and understandings. It is also necessary to slow the hasty drawing of conclusions that are sometimes made when limited data from an investigation seems to invite a particular meaning. Being critical is not about attacking or undermining the viewpoints or beliefs of others in the field, it is about questioning, probing, pushing for deeper explanation or greater detail. The word critical has a negative association for many of us, reminding us of how it feels to be criticised, sometimes unfairly and when we are not able to defend ourselves. Sometimes the word "critique" is used to describe this mode in academic writing – a process of rigorously examining ideas to move thinking forward.

Writing assignments and dissertations

The assignments in your course have two important purposes. The first is to provide an opportunity to practise academic writing at the appropriate level for your course. The second is to enable us to discover, organize and report the evidence that supports our arguments.

Purposes

The best way to begin work on an assignment is to formulate a clear purpose. Once the initial thinking around the subject has been carried out, and the focus selected, it is important to decide what it is we are doing, why we are doing it and what the assignment will look like when it is completed. A useful way to achieve a clear sense of purpose is to complete the following sentence stems:

1   This assignment is designed to . . .
2   I am undertaking this assignment in order to . . .
3   What I will end up with is an assignment consisting of . . .

It is worth spending some time on formulating and reformulating these statements. Aim to be clear, specific and detailed to feel purposeful and focused.

Structure

There is some flexibility in the structure of assignments, and your tutors will guide you with any specific requirements. Sections usually required in an assignment are the following:

1   Title page, without your name due to anonymization requirements
2   Contents with page numbers
3   Introduction and context: an introduction to the assignment and your professional context, considering the subject matter of the assignment. For instance, in an assignment about "working with parents," the focus of your professional context will be about your past experience of working with parents, and your values and beliefs about this particular aspect of your work.
4   Methodology and ethics: a description of the methods employed to gather, organise and analyse the data. An outline of the ethical considerations you have made during your research, drawing on a recognised code of ethics in the Early Years field.
5   Findings and analysis: a discussion of the data produced and what you believe it means and demonstrates.
6   Conclusion and implications for practice: a proposition or argument related to the analysis of the data. This is the section that makes connections between what was looked for, what was found and what it means. You should outline what you will do differently in your practice as a result of what you have found.
7   References: a list of all the materials cited in the report.

Presentation

Consideration for the reader is important if we want the fruits of our enquiries to make an impact. We need to be thoughtful about layout and presentation, and our aim should always be to make it easy for the reader to understand what we are saying.

Each of us has our preferences for different styles of visual presentation, and it is worth planning to ensure clarity and consistency and that you are adhering to the formatting guidance provided.

This plan should give attention to:

1 Margin size and line spacing.
2 A convention of main headings, section headings and sub-headings.
3 A consistent approach to:

- Font size and style – the university requires you to present your final version of an assignment/dissertation in Arial size 12 with 1.5 point spacing.
- Bullet points and numbered lists.
- Quotations from other writers.
- Direct quotations from research data from field notes, interviews etc.
- Diagrams, photographs, or other illustrations.
- Page numbering.
- Use of italic or bold font.

Three types of proofreading are vital prior to submission:

1 The text

- Simply reading the text through rarely identifies all the typographical and other errors. It helps to proofread line by line rather than sentence by sentence (the meaning can interfere). Moving a ruler down the page can help.
- Spell checkers only identify words not in their thesaurus and will not distinguish between words that sound the same but mean different things such as "there" and "their."
- Reading aloud can often help to identify punctuation problems and where your meaning is not as clear as you think it is.
- Asking other people to critically read the assignment, both for meaning and for errors.

2 Layout

- Check for consistency in use of spacing, fonts, headings etc.
- Check that there are no headings at the bottom of a page with the text to which it refers at the top of the following page.
- Add page numbers to the contents list before final printing.

3   Citations and references

- Check that all references to the work of others are cited in the text where they occur (see next section).
- Check that all works referred to in the text are included in the list of references after the final section of the report.

Referencing

While consistent failure to reference correctly can lose marks, consistently applied correct referencing can win them. Referencing is a way of identifying the source of the knowledge we use in our own writing. Since we are always building on what has gone before, we will spend a lot of our academic time examining and becoming familiar with the thinkers, enquirers and writers who have gone before us. It is important to acknowledge with respect the contributions that others have made to the discourse in which we have now become participants. We can do this by mentioning by name anyone whose ideas we use during our own investigations and assignment writing.

Mentioning sources has two purposes:

1   It acknowledges our inspirations and influences. It shows that we place ourselves in the rich tradition of scholarship and debate about the knowledge and practice of our professional field.
2   It enables others who read our work to be able to trace the knowledge and ideas of those we have drawn on. This means that we must show who has influenced us, where we found the idea, we are now commenting on and when and where it was published.

We serve this second purpose very simply by carrying out two tasks:

1   Placing the name of the writer whose ideas we are using in the main body of the text nearest to the idea that is being commented on. This is called a citation and the convention has the following elements:

- Brackets to separate the citation from the text.
- The surname of the writer.
- The date of publication of the document in which the idea occurs.
- The page number or numbers where the idea can be found.

2   Putting the details of the document containing the idea in the References list at the end of the assignment. This needs to contain the following information:

- Name of the author
- Date of the publication
- Title of the document
- Place of publication
- Name of publisher.

There are many guides to referencing, however the University of Hertford-shire's "Guide to Referencing in the Harvard Style" is both comprehensive, easy to follow and a course requirement. Your References list should contain only citations that you have used in the text of your dissertation, and you should ensure that it does not contain anything which does not appear there.

Disregarding these important conventions in academic work is called pla-giarism. This is defined as the act of taking someone else's ideas and present-ing them as your own. This is a serious offence in the academic world and is penalised in most academic institutions. Where the intention is to mislead, a writer's reputation is disgraced. When it is an error or omission, corrections must be made to a draft before circulation of the material.

Plagiarism may be committed because the writer wants to appear more academically capable than they really are. This is to misunderstand the nature of academic capability. The mark of a true academic is their painstaking deter-mination to plot the journey of an idea and to place it within a category of ideas that characterise the history of that field. Citing sources and generating a substantial range of references demonstrates how well we have engaged with the knowledge and thinking of our field, and how well equipped we are to offer comments on these ideas and begin to contribute ideas of our own.

As you begin to see yourself as an academic writer, we hope these tips and techniques will help you to develop and refine your own academic style.

As I draw this chapter to a close, I want to ask you to consider your own experiences, your own fears and your own needs as an adult learner.

The coming chapters will take you through each of the themes from Image 1.1. You will read extracts from assignments produced by some of our adult learn-ers, who have generously shared their work for this publication. You will read about the way each theme has been developed and the approaches and andra-gogical strategies that have been used.

I want to remind you how being "academic" is about being a specialist – you choose the specialism, you choose the approach and, most importantly, you can choose to reclaim your education.

Endnotes

1 Pedagogy means the method and practice of teaching.
2 Andragogy means the method and practice of teaching adult learners.

References

Aldridge, F. & Lavender, P. (2000) *The impact of leaning on health*. Leicester: NIACE.
Allman, P. (1983) The nature and process of adult development. In *Adult learning and education*. Kent: Open University.
Bion, W. R. (1959) Attacks on linking. In E. Bott Spillius (ed.) *Melanie Klein Today: Develop-ments in theory and practice*. Volume 1: Mainly Theory. 1988. London: Routledge.
Bion, W. R. (1961). *Experiences in groups*. London: Tavistock.
Clance, P. R. & Imes, S. (1978) The imposter phenomenon in high achieving women: Dynamics and therapeutic intervention. In *Psychotherapy Theory, Research & Practice, 15(3)*.

Clare, S. & Clark, K. (2021) "Virtually Pen Green": Developing a synchronous teaching response for adult learners studying early childhood degree programmes during COVID-19. *European Early Childhood Education Research Journal*, DOI:10.1080/13502 93X.2021.2016882.

Dweck, C. S. (2006) *Mindset: The new psychology of success*. New York: Ballentine Books.

Formosinho, J. & Formosinho, J. (2005) *National Professional Qualification in Integrated Centre Leadership (NPQICL) Pilot Programme*. An Evaluative Research Study. Corby: Pen Green Leadership Centre.

Formosinho, J. & Oliveira-Formosinho, J. (2012a) *Pedagogy-in-participation: Childhood Association Education Perspective*. Braga, Portugal: Sponsored by the Research Centre on Child Studies of the University of Minho.

Formosinho, J. & Oliveira-Formosinho, J (2012b) Towards a social science of the social: the contribution of praxeological research, *European Early Childhood Education Research Journal*, *20*(*4*), 591–606.

Freire, P. (1970) Cultural action for freedom. *Harvard Educational Review*.

Freire, P. (2006) *Pedagogy of the oppressed*. London: Penguin Books.

Freire, P. & Macedo, D. (1995). A dialogue: culture, language, and race. *Harvard Educational Review*, *65*(*3*).

John, K. (2019) Holding the baby: Leadership that inspires and contains ambition and anxiety. In Whalley, M., John, K., Whitaker, P., et al. *Democratising leadership in the early years*. London: Routledge: 38–86.

Kirkwood, G. (1991) Freire methodology and practice. In *Roots & Branches*. (Series of occasional papers). Vol. *1*: Community Development and Health Education. Milton Keynes: Open University Health Education Unit.

Knowles, M. S. (1950) *Informal adult education*, New York: Association Press. Guide for educators based on the writer's experience as a programme organizer in the YMCA.

Knowles. M. S, (1970) The modern practice of adult education: From pedagogy to andragogy. Cambridge Book Company. Cambridge. In Tight, M. (1983) (ed) *Adult learning and education*. London: Groom Helen.

Kolb, D. A. (1984) The process of experiential learning. In Thorpe, M., Edwards, R. & Hanson, A. (ed). (1993). *Learning through Life: Culture and Processes of Adult Learning*. London: Routledge/Open University.

Kolb, D. A., Rubin, I. M. & McIntyre, J. M. (1971). *Organizational psychology: An experimental approach*. Englewood Cliffs: Prentice Hall.

Lawrence, P. & Gallagher, T. (2015). "Pedagogic Strategies": A conceptual framework for effective parent and practitioner strategies when working with children under five. Early *Child Development and Care*, *185*, 1–17. 10.1080/03004430.2015.1028390

Marshall, J. (1999). Living life as enquiry, *Systemic Practice and Action Research*, *12*(*2*), pp. 155–171.

Mezirow, J. (1981) *Adult education*. Washington, Adult Education Association of the USA.

Mezirow, J. (1997) Transformative learning: Theory to practice. In Cranton, P. (ed) *Transformative learning in action: Insights from practice. New Directions for Adult and Continuing Education*. No 74. San Francisco: Jossey-Bass.

Mezirow, J. (2000). *Learning as transformation: Critical perspectives on a theory in progress*. San Francisco: Jossey-Bass.

NCSL (National College for School Leadership) (2004) *National Professional Qualification for Integrated Centre Leadership (NPQICL) Programme Document*. Nottingham: NCSL.

Pascal, C. & Bertram, T. (2012): Praxis, ethics, and power: developing praxeology as a partici-patory paradigm for early childhood research, *European Early Childhood Education Research Journal*, *20*(*4*), 477–492.

Podmore, V., May, H. & Carr, M. (2001). The "child's questions." Programme evaluation with Te Whāriki using "Teaching Stories." *Early Childhood Folio*, *5*, 6–9.

Rogers, M. & Tough, A. (1996). Facing the future is not for wimps, *Futures*, *28*(*5*), 491–496: Great Britain: Pergamon.

Taylor, E. (2008) Transformative learning theory. In Merriam, S. B. (ed), Third update on adult learning theory. *New Directions for Adult & Continuing Education*, *119*. San Francisco: Jossey-Bass.

Weil, S. (1993) Access; towards education or miseducation? Adults imagine the future. In Thorpe, M., Edwards, R. & Hanson, A. *Culture and processes of adult learning*. London: Routledge/Open University.

Whalley, M. & The Pen Green Centre Team (2001). *Involving parents in their children's learning*. London: Paul Chapman Publishing.

Whalley, M., John, K., Whitaker, P., Klavins, E., Parker, C. and Vaggers, J. (2019) *Democratising leadership in the early years*. London: Routledge.

Winnicott, D. W. (1964) *The child, the family and the outside world*. Cambridge, Massachusetts Perseus Publishing.

2   The self as a learner and reflective practitioner

Dr Christine Parker and Sandra Clare

[In collaboration with Charlotte Richardson, Billie Fox-Barkshire, Ben Powley and Sam Butterwick]

In this chapter you will find:

- A consideration of what it means to be a reflective practitioner
- The value of journaling to support reflective practice
- Assignment extracts that illuminate how students have considered the benefits of reflective practice.

Why allocating time to think about being a learner and a reflective practitioner matters to adult learners

This chapter begins with an introduction to the context of reflective practice and insights into why it is significant in current practice. When considering the education of others, a useful starting point is a thorough consideration of our own experiences of learning and education. Many early experiences of learning include tales of shame and embarrassment, so putting your head above the parapet and saying to the world "I want more" takes real courage. Studying towards a degree involves deciding you want more; for yourself, for your family, for the children you work with and the communities you serve. Like David (1984:29) we think of "education" and the term "educator" broadly, underlining the educative significance of not only teachers but all those within educative environments amongst children and throughout communities; the social workers, Early Years professionals, health visitors, family visiting volunteers, foster carers, 1:1 support staff, midday supervisors and local authority officers.

Kolb (1984) suggests our survival depends on our capacity to learn and to make sense of the complex environment around us. To engage successfully in studies, and develop into reflective practitioners, students require the ability to think deeply. Schön (1983) argues the successful development of professional capability depends more on the ability to learn from one's own experience of practice than from theory and research. Individual experiences, either in school or previous learning environments, will always have an impact on feelings about beginning new learning.

DOI: 10.4324/9781003271727-2

Reflective practice is the process by which you set aside dedicated time to think carefully through what has been happening in the workplace and in your studies. Lines of inquiry such as, "How effective have I been in supporting a child?," "What happened in that encounter?," "Is there a theory that underpins my practice here?" and "How am I managing this work situation?" come to mind. Educators have a tendency to grasp the "what went wrong" first. What reflection provides is the time to go deeper and acknowledge that "what went well" is equally important to consider and articulate (Whitaker, 1993). As an educator you need to be able to articulate your work and study experiences in a way that has been thought out. Identifying dilemmas that need to be addressed as well as aspects of work to be celebrated. Reflective practice enables more precise and detailed explanations. The notion of Imposter Phenomenon (Clance & Imes, 1978), as referred to in Chapter 1, has a relevance here, in that a sense of being an "imposter" in a professional role can be revealed through this process. However, with further reflection, the aim is for you to be more confident in positioning such feelings.

Broadening out your reflections to include where you see yourself in wider society is important (Bronfenbrenner, 1979), as well as being confident to describe your workplace locality and the families and community you serve. Showing curiosity for others and creating safe spaces to articulate what challenges you face strengthen your position as self as learner. bell hooks (2003) talks about the dominance of the White, capitalist, colonial education agenda, and though many will argue against racist dogmas within teaching, the reproduction of oppressive education structures takes some real unpicking, as does the origin of your thoughts and attitudes. It is deeply unsettling to do sometimes and requires honesty and vulnerability. Assumptions about family income, structure, educational achievement and religion all need reflecting on – as do responses to those who are different to us.

The process of reflection is likely to raise challenges, tackling contentious areas, both personal and from practice. It is likely to raise information rich assignments but also anxiety. It is not possible to guarantee that reflection will not stir negative emotions in either the short or long term. An insight into your own preferred ways of learning, hang ups and preferences can be the most helpful tool to guide and shape you as both a learner and teacher, being both at the same time takes real humility but leads to greater outcomes.

Pen Green perspective

Every course at Pen Green begins with the opportunity for students to capture their experiences of learning and reflect upon the impact of them. There are assignments throughout all levels of the courses on offer at Pen Green, and indeed other educational settings, that require reflection upon the self, either as a learner or in practice. The first module at Level 4 is entitled Self As Learner, the belief being that before we can "teach" we need to think about how we "learn." Whether as an educator or learner it is important to pay attention to your own needs and grow from your own experiences.

During study weeks and tutorials, time is invested in the process of reflection and journaling. For many adult learners, but not all, writing is a helpful process, whereas for others visualising their ideas through the use of pictures can help to express and communicate, all of which support reflexivity. These quiet and contemplative processes are not always highly regarded in our action-focused society, yet it is through reflective thinking that it is possible to create visions and forge beliefs about how we would like to practice and who we want to be. You may find the idea of freefall writing useful (Marshall, 2007). This is a process where you write what comes to mind without thinking too much about grammar and punctuation. It is a personal process, that allows that outlet of emotion, ideas and concerns. The mechanism for reflective practice works well when you have the time to journal first, and then talk through your ideas with trusted others.

A reflective journal is personal to the individual, and extracts are only shared if the learner is comfortable with doing so. Tutors encourage students to draw on journal entries, reflect on incidents from practice and consider the impact of their own practice wisdom on their current value base. Being authentic in your reflective practice means you are prepared to think about those aspects that may be challenging you intellectually and emotionally.

We have selected student work where adults have reflected deeply on themselves as learners. Assignment extracts have been chosen to illustrate the validity of reflective journaling as a research methodology. Students have been able to articulate challenges, how barriers to learning have been overcome and the subsequent impact on children, the children's families and work colleagues. There is a fine line between the personal and professional aspects of an adult learner's life. Through the extracts we hope to demonstrate the importance of the first-person inquiry (Marshall et al, 2011) and the relevance of it within practice and academia, understanding that it is the interplay between the personal and professional that is at heart of most struggles.

Foundation Degree (year 1) Level 4 assignment extract

Charlotte Richardson

Assignment brief

In this first assignment, the Level 4 learners are invited to introduce themselves and their learning journey to date. They identify an incident that has evoked an emotion within them and systematically analyse their narrative, applying a reflective cycle.

Introducing Charlotte

My career in Early Years began in 2009 as a volunteer in a local nursery and afterschool club. Having experienced significant loss I decided it was time to make a meaningful change and a spark was ignited. I was supported through NVQ Levels 2 and 3, and have since become a parent. Adopting our son shifted my perspectives of child development, and I have undertaken many roles in a variety of settings. Currently I am a Family Support Worker for local government in the East of England.

Assignment extract

Introduction

I am a Nursery Practitioner with ten years' experience. I will be drawing on Kolb's (1984) Experiential Learning Cycle and Clance and Imes' (1978) Imposter Phenomenon. I will explore my learning journey, identifying values and practice wisdom and how they have evolved through professional development and personal experiences.

Reflective practice

Reflective practice is "the conscious examination of past experiences, thoughts and ways of doing things" (Gibbs, 1988; Gibbs, 2019) (see Figure 2.1). However, there is a difference between unconscious thought processes and reflective practice.

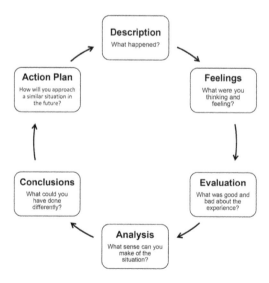

Figure 2.1 Gibbs' Reflective Cycle

Kolb (1984:51) believed "knowledge is created through the transformation of experience" and developed a reflective cycle. This includes two continuums; 1) how individuals approach tasks; processing continuum and 2) how individuals feel about tasks; perception continuum (see Figure 2.2). Kolb (1984) believed the cycle could begin at any point, but I believe reflection starts with concrete experience and states that experiential learning links work, education and personal development.

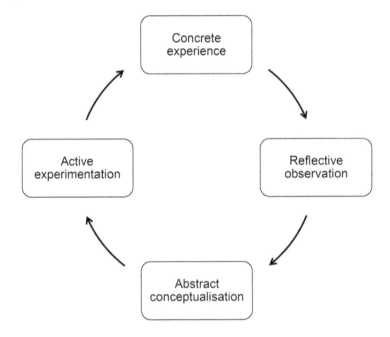

Figure 2.2 Kolb's Model of Reflection

Clance and Imes (1978) suggest some women experience feelings of inadequacy – "Imposter Phenomenon." They found high-achieving women believed success was through deception or luck rather than intellectual ability. Social stereotyping, along with family dynamics, contribute to the development of self-doubt. They identified two categories; those who had been labelled "sensitive" implying not intelligent and those labelled as "bright" who develop distrust if unable to achieve. I could identify with this and have developed strategies to overcome self-doubt.

Ethics

According to the British Educational Research Association (British Educational Research Association, BERA, 2018:6) "any researcher should operate within an ethic of respect." I will ensure that references to anyone remain anonymous, protecting their identity. I do not require informed consent as the focus is my own learning journey, opinions, thoughts and feelings. Therefore, I will safeguard myself by upholding confidentiality.

Reflective learning journey

Attending my first school I was an anxious child, I found it difficult and confusing. Later I underachieved throughout high-school, and during this time, my family moved to Argentina, where I sat my GCSEs before returning to England. I wanted to travel, so I completed NVQ Leisure and Tourism, spending two years in the travel industry before realising it was not right for me. I then secured a position in the Motor Industry for 10 years.

A close family member was having a difficult time in school and I could identify with her experiences which I discussed with my father. My father's untimely death encouraged me to pursue my dream of a career in child-care. I began volunteering in a Children's Centre. The manager encouraged me to do NVQ Childcare Learning and Development. I became a Nursery Practitioner until the adoption of my son, when I took a year off. I loved time with my son, but sometimes found it isolating and I became interested in family support.

Experience from practice: I knew undertaking the Foundation Degree would require me to be academic and felt anxious and excited. On the second day, self-doubt washed over me. During "check-out" I was unable to control my emotions. I felt overwhelmed by the enormity of the task ahead. I felt frightened that I was not going to be able to complete the assignment or degree. I used Kolb's framework (1984) and the Imposter Phenomenon concept (Clance & Imes, 1978) to unpick my reaction.

Concrete Experience: I observed other students who appeared fully engaged and seemed to have understood the tasks. After releasing my emotions in front of everyone, I felt I had let myself down and felt vulnerable.

Reflective Observation: Once emotions settled, I reviewed my feelings and the cause of my anxieties. I assumed other students were feeling relaxed and had complete clarity of the module and assignment. I let the thought of writing an assignment become my focus, rather than the learning process. The learning journey task provoked a memory. I remember feeling confused and inadequate at school. I was eight years old and set a mathematical task to complete in my workbook. I was unable to make sense of it. Eager to please, I wrote what I thought the answers were. My teacher put a big cross through the page and berated me. I vomited over my work. I was reprimanded and sent to get changed into my PE kit. I spent the day feeling humiliated.

Abstract Conceptualisation: Reflection brought clarity; I have learnt to disguise my anxiety by becoming socially adept. Forming relationships with peers meant support and hiding academic inadequacies. Thirty years later I was fearful my academic deficit would be exposed and had not yet formed friendships for reassurance. Pen Green's approach to adult learning is very different – actively learning, researching, discussing and sharing ideas. By allowing myself to "trust the process," the learning continues. From exposing my emotions and vulnerability, I trust students and tutors will not humiliate me or tell me I am not good enough.

Active Experimentation: The opportunity to put my learning into practice came in the form of a presentation. Usually, this would provoke feelings of anxiety, but knowing the group had already seen me at my most vulnerable and shown empathy and reassurance, I was in a safe environment to expose myself as a student.

I was able to identify with the Imposter Phenomenon (Clance & Imes, 1978). Although I had a loving, stable childhood, I was often referred to as "the sensitive one," not intellectual. Self-doubt gained momentum as I started school. When my teacher crossed out my work, I was exposed, my stupidity discovered and revealed to my peers.

Summary

Kolb's (1984) work gave me the opportunity to process feelings, thoughts and emotions that have accumulated since I began education. I have gained insight into my own learning style and found this assignment extremely insightful to rebuild and move forward with my own personal development.

Charlotte's reflections on the assignment

I remember every moment of my first study week. I distinctly remember wondering what on earth I thought I was doing, telling myself off for even thinking about the possibility of completing a degree. I recall the Learning Journey task and looking at it in black and white, evidence I am not academic, I should not be here, I cannot hide behind the social mask I had engineered for myself over the years.

Then I remember the compassion and the encouragement that the tutors extended to me. They talked me through the process and asked me to trust them in guiding me through it. This first assignment was the beginning of a new chapter in my learning journey. Through this assignment, the theories I was introduced to, the reflective cycle and the guidance from Pen Green, I completed this assignment and the assignments that followed, which led me through a continuous learning journey.

Indeed, for every assignment I have learnt about children, I have learned twice as much about myself.

Tutor comments on Charlotte's work

I recall Charlotte's first week with huge amounts of admiration. She was filled with nervous anxiety, fear that she was not good enough, and most definitely concerned she would be exposed as an "imposter." Her assignment was one that stuck in my mind, she took her fear, she processed it and she went on to learn such a lot about herself. Academically she had started to work out what her writing style would look like, and she engaged with some complex reading.

In the short excerpt, you will note her introduction is succinct but clearly outlines what she hopes to achieve. She shares a brief summary of theories she later relies on. Though this assignment is very personal, she demonstrates a good ethical stance by clarifying her responsibilities to herself and anyone who may be connected to the stories shared. The findings and analysis are raw and brave. In assignments such as this, the marker is not marking the event but the student's authenticity in reporting it and their ability to analyse it making effective use of theory.

Foundation Degree (year 2) Level 5 assignment extract

Billie Fox-Barkshire

Assignment brief

Level 5 students complete a "leaderful learner" assignment through self-reflective accounts. Much like we encourage reflections on how we learn to inform how we educate others, reflections on how we feel about leading are useful when becoming leaderful. The expectation is that students will know and understand how to assess and critique their own capability, including the use of feedback from others, to reflect on actions, thoughts and feelings, and a review of personal learning.

Introducing Billie

I am a second-year student participating on the Pen Green Degree programme. I started my journey into Early Years development quite a few years ago when my eldest child was a toddler. I have two children; one is now an adult and the other a "pre-teen." I work full time as an Early Years practitioner and am very passionate about my role. I knew when I started this journey that I wanted to continue to progress, and I had many aspirations. It has taken me much longer than I anticipated to continue into higher education. In part this is due to the many commitments I had as an adult and a mother. I kept waiting for the right time and opportunity to arise. The truth was, there was never going to be a right time. I had to take the "bull by the horns" and go for it, and I am so glad I did. When I began, I had many doubts about whether I could complete the degree. And obviously, fear of failure sat heavy with me.

Assignment extract

Introduction and context

I am going to be exploring and reflecting upon my personal journey with leaderful experiences within my professional context. I believe this to be an important subject for me to broach, since I have found it hard to look upon myself as a leader. I have questioned my abilities many times, albeit in silence. I will use literature, alongside my personal thoughts, to link reflection, implications and improvement of my practice. At the time of writing this paper, I had been promoted from Early Years Teaching Assistant to Lead Early Years Practitioner. I had wanted to progress for a long time, but a fear of failure stopped me. The promotion came at the right time, and I was keen to begin a new journey that would challenge me. However, the title of "Lead Early Years Practitioner" did concern me. I did not enjoy the thought of being placed within a hierarchy. I also worried that the promotion would perhaps change my relationships with some colleagues. This assignment will give me the opportunity to look inwards and discover where my confidence loss and fear of perceived hierarchy was stemming from. I had not experienced feelings of being undervalued. In fact, my opinion was often sought and held in high regard. Communication was open and collaborative (Raelin, 2004). I felt that I was valued.

Methodology and ethics

Research involved a focus group (Gibbs, 1997), anonymised feedback forms and journal entries (Fulwiler, 1980). I led a focus group with my team to gain the thoughts, feelings, experiences and reactions of respondents. Gibbs (1997) suggests a person is better able to gain holistic viewpoints through the social gatherings and interactions that this method offers. I needed to organise the group within the normal working day, which was difficult. I was aware of the different personalities within the group, and considered those that may be reluctant to speak, as this could lead to "difficulties in distinguishing between an individual view and group views" (Gundumogula, 2020:301). I used anonymised feedback forms to ensure participants unconfident to express themselves had the opportunity to give honest feedback. This opened a dialogue between participants, where they were able to debate, collaborate and share experiences and differences.

I used journal entries (Fulwiler, 1980) throughout to reflect upon my learning, thoughts, feelings, experiences and assumptions. Moon (2013) explains that journal writing can be used to provide "a means by which learning can be upgraded" (:187) and suggests that deeper meanings emerge. I considered how to balance what the reader needed to know and what must remain private, as such, there will be gaps in my findings and analysis. The process would be "transparent" (Halej, 2017) so participants would know and understand what the research was in aid of and how information would be gathered, stored and disposed of. Participants were aware they could withdraw at any point, and how. Anonymity meant they could not be identified within my writing. Each participant was verbally briefed before being given consent forms.

Findings and analysis

The assignment has enabled me to understand that leaderful behaviour is about the way a person presents themselves positively, with both intrapersonal (with self) and interpersonal (with others) relationships in mind (Whalley et al, 2019; Raelin, 2004). As I explored my journal entries, I synthesised my thoughts regarding my abilities as a leader. It was clear that I hold myself in low regard, whilst setting myself high standards that I would not expect of others (Hibbert, 2019). I also had conflicting inner beliefs. I realised my own assumptions did not match those of the group. There was positive collaboration taking place, and at the end participants thanked me for the knowledge I shared and they had gained. I realised participants saw me as a leader and a knowledgeable other. I needed to understand why I do not regard myself in this way. Raelin (2004) believes leaderful behaviour begins when a person can be self-aware and comfortable with their inner self. A leader must be able to question and reflect upon themselves to "gain some self-awareness of their actions" (Raelin, 2004:66), especially regarding participation and control. A leader must be able to know their limitations and be humble that they (the leader) do not know all the answers, being able to collaborate. Individual leaders must be behaviour and cognitively focused, engaging in self-criticism, self-observation, self-set goals and self-reward: "it's important to first understand and observe oneself before advising others" (Raelin, 2004:67). John (2019:38) believes leaders must "recognise and overcome internal and external obstacles that interfere with their healthy and socially responsible functioning," suggesting leadership skills are influenced by previous experiences of being led from infancy through to adulthood.

Reflections

This assignment has been very personal to me, I have recognised I am already seen as a leader by my colleagues. As I began to understand Raelin's (2004) definition of leadership, I recognised my team make me feel supported, respected, believed in, trusted and able. I realised fear of failure has kept me from progressing to roles I desire. Perhaps then, the worst part is that my silenced inner-self knows I can achieve, whilst acknowledging failure is part of growth.

Implications for practice

I was under no illusion that changing my own mindset would be an easy task. I need to dedicate time to myself to uncover some uncomfortable truths and set myself boundaries. I am also aware knowledge can be empowering. I am choosing to learn how to accept both positive and negative feedback from trusted people within my life in a humble and active manner. I am aiming to continue developing my role and leadership qualities, using the knowledge I have gained. I feel I do not need to focus on hierarchy/dominating others to fulfil my role. I can continue being a leader, without needing to change my persona. I feel that I can now say I am a leader, with leaderful behaviours, whilst continuing to develop my inner self (Raelin, 2004).

Billie's reflections on the assignment

I went into the assignment with a clear vision of what I intended to write about. However, as I began my literature review and compared my findings to that of my personal journal entries, it was apparent that I was crafting something much more reflective and personal. I felt the common themes that were emerging needed further exploration for me to grow and develop my practice. I realised that I could not move forward if I did not address this. I did feel unsure of the outcome and apprehensive regarding the discoveries I may find. My tutors were a brilliant source of support and guided me through. "Trust the process and yourself" were words that I recollect and kept reminding myself of. It was crucial that I kept myself safe and did not over share, I was very conscious of this. My work remained true and authentic throughout.

The assignment has led me on a real journey of self-reflection and discovery. I have been able to unpick factors that were unconsciously affecting my growth, confidence, and practice. Once I realised this, it was like a light bulb moment. I knew where and how to target changes relevant to my personal practice. This has led to greater self-belief, enabling me to perform better in a humble and holistic way. This is particularly true regarding my academic abilities. I have developed the skills to trust myself and self-reflect effectively. The process was hard and long, with the need to be mentally ready, motivated and secure in what I was uncovering. I had the right means and mindset to achieve good outcomes safely. I knew this process was crucial. The research I embarked upon was broad and heavy, but imperative. I have a much deeper understanding of effective leadership and of myself.

Tutor comments on Billie's work

Billie has applied her self-reflection skills to unpick her understanding of leadership. She demonstrates a significant shift in her thinking in terms of her own leaderful practice. To begin with, Billie explains how fearful she felt with her promotion and finds Raelin's (2004) writing to be especially supportive. In her methodology and ethics section, Billie identifies her three research methods which include entries in her reflective journal, as well as focus groups and anonymised feedback forms. Her journal entries (Fulwiler, 1980) provide a rich resource from which she develops her authentic voice. She identifies her learning from Moon (2013), which gave her the courage to explore more deeply her inner feelings about leadership. Billie recognised that through the process of gathering data in her journal she was able to make the links between the theories and her practice. She discovered that she did demonstrate leaderful behaviours, including being self-aware, in order to pursue a collaborative approach to her leadership.

Bachelor's Top-up Degree Level 6 assignment extract

Ben Powley

Assignment brief

The Level 6 Leadership assignment requires students to reflect on their experiences of leadership in the workplace, either being led, or how they lead. Leadership as a concept within the early years and beyond will be more thoroughly explored in Chapter 6, however, it does have a relevance to the notion of self-reflection. When students reflect on their professional role, aspects of leadership within the organisation arise naturally.

In his assignment, Ben finds himself having to take on an unexpected leadership role, and in doing so uses self-reflection as a tool for problematising his way through this experience, ensuring that ultimately, it is the children he teaches who benefit. He is consistently mindful of the ethics of his situation as he processes his lived experiences in school.

Introducing Ben

When I attended the open evening of my local sixth form, I happened upon the childcare classroom and I remember stepping down into the classroom and seeing board games, toys and a baby doll. I thought to myself, "Well, can't be that hard, it's just playing." A phrase that now conjures the same feeling as nails on a chalkboard. I began work experience in a local preschool where I was offered a job twice, the first time I wasn't sure it was what I wanted to do with my life and the second time I couldn't have been surer! In my eight years there I worked my way up the ranks to senior supervisor, completed my foundation degree, met my wife and fell out of love with the job. I decided to complete my teacher training, firstly needing to complete my degree. I heard from a friend that Pen Green were offering the BA (Hons) top up and from then no other provider was good enough. Subsequently, I found myself in an unqualified teacher role in the school I attended when I was little.

Assignment extract

Introduction and context

In this assignment I will evaluate a change in my setting through self-reflection, taking into account how to process my feelings and events ethically. I have worked at my local infant school for half an academic year, and although it could be perceived my job description does not allow for leadership, I believe there are ways of being a leader without being at the top of the hierarchy. Recently I had to take on the role of leader supporting both children and staff through several transitions, and it is this change that I would like to explore further.

Ethical considerations

I decided to engage in a reflective account and utilised autoethnography to support these reflections. It has been written that it is easier to research a topic that you are interested in, it feeds a desire to get something from the research, giving it meaning and a purpose (Sanduliak, 2016). Auto-ethnographies are very personal reflections that consider the experiences, thoughts and feelings of the practitioner, which lead to deeper understandings (Sparkes, 2000). I had hoped that this deeper understanding would lead me to findings that would inform my practice later in my career.

Autoethnography is similar to autobiography in the sense the writer talks about themselves, however, autoethnography focuses on the self in context rather than only focusing on the self (Cohen et al, 2018, Denshire, 2014). I have reflected on myself in terms of not just my personal views, feelings and opinions but in the context of my setting. Although my research was reflective, I still had to make ethical decisions, I ensured any notes written about my assignment or reflections were kept safely and made sure they were not accessible to anyone else. I made sure that I did not use people's names in my reflective account, nor did I use any terms that would identify the members of staff in my setting.

Change in the setting

In the middle of the autumn term, the school appointed a newly qualified teacher with little prior experience of leading a class. A term later it became apparent they may have been overwhelmed by their role and decided to take a support position elsewhere in the school. I was approached by the head teacher to replace the teacher by taking on an unqualified teaching role. I implemented changes I knew would benefit the children. Feedback from learning walks conducted by the school's Early Years lead and head teacher was that my influence and leadership meant the children were using the space better and getting more from their time at school, and that I have built a good bond with them and encouraged a culture of respect and community in the classroom.

Analysis

Part of my role as a class teacher is to coach the children "coaching focuses primarily on personal development . . . coaching improves results" (Goleman, 2000:87). He talks about the coaching being leadership style, one that says, "I believe in you, I'm investing in you, I expect your best efforts" (Goleman, 2000:87). In order for me to get the best from the children, I had to get to know them again. Carter (2003) describes this as "coaching as inquiry," used to plan activities, lessons and experiences I knew they would benefit from.

By making changes to the classroom, I felt the children achieved a deeper level of engagement with the provision available. I believe in the notion of the classroom being the third teacher. I am confident "the classroom" is now responsive and available to foster high quality learning for all children, no matter their ability. I have done my best to make the changes exciting and positive for everyone, I ensured change happened slowly for children who do not cope well with change and kept some aspects of the classroom familiar. I feel my actions were just, given the nature of the situation. Raelin (2011) says: "No one knows the practice better than the practitioner who must in relation to others negotiate and arrange the objects of his or her own practice."

I set up a social network group chat for future communications of changes or messages that need to be passed on. "Successful leadership in the early childhood field is a matter of communication more than anything else" (Rodd, 1994:21). I disclosed that I struggled to understand the teaching because I was still learning, an "expression of human solidarity" (Heron, 1976:154). I had to be sure the positive change forces or reasons for change were greater than the negative change forces or reasons not to change. I am also aware there is constant room for improvement, while the first set of changes are fresh, new and exciting, it is important to bear in mind changes may be short lived (Lewin, 1947).

Implications for practice

I have learnt I can adapt my practice and style of leadership to the requirements of a situation, drawing on my knowledge of what has worked in the past in similar situations and what I have learnt from taking part in the study week. I realise the importance of maintaining my own well-being and the link between this and the quality of provision I provide for children. I have to monitor my well-being so I do not become overloaded. With my new role and added responsibilities and the pressures of writing my assignment I have had to ensure my work-life balance has been appropriate, and that I have the "courage to be imperfect" (John, 2019).

I am fully aware of room for improvement in my role both as a teacher and as a leader, however I know I have a team around me who have certain strengths that counterbalance my weaknesses. Ancona et al (2007:92) discuss the "incomplete leader," stating: "no leader is perfect. The best ones don't try to be – they concentrate on honing their strengths and find others who can make up for their limitations."

Ben's reflections on the assignment

One of my favourite things about Pen Green is the study blocks. It is a really valuable time to spend reflecting and analysing your own practice as well as having time to research and share ideas that benefit yourself and the rest of your cohort. Writing this assignment came fairly fluently because the content had already been discussed during the study week and so it was just a matter of pulling the ideas together after the week. It was important for me to be mindful of the children in my class as they had already had a turbulent start to their academic lives. I was the third teacher they had in their five months in school; little did I know they were going to suffer further disruptions due to a global pandemic. Having worked with the children before taking on the role of class teacher meant I had already built strong relationships with the children and knew what they needed from both myself and their classroom environment.

Tutor comments on Ben's work

Ben uses self-reflection to understand the impact of changes to provision he made when asked to teach a class of reception-aged children. Through the reflection process, he unpicks the notion of leaderful practice and how to be mindful of the children's needs alongside those of the adult team members. He was aware that some children would struggle with the change more than others, and this was true of adults too. He expertly interweaves theories with the judicious use of quotations to support his arguments.

Masters' Degree Level 7 assignment extract

Sam Butterwick

Assignment brief

The Master's degree programme does not have a standalone "self as learner" assignment but the process of self-reflection is very much emphasised throughout the course and especially in the Leadership module. Here, students are expected to consider their own role and responsibilities within the notion of leadership, whether they have a designated leadership role or not. This reflection involves students identifying what are the constraints and driving forces for their practice.

The leadership chapter (Chapter 6) explores the notion of leadership within Early Years in greater depth, but it has a relevance here, too, because a proportion of MA students have designated leadership roles or experience leadership as one who is formally "led." Here, Sam applies self-reflection to support her in unravelling aspects of her role as a nursery owner and designated leader. Although initially reluctant to journal, she eventually finds writing in her reflection journal to be a source of comfort, an opportunity to grapple with work dilemmas and to recognise the impact of family history.

Introducing Sam

I am a mother to three children. I am also an owner of a small day nursery in a rural location. My job role involves leading a team of eighteen staff whilst supporting the children and families who attend. My theoretical approach fosters a deep respect for children and staff's emotional well-being and I am influenced by theories of emotional containment (Bion, 1959).

   I found studying for my Master's a pivotal point in my career. Whilst my initial aim of studying was to gain an academic qualification, I found that my Master's became more about my personal journey. At times the process felt therapeutic and as a result I grew holistically. My leadership assignment was met with the most trepidation, feeling that I would be caught out as "not good enough to lead." I felt vulnerable that my leadership skills did not match the stereotypical image of who a leader should be. I was trapped in a state of insecurity. Using reflective journaling as a methodological research tool allowed me to unearth my vulnerabilities and take hold of my life story. Instead of exposing my perceived weaknesses, the process allowed me to feel proud of who I am as a person and gave me the confidence to lead authentically.

Assignment extract

Finding myself – An introduction

I am a mother and a partner. I also own a small day nursery in a rural location, a position I have held for ten years. During my role as owner and manager, my feelings towards leadership have changed. Through the process of reflection (Schön, 1983) I have naturally moved from a "top down" leader who believes that personal issues should be "left at the door," to a leader who understands the need to lead with "authenticity" and "flaneurial" spirit (O'Connell, 2014).

   The focus of this assignment is my leadership journey. I share personal reflections about some of the complexities I face. I have tried to write authentically whilst also understanding the ethical need to protect myself and those around me (BERA, 2018). It is inevitable that my reflections are going to mention others, including members of my family and staff within my team. I have referred to my family as how they are related to me, and staff as their job title to ensure anonymity is maintained.

Using reflecting journaling as a methodological research tool (Robert-Holmes, 2011; Clough & Nutbrown, 2012), I have been able to see my leadership as an ongoing journey that has its roots in childhood (Marshall, 2001; Shamir & Eilam, 2005). Before this I had seen my life in distinct and separate phases. I now understand the importance of allowing my life narratives to flow and how important it is to find the time and space to develop and engage in reflective practices (Schön, 1983; Ruch, 2007; O'Connell, 2014:198). Reflection has allowed me to understand how the phases of my life story interact and how the skills required to lead have developed over time (Pearce, 2013; Shamir & Eilam, 2005; O'Connell, 2014).

I have found self-reflection both powerful and emotional. There have been times when I have needed to write and times when I could not add to my journal. I have found the blank pages as important as the full ones, as it signifies an emotional block, a time that is needed to "just be" and re-visit when I am mentally and emotionally able to. Like Parker (2019:142), I have found comfort in finding other ways to express myself when the words could not be found. In my journal I use the weather to describe and illustrate my feelings. I find thinking about the weather as a metaphor for leadership helps me to make sense of the complexity surrounding my role as a leader.

Leadership theories that have influenced my thinking

Having found myself with supervisory titles early on in my career based on my performance as a childcare practitioner, I identified strongly with Rodd's (1997) work. O'Connell (2014) adds depth to the notion of leadership being a skill that progresses through the development of the "self." She argues that through life and leadership experience, individuals develop cognitive webs of belief – "learning," "reverence," "purpose," "authenticity" and "flaneur." I agree with the notion of life and leadership experiences interacting through lifelong learning (Shamir & Eilam, 2005), and Lambert (2003:423) argues that learning and leading should be understood as "intertwined."

I have been continuously drawn back to the theory of emotional containment (Bion, 1959) and the need to create emotionally safe spaces. Toasland (2007) illustrates parallels between the relationship of mother and baby and professional relationships, and how the process of supervision enables containment. Ruch (2007) adds that settings need to offer "holistic containment" for reflective practice to flourish, and I have come to recognise how a lack of support for leadership development within Early Years has caused barriers in my setting for supervisions to be carried out to a high standard.

My leadership journey – Finding the Rainbow

Throughout my career there have been significant points of change, and I had one of these moments in my study week. During a session with Dr Margy Whalley, we were asked to create our leadership journey on paper. The instructions were open, and we were free to put on paper what we felt was relevant. I felt a little lost and did not know where to start.

Journal extract – 11th February 2019

Today I completed a leadership journey. I started at the beginning but could not find the words, so I drew. My journey started from my first childhood memory of me and my three siblings at our first house. I created the sunshine above the roof, I took a deep breath and I felt happiness. As I continued, I realised that using the weather to describe the times of my life helped me to make sense of my journey.

Figure 2.3 Author's journal extract

My drawing, like the weather, flowed in a cyclical way, and for each stage weather was assigned to illustrate my feelings (see Figure 2.3). Sunshine has been used for happy times, rain for times of uncertainty, thunderstorms for times of loss and rainbows for times of progress.

My journal helped me find my life story (Shamir & Eilam, 2005) and understand how my past interacts with my leadership experience. Shamir and Eilam, (2005) demonstrate how important it is for leaders to understand and interact with their life stories in order to become authentic. Pearce (2013:15) states "every idea you hold passionately has a background in your personal experience." Change experienced in my childhood created a need for me to feel secure, seeing the importance of gaining qualifications and having the ability to support my family independently.

Creating shelter from the rain – The need to create safe spaces

I have come to realise safe spaces are not just about the physicality of a shelter, but also an ethos which is embedded in supportive leadership environments. In my role as a leader, I can become lost and absorbed in putting the children first and I can forget about the adults who are so fundamental to supporting the children. The art of checking in and out (Vaggers, 2010; Parker, 2016) is a well-established practice at Pen Green, and I recall how I felt following my first study week.

Journal extract – 17th October 2017

> At first I brushed off the emotional need to check in and out each day. I felt that this was a waste of time, after all we had work to be getting on with. Today after my final check out I felt the need to drive to work to ask how everyone was. Checking in and out each day had felt so great. How have I missed the need to ask everyone how they are each day?

I remember feeling a plethora of emotions as I felt a sense of containment (Bion, 1959) from my study group. Driving straight to work was highly emotive but a significant act as I realised such an error in my leadership ethos. It had felt so good to have a time to check in and discuss what had happened previously. Each staff member had a story to tell; I needed to find a way for story sharing to happen (Gardner, 1995; Pearce, 2013).

When the thunderstorm strikes: Emotional blocks and mental overload

Journaling allowed me to delve deeper into myself, which in turn enabled me to empathise with the staff team when they find something challenging, either on a personal or a professional level. During this assignment

I had emotional blocks which were times when I just could not write in my journal. I understood the benefits and really wanted to but I just could not write. At these times I felt frustrated and angry, but also scared and alone; the blank pages spoke volumes. I was not ready to write, I was not ready to learn any more, I needed to switch off and re-visit. Mentally I was overloaded.

At work I can be guilty of becoming task orientated. My thought processes become almost military as external pressures to complete tasks build up.

Journal extract – 14th April 2019

I had a phone call from work today when a staff member was identified as needing support and a supervision. I agreed with this and suggested the room leader and manager both support the supervision process. My manager explained the room leader expressed that she felt she could not do it. My first reaction was that she must as it is part of her job. As I reflected, I realised she was just not ready; we must collaborate to get a plan, I must not force.

Within this extract there is an external and internal tension between a task to be completed and the understanding that time for staff development is needed. It was beneficial for me to find empathy and not jump in to try to control the room leader. I could feel my internal and external tensions fighting each other. Ryan (1995) illustrates how adults experience internal tension and display resistance in situations that do not acknowledge their need for self-direction. The room leader showed resistance to a situation she did not feel ready for. I felt tension not being able to control staff. Toasland (2007) illustrates the need for leaders to hold anxiety for staff, cautioning there is "a tightrope walk between managing busy teams and inappropriately allocating staff to overload workers" (:200). It was important to make sure the room leader received the support she needed and ensure my manager and I supported each other.

That evening I reflected on how I felt.

Journal extract – 28th April 2019

I am beginning to see my role as leader differently. My job is not to control the journeys of my staff but to equip them with the skills needed to complete tasks. When staff are not ready to do something, it is not just a reflection of them but also a reflection of the training I offer. I do not equip staff with any leadership skills, I do not give any consideration to supporting leaderful practices, yet I expect staff to lead. This causes tensions, I must do more.

I can see there are gaps in how I prepare and equip staff for leadership. When staff are unable to complete a task, my initial reaction is to try to exert control to get the task done. I have come to realise that this need to control can cause workplace tensions, staff to have mental overload and for their well-being to be crushed. Ryan and Deci (2000), through their Self-Determination Theory, illustrate how excessive control within a work place causes a lack of responsibility and distress.

Sunnier times ahead: Continuous professional development and the need for supervision

Through my studies I have been able to see the link between theory and practice. Before starting this module, I felt a little lost in my role as a leader and had underestimated how much I was containing my emotions (Bion, 1959; Ruch, 2007).

Journal extract – 12th February 2019

> I have found it hard in my role to feel that I am not liked by others and at times I feel vulnerable, but I never show it; I create a persona of strength. I need to open up and allow myself time to explore my emotions which will allow others to access me as a person, not just as a leader. During this morning's discussion someone asked who supervises me? I was silenced. I had not realised that I needed supervision.

Prior to this module I had struggled to understand the need for me to off-load and share my emotions (Ruch, 2007). I had always stuck by the stereotypical vision of leadership which was to remain strong (Lambert, 2003). I have come to realise that strength does not mean not feeling, and that power does not mean to control. My tutorials during this course have been invaluable not only to my studies but as a means of identifying my need to discuss my feelings.

Journal extract – 17th April 2019

> My tutor came to see me today. I could not access the research base, so she home visited; she brought me an orchid. I feel supported and I feel cared for. I feel like I can do this.

From this tutorial I realised how much I needed someone to talk to and it helped me to feel motivated to continue. The tutorial was open, it was individual, and it focused on me; at times it felt therapeutic. Rogers (1957) argues to support individuals certain conditions must exist including "unconditional positive regard," "empathy" and "communication."

Meeting with my tutor, my emotions changed from feeling vulnerable to feeling positive. I realised how beneficial a supportive approach is and how valuable it is to feel listened to. I also realised by not taking time for myself, I ran the risk of burning out, which in turn limits my ability to be there for others (Morrison, 1996). O'Connell (2014) identifies the need for leaders to develop a work–life balance. I now know a good supervision process is not just about supervising others, but it is about us as a team possessing the skills to supervise and mentor each other (Lambert, 2003).

Conclusions – The end of the rainbow

Creating a learning journey enabled me to see myself as a whole. This in turn led me to see my three main roles – as a mother, partner and leader – as overlapping entities that can interact and benefit each other. This connectivity has allowed me to remove the barriers that were causing me to spread myself too thinly in separate and segregated roles. For me it signifies growth in my confidence to find "me," I have let the personal and the professional interact (Elfer, 2007).

I have been able to use weather as a metaphor for describing feelings and emotions. Using "a rainbow of understanding" as a leadership tool creates space for staff and me to view issues as multifaceted (O'Connell, 2014) and find mutual solutions (Lambert, 2003).

Whilst I cannot always prevent turbulent times, I leave my team a promise:

> A rainbow is a promise
> of sunshine after rain
> of calm after storms
> of joy after sadness
> of peace after pain
> of love after loss

Sam's reflection on the assignment

The reflections are honest accounts of how I was feeling at the time. Submitting such personal reflections, I was able to feel for the first time "I am enough." Journaling became a powerful tool in the re-discovering of who I am, and a safe space to organise my thoughts. Journaling continued to impact my studies throughout my dissertation, where I mentored two staff members in their own leadership journeys. It felt powerful to continue to drive forward my passion for emotional containment to be a part of our leadership practice.

Although my studies have ended, journaling is a process which has stayed with me and helped me during times of crisis. The period that followed my Master's was particularly challenging, both personally and professionally. Reflection has helped me to always see the viewpoint of the "other" and continues to allow me to grow as a mother and a leader. I will be forever grateful for the experience I had at Pen Green, and look at my period of study as a time which enabled me, for the first time, to be proud of my authentic self.

Tutor comments on Sam's work

Sam's assignment is highly original and deeply personal. She is able to critically analyse and reflect on her practice as a leader, identifying how her leadership style has developed over time. She writes authentically and displays a degree of vulnerability in unpicking how she has moved away from an autocratic style. Sam is creative in identifying the metaphor of "weather" to help her understand what is happening for her as an adult learner, in her role as a nursery owner and leader. This imagery guides and supports the readers understanding of different incidents within her workplace. Simultaneously she demonstrates a robust theoretical knowledge interweaving concepts concisely, yet accurately, into her writing to enrich her self-reflections.

Conclusion

To summarise, reflective practice is a process of continual questioning, identifying dilemmas and seeking better ways forward. Reflective practice informs future actions and helps you to articulate the reasoning behind why you do what you do. It makes you stronger and supports you to unpick what is happening for children in a range of different contexts. Sometimes reflective practice throws up more questions than answers.

Reflecting on what you want from and for education is important, but it is also critical to establish your ontological and epistemological positions. These may sound like long and complicated words, but they are floating around higher education and take some consideration. Your ontological position will be what you believe to be true, this may be that all children have a right to schooling or that learning through play is possible. It may be that as an adult you are keen on social constructivism and believe people learn best in the company of others. This would then inform your epistemological position, you may believe that knowledge is constructed in communities of learners, and this will then shape how you conduct research and what you are willing to believe is truth.

The notion of reflective practice has been critiqued (Bradbury, et al, 2010) in that there is a perceived limitation when reflections are held by the individual and do not necessarily impact on practice. How reflections are shared is a process where educators need to be mindful of the emotional landscapes of workplaces (John, 2019), the vulnerabilities that can be experienced and frustrations can become barriers to sharing work dilemmas. There is a connectivity between how you perceive yourself as a learner and the learning process. This is a concept that is given time at Pen Green, whatever the level of qualification. To understand young children as learners, in partnership with parents and carers, educators need to be able to articulate their own learning. The theory of andragogy, as described in Chapter 1, is useful here. Adult learners bring experience, theories of life lived, and knowledge and understanding to the learning space. For adults who have been away from formal education, for maybe decades, being in a reflective adult learning space can be challenging as well as exhilarating.

Further reading ideas

Table 2.1 Further reading ideas

Reflective practice	Learning theories	Imposter phenomenon	Nature of inquiry
Schon	Kolb	Clance & Imes	Heron
Raelin (Leaderful)	Mezirow		Reason
Whitaker	Maslow		Marshall
Arnold et al	Vygotsky		Fulwiler
Klein & Bloom (Wisdom)	Knowles		
	Rogers		

References

Ancona, D., Malone, W. M., Orlikowski, W. J., & Senge, P. M. (2007) *In praise of the incomplete leader. Harvard Business Review, 85* (2), pp. 92–100.

Bion, W. R. (1959). Attacks on linking. *The Psychoanalytic Quarterly, 88,* September. pp. 285–300.

Bradbury, H., Frost, N., Kilminster, S., & Zukas, M. (2010). *Beyond reflective practice – New approaches to professional lifelong learning.* Oxon: Routledge.

British Educational Research Association (BERA) (2018) *Ethical guidelines for educational research* (4th edition). London: British Educational Research Association. https://www.bera.ac.uk/researchers-resources/publications/ethical-guidelines-for-educational-research-2018

Bronfenbrenner, U. (1979) *The ecology of human development: Experiments by nature and design.* Massachusetts & London: Harvard University Press.

Carter, M. (2003) *Supervising or coaching – what's the difference?. Childcare Information Exchange,* 5 (03), pp. 20–22.

Clance, P. R. & Imes, S. (1978) The imposter phenomenon in high achieving women: Dynamics and therapeutic intervention. *Psychotherapy Theory, Research and Practice, 15,* 1–8.

Clough, P. & Nutbrown, C (2012) *A student's guide to methodology* (2nd edition). London: Sage.

Cohen, L., Manion, L. & Morrison, K. (2018) *Research methods in education,* (8th edition), New York, Routledge.

David, M. E. (1984) Motherhood and social policy–a matter of education? *Critical Social Policy,* 4 (12), 28–43. doi:10.1177/026101838400401202.

Denshire, S. (2014). *On auto-ethnography. Current Sociology, 62* (6), pp. 831–850.

Elfer, P. (2007) What are nurseries for?, *Early Childhood Research, 5, 2,* pp. 169–188.

Fulwiler, T (1980) Journals across the disciplines. *The English Journal, 69 (9),* pp 14–19.

Gardner, H. (1995) *Leading minds: an anatomy of leadership.* New York: Basic Books.

Gibbs, A. (1997). Focus groups. *Social Research Update, 19 winter.*

Gibbs, G. (1988). *Learning by doing: A guide to teaching and learning methods.* Further Education Unit. Oxford: Oxford Polytechnic.

Gibbs, G. (2019) *Reflective cycle reflection toolkit.* University of Edinburgh. https://www.ed.ac.uk/reflection/reflectors-toolkit/reflecting-on-experience/gibbs-reflective-cycle

Goleman, D. (2000) *Leadership that gets results. Harvard Business Review, 78 (2),* pp. 4–17.

Gundumogula, M. (2020) Importance of focus groups in qualitative research. *International Journal of Humanities and Social Science* (IJHSS), *Centre for Promoting Ideas, 8 (11)* pp. 299–302. https://hal.univ-lorraine.fr/hal-03126126/document

Halej, J. (2017). Ethics in primary research (focus groups, interviews and surveys). Equality Challenge Unit (EEU). https://warwick.ac.uk/fac/cross_fac/ias/schemes/wirl/info/ecu_research_ethics.pdf

Heron, J. (1976) A six-category intervention analysis. *British Journal of Guidance & Counselling, 4 (2),* pp. 143–155.

Hibbert, J. (2019). *The imposter cure.* London: Aster.

hooks, b. (2003) *Teaching community: a pedagogy of hope.* London: Routledge.

John, K. (2019). Holding the baby: leadership that inspires and contains ambition and anxiety. In Whalley, M., John, K., Whitaker, P., Klavins, E., Parker, C. & Vaggers, J. *Democratising leadership in the early years.* London: Routledge.

Kolb, D. A. (1984). *Experiential learning: experience as the source of learning and development.* Englewood Cliffs, N.J.: Prentice-Hall.

Lambert, L. (2003) Leadership redefined: an evocative context for teacher leadership. *School Leadership & Management, 23 (4),* pp. 421–430.

Lewin, K. (1947). Frontiers in group dynamics: Concept, method and reality in social science; social equilibria and social change. *Human Relations (New York), 1 (1),* pp. 5–41.

Marshall, J. (2001) *Self-reflective inquiry practices.* In Reason, P. & Bradbury, H. (eds) *Handbook of Action Research* (2nd edition). London: Sage.

Marshall, J. (2007). *Finding form in writing for action research.* In Reason, P. & Bradbury, H. (eds) *Handbook of Action Research* (2nd edition). London: Sage.

Marshall, J., Coleman, G. & Reason, P. (Eds) (2011). *Leadership for sustainability. an action research approach.* Sheffield: Greenleaf Publishing.

Moon, J. (2013). *Reflection in learning and development.* London: Kogan Page.

Morrison, T. (1996). *Staff Supervision in social care: an action learning approach.* Brighton: Pavilion Publishing.

O'Connell, P. K. (2014) *A simplified framework for 21st century leader development. The Leadership Quarterly, 25,* 183–203.

Parker, C. (2016) *Leadership narratives: A learning community develops a systemic approach to primary school leadership.* Thesis submitted for the degree of Doctor of Philosophy, University of Leicester, School of Medical and Social Care Education.

Parker, C. (2019) We all have the potential to lead because we all have responsibilities. In Whalley, M., John, K., Whitaker, P., Klavins, E., Parker, C. & Vaggers, J. *Democratising leadership in the early years.* London: Routledge. pp. 139–170.

Pearce, T. (2013) *Leading our loud.* San Francisco: Jossey-Bass.

Raelin, J. (2004) Don't bother putting leadership into people. *The Academy of Management Executive, 18 (3).*

Raelin, J. (2011) From leadership-as-practice to leaderful practice. *Leadership, 7 (2),* pp. 195–211.

Robert-Holmes, G. (2011). *Doing your early years research project: a step-by-step guide* (2nd edition). London: Sage.

Rodd, J. (1994) *Leadership in early childhood* (1st edition). Buckingham: Open University Press.

Rodd, J. (1997) Learning to be leaders: perceptions of early childhood professionals about leadership roles and responsibilities. *Early Years: An International Research Journal*, *18 (1)*, pp. 40–46.

Rogers (1957). The necessary and sufficient conditions of therapeutic personality change. *Journal of Consulting Psychology*, *(21)*, pp. 95–103.

Ruch, G. (2007). Reflective practice in contemporary child-care social work: the role of containment. *British Journal of Social Work*, *(37)*, pp. 659–680.

Ryan, R. M. (1995). Psychological needs and the facilitation of integrative processes. *Journal of Personality*, *(63)*, pp. 397–427.

Ryan, R. M. & Deci, E. L. (2000) Intrinsic and extrinsic motivations: classic definitions and new directions. *Contemporary Educational Psychology*, *25*, pp. 54–56.

Sanduliak, A. (2016) Researching the self: the ethics of autoethnographic and aboriginal research methodology. *Studies in Religion/Sciences Religieuses*, *45 (3)*, pp. 360–376.

Schön, D. (1983) *The reflective practitioner: how professionals think in action*. Farnham: Ashgate.

Shamir, B. & Eilam, G. (2005) What's your story? A life-stories approach to authentic leadership development. *The Leadership Quarterly*, *16*, pp. 395–417. www.sciencedirect.com.

Sparkes, A. C. (2000) Autoethnography and narratives of self: reflections on criteria in action. *Sociology of Sport Journal*, *17 (1)*, pp. 21–43.

Toasland, L. (2007) Containing the container: an exploration of the containing role of management in a social work context. *Journal of Social Work Practice*, *21*, *(2)*, pp. 197–202.

Vaggers, J. (2010) *My personal experience of the PhD learning community at Pen Green in transformative dynamics in doctoral studies: disrupting traditional trajectories*, Presentation at EECERA, 03.09.2010.

Whalley, M., John, K., Whitaker, P., Klavins, E., Parker, C., & Vaggers, J. (2019). *Democratising leadership in the early years*. London: Routledge.

Whitaker, P. (1993) *Managing change in schools*. Buckingham: Open University Press.

3 Child study "Children as learners"

Sandra Clare

[In collaboration with Hayley Coleman, Shafia Chowdhury, Lucy Sherman and Katherine Clark]

In this chapter you will find:

- Early Childhood Education pioneers
- Concepts and theories from the Pen Green Centre about children as learners
- Extracts from assignments adopting differing observation techniques and research methods to illustrate what can be learnt from children and their families
- Provocations about contemporary Early Years education.

Why thinking about how children learn matters to adult learners

Early Childhood Studies degrees advocate for social justice by drawing on the knowledge and understanding of the holistic nature of young children's development, well-being, participation and learning, and young children as active participants in the lives and practices of families, societies and cultures (QAA, 2022).

Early childhood is the time during which the most remarkable learning occurs. The evolution of education systems in the UK, and the experiences of children within them, have been profoundly influenced by family income, gender, race and health. The Early Years offers a time to facilitate opportunities for children to make sense of the world around them, in the company of others. The Early Years Foundation Stage (EYFS) (Department for Education, (DfE), 2021) asserts *every* child deserves the best possible start in life, and thanks to the hard work and campaigning of many, it now seems inconceivable that a child would be unable to attend an Early Years setting because of their class, sex, ethnicity or ability.

The socio-political-historical context within which concepts about education, learning and early childhood were developed is important; it is worth noting early western theorists (Froebel, 1968; Pestalozzi, 1912; Rousseau, 1780; Locke, 1968; Piaget, 1950; Vygotsky, 1978) were writing at a time when education was exclusive, mainly for the affluent and mostly for boys. For adults undertaking

DOI: 10.4324/9781003271727-3

further and higher education, it is an essential endeavour to comprehend who was writing and for whom. Consideration should also be given to how ideas have developed over time, and before dismissing seemingly outdated concepts completely, time should be taken to think about what the more recent theories have replaced. Within less than a century, children's access to school, and entitlement to an Early Years education, has improved significantly. Pioneers such as the McMillan sisters (1919), Susan Isaacs (1930) and Robert Owen (1969) were concerned about children growing up in challenging circumstances. They explained the importance of play, the outdoors and relationships in the Early Years, and the potential each has to counter disadvantage.

One view is that children enter this world defenceless beings who rely upon the adults around them in the process of learning what it means to be members of society. An alternative view is children are born into a set of relationships and are therefore not vulnerable. Learners need to understand theories from different fields of study and *how* children are supported in the process of learning. Educational policy, curricula and external expectations are prone to change, but children always learn and develop in their own ways with their own trajectories. The EYFS (DfE, 2021) sets out a flexible framework that supports practitioners in planning a fluid and responsive curriculum, inclusive for all children, reflecting their neighbourhood and community. A solid theoretical understanding of how to watch children learn, and what they need to be in a position to learn, will support graduates to advocate for early childhood education.

Ideas from the Pen Green Centre about how children learn and how this can best be captured

At Pen Green children are recognised as independent learners. Time is spent with parents, staff and adult learners discussing theoretical concepts about early childhood, identifying how these can further understanding of individual children and Early Childhood Education and Care practice more generally. Young children are not empty vessels waiting to be filled, they are powerful thinkers. Children are naturally curious about the world around them and come with their "plans in mind," even if they are not yet able to articulate these plans. Whalley (1994) explains that all children in Early Childhood Education and Care settings should feel strong, in control, able to question and able to choose.

Environments need to be emotionally warm where adults are thinking carefully about each child and responding flexibly. An understanding of children's social and emotional worlds is critical. Within settings and schools many "wellbeing assessments" rely on the subjectivity of adults, or children themselves (Emery, 2020). At Pen Green and for adult learners through research assignments, those caring for children are encouraged to adopt a broader set of ways to evaluate how children may be feeling. Practitioners have made adaptations to approaches such as the Bick method (1964), a form of non-participant observation which involves the Practitioner (the observer) to "be present" and become aware of the feelings evoked in themselves as observers. The observation is carried out, with no notes taken and then as soon as possible after the observation the observer writes up their narrative account. The focus is not on "happiness" but on how children display a full range of emotions that are indicative of the context and scenario. The observation also includes the description of the personal feelings evoked for the observer. This method of observation can give insight into the child's emotional world and provide an opportunity for practitioners to develop his or her own internal reflective space (Ringer, 2002:231) and reflect on a child's whole experience in the setting.

Staff at Pen Green are encouraged to slow down their pedagogy, not rushing children inappropriately or cutting across their play. Children need time to revisit experiences, experienced staff and well-informed parents afford them time to consolidate and apply their ideas and develop their learning. The youngest children require variable resources within environments supportive of the notion that children are born explorers, scientists and academics.

It is unhelpful to define children by their ability or assessed levels of development; it is important to *know* individual children and nurture their individuality, being courageous and aspirational and encouraging them to be all that they can be. In New Zealand Early Years settings use the questions proposed by Margaret Carr and her colleagues. The questions are used to shape reflections on how well known, related to and understood children are.

- Do you know me?
- Do you hear me?
- Can I trust you?
- Is this place fair for me?
- Do you let me fly?

(Carr et al, 2002).

At Pen Green the underpinning theoretical concepts (Schema (Athey, 2007; Arnold, 2010), Involvement (Laevers, 2011), Well-Being (Laevers, 2011) and Adult Pedagogic Strategies (Whalley & Arnold, 1997; Lawrence & Gallagher, 2015)) are shared with staff and parents creating a shared language through which individual children's development can be thought about. These same concepts are also shared with Further Education and Higher Education learners, and through writing assignments the adult learners have a chance to try out sharing and applying them in their own settings.

Many years ago, at Pen Green, the team conceptualised The Pen Green Loop (Figure 3.1). This was devised to illustrate a way of honouring the contribution of the child's learning in the setting and their home learning. At Pen Green the staff closely observe children in the Centre to see what interests and motivates them. Parents and carers are also asked to closely observe their children at home and see what interests and motivates them there. The parents, carers and staff develop a reciprocal exchange of information.

When considering the exchange of information between parents and staff, we have been influenced by the work of Patrick Easen et al (1992), who

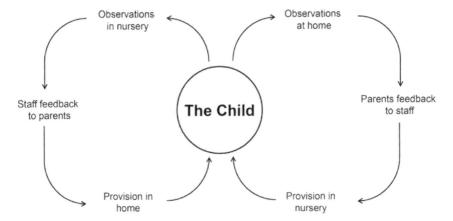

Figure 3.1 The Pen Green Loop

describe practitioners as having expert knowledge of the "public" theories of child development, while parents and carers have "personal" theories about the development of their child. It is the interaction between both theories that produces a far deeper understanding of what intrinsically motivates the child and how best to plan a unique and responsive curriculum that will excite and challenge them within the nursery and the home.

All children deserve to have an advocate who will champion their wants, needs and rights. In 2014 staff from our Special Educational Needs and Disability (SEND) team joined other professionals from around the UK to develop a celebratory assessment tool for children with special educational needs and/ or disability (Prodger & Smith, 2018). Following the recent EYFS reforms (DfE, 2021), this was subsequently updated (Prodger & Devine, 2021). The principles outlined below are reflective of fundamental principles about the role of assessment for all children.

1   Assessment must honour both the child and their family.
2   Every child's progress should be demonstrated and celebrated and that, where possible, the assessment process adopted should be applicable to all children.
3   The voice of the child must be represented clearly and must inform and remain central to any assessment.
4   The voice of the family must be represented clearly and where appropriate the voice of peers and siblings should also be heard.
5   Assessment is done in collaboration with, rather than to, the family, and that it reflects their views and comments.
6   Assessment is accessible and can be understood by the family.
7   Assessment celebrates achievement rather than identifies "underachievement" and that its language and style of presentation stays true to this principle.

8   Assessment process offers a powerful means of identifying how the child can be best supported in their development and learning. This may be done through the consideration of next steps or "Possible Lines of Direction" for an individual child.

9   Assessment provides insight and information that can be understood and used by others including external agencies and schools to which children may transfer.

10 As the Rochford Review states, "Equality is not always about inclusion. Sometimes equality is about altering the approach according to the needs of the child" (Prodger & Devine, 2021:11).

A former Pen Green tutor and current colleague Cath Arnold (2015) stated that those who know how to observe children can withstand any imposed changes to curricula. Those caring for children learn, through observation *and trusting their own practice wisdom*, what it is that captures their interest. The EYFS (DfE, 2021) encourages the use of professional judgement, building on a deep understanding of each unique child. It is not necessary for all observations to be written or recorded. It is, however, important for staff to invest time in carefully watching and sensitively noticing the children around them, what they are curious about and intrinsically motivated by. The environment, resources and relationships available to children needs to be the best possible for each and *every child*, each and *every day*.

A child study at Pen Green

At Pen Green, the adult learners engaging in Further Education and Higher Education courses participate in studies with, about or for babies and young children. The use of a child study offers a chance for the learners to engage in using different observation techniques and apply theoretical concepts. There are also practice-based assignments which involve presentations of legal responsibilities or international curricula to deepen understanding of social policy and how it impacts the lives of young children on both a local and global scale.

Learners are encouraged to unpick the ethical implications of studies involving children, over and above the university requirements to "do no harm." Bertram et al (2015) remind us, all participants in the research process need to be viewed as subjects, not objects. For a child to be studied, consent needs to be sought from their parent or carer who needs to be fully informed about the purpose and potential reach of the research. Parents and carers need to understand the right to withdraw, and that withdrawal from research will not affect their experiences, the experiences of the children in their setting or the service through which the adult learner knows them.

Learners also need to ensure they have "informed" and "ongoing" consent from the child. Sometimes referred to as assent. Ensuring a child has given their consent relies on the adult learner's understanding of what is age appropriate and what consent may look like for an individual child. For example, babies that turn their head away or children who run and hide when being filmed may be conveying a message that they do not want to be filmed. These actions of the young children, as research participants, must be taken seriously.

Anonymity is an essential tenant of research and as many assignments encourage the use of photography or filming; this also needs careful consideration, the modification of pictures of children feels disrespectful and as such learners are asked to be explicit in the seeking of consent of the potential reach of the images gathered. Similarly, assigning a number or letter to replace the child's name inhibits the flow of beautifully rich stories about children and their learning and is largely discouraged. As Arnold (2015) states, a far more authentic way to write about children is to adopt a pseudonym, and to provide the family with a copy using their child's real name. (For further information on Practitioner Research see Chapter 5.)

The purpose of this chapter is to consider why we need to know about how children learn, why we need to understand the context within which children are learning and how this can inform ongoing practice. The work of the adult learners featured here takes account of the totality of childhood and how learning is experienced within the lived life. The assignment extracts included cover a range of topics including play, parental involvement, home learning environments, emotions, communication and physical, cognitive and social development.

Foundation Degree (Year 1) Level 4 assignment extract

Hayley Coleman

Assignment brief

Adult learners observe a child, looking at "lines of enquiry" over a three-week period in a setting or their home. They need to know and understand about their own beliefs and articulate their knowledge of child development theories, identifying strengths and areas for development.

Introducing Hayley

I am an Improvement Adviser, based in my local authority's Early Years Learning team. I wanted to further myself, learn new skills and add extra strengths to my practice wisdom to offer more to the professionals I support. As well as my advisory role, I worked part-time as a private nanny during my studies. The hands-on practice was invaluable and enabled me to approach the foundation degree from two perspectives. I could draw upon my experiences of supporting Early Years settings with their professional development, alongside the experiences of being an Early Years practitioner and collaborating with parents.

Assignment extract

Introduction

This assignment was a child study of Annabelle whom I privately nanny for. I observed her; *noticing* what she was interested in, *recognising* what she might be learning and *responding* by considering how I could plan future opportunities for her (Carr, 2001).

Methodology

I undertook three observations, employing the use of written narratives, video recordings and photographs. Videos are particularly useful being multimodal and offering the ability to relook at interactions, noticing subtle gestures, movement and language. Learning Stories (Carr, 2001) were developed addressed to Annabelle; I had never used these before but found it ensured my observations were personal.

Ethics

I prepared specific consent forms explaining the purpose of the study and about anonymity and confidentiality. Videos and photographs were taken using a password-protected smartphone and stored on a secure laptop.

Anonymity is difficult to achieve when photographs are included within the assignment, however, Annabelle is a pseudonym her mother chose, and Annabelle's parents have a copy of this assignment using her real name.

Learning story

I care for Annabelle, aged 3 years 6 months, in her own home, one day a week. She attends pre-school two days per week. I am friends with Annabelle's mother; we have a strong bond, like that of a Key Person (Elfer et al, 2012) sharing a special kind of relationship.

I have applied schema (Athey, 2007), well-being and involvement (Laevers, 2011) theories to explain and understand elements of Annabelle's play.

The first observation of Annabelle was walking to the park. She noticed my hair and described it as "like Elsa's" (from the Disney movie *Frozen*) and "yellow." She continued to talk about hair the whole time at the park.

The second observation we "played hair" with dolls, brushes, clips and bobbles. She concentrated for around 30 minutes, then autonomously decided to use hair bits to make floor art, initially explaining she was "making a triangle," then changing it to "a heart" when one of the lines went wonky.

The third observation involved the construction of a marble run, then repeated efforts of getting different sized marbles and balls to complete the course. She moved on to building a tower from blocks, getting the structure as high as possible until all the blocks were used.

Having completed the observations, I noticed Annabelle's fascination with "trajectory." She first noticed and commented on my long hair. That interest revealed itself again when she made lines with her hair accessories and also the lines made with the marble run and vertical tower. It is clear that both the figurative and dynamic aspects (Athey, 2007), of trajectory were being explored from the static art and tower, to the balls moving along the run.

From the initial observation of Annabelle's interest in hair, I expected the movement of brushing hair, or plaiting for example, to be the intrinsic motivation. I was not expecting "connecting" and "positioning" to be seen as repeated patterns of play. Brushing hair or styling was not enjoyed for long, it was the function of adding clips, hairbands and bobbles to hair that was relished. Arnold (2015:86) explains:

> Play can be initiated by a child or an adult, but adults need to bear in mind that every player has his or her own personal play agenda (which he/she may not be aware of), and to respect this by not insisting that the adult agenda should dominate the play.

Seriation was frequently explored as Annabelle sorted hairclips by colour, when she assembled all the flower parts together for the marble run scene and also when grouping the marbles and balls by size. Arnold (2003:100) explains seriation play as children noticing the similarities and differences between objects, helping them to understand numbers and related subjects.

Observing Annabelle led me to identify particular patterns of play and, in turn, offer activities that may interest her. Some people may not see the benefit or learning opportunities that arise with "hair play," however, I believe in allowing and encouraging the child to lead: Arnold (2015:22) says:

> I wonder how often, as parents and workers, we ignore children's interests in favour of something we consider more worthwhile. Part of behaving ethically is to listen to children and understand what is of concern or interest to them.

Reflection and implications for practice

Undertaking this series of observations allowed me to analyse how to encourage innate creativity, playfulness and the urge to have a go. Watching

Annabelle strategising and persevering taught me much about the role I play in enabling "deep level learning" (Laevers, 2015) to occur.

I reflected that I had been missing opportunities to support Annabelle's schemas outdoors. Conscious of this, we have since enjoyed activities that do, all enjoyed with the same enthusiasm as indoors but with the benefit of play on a bigger scale, encouraging larger motor skills and developing Annabelle's physicality. Learning Stories (Carr, 2001) are a method of observing I will continue to use. Feedback from Annabelle's parents confirmed that they valued the personal nature of the records and that they would be lovely mementos to keep and one day look back on together.

Hayley's reflections on the assignment

Although I have been in the Early Years sector for 18 years, I have learned a great deal whilst studying. I have developed confidence personally and professionally, and by regularly drawing on reflective practice at work, I am able to better understand my own strengths and development needs.

Tutor's comments on Hayley's work

Hayley has explained her role and demonstrated her understanding of the differences of her professional responsibilities dependent on the different roles. She demonstrates a real curiosity about Annabelle's learning as an educator and makes good use of theories introduced in the study weeks to analyse her observations. She communicates well her appreciation of play, and how it is through play that children develop a sense of who they are, what they know, what they are curious about and who they can learn what from. In illustrating how her own learning has shifted, we can glean an understanding of how practice in her dual roles will shift.

Foundation Degree (Year 2) Level 5 assignment extract

Shafia Chowdhury

Assignment brief

At Level 5 students can choose to design their own practitioner research study, and many conduct research with a focus on children's learning. This extract is a research project designed by Shafia to explore how Bangladeshi families facilitate learning at home.

Introducing Shafia

I am a Bangladeshi women born in 1975 in the UK, the youngest of five. My father came as an economic migrant, once settled brought my mother and eldest sister to join him. He worked in the textile industry while my mother stayed at home.

English was not my parents' first language; my dad was able to get by, but my mother spoke no English. As a result, I attended a language school. My earliest recollection of schooling was fighting against the force of the rain and wind whilst being held by my mother's hand while walking very briskly up a road.

The first school I attended predominantly had Asian pupils. Three of my siblings attended a different school "bussing" out of the area. I also attended summer playschemes where I was cashier for the sweet shop and banked money on a weekly basis at the book club which allowed me to purchase a book at the end of each month. My parents never read to me; however, I loved reading and would also use my pocket money to buy second-hand books.

When attending middle school, I had a blue table where I would sit to do my homework. My mum did not need to tell me to do my home-work, this was a natural routine for me. I attended any afterschool clubs I was able to and was average academically. As my parents did not speak or write English, I filled in my own Upper School application.

I completed my GCSE and started to do my A-Levels. However, after my first year, I left school to undergo an arranged marriage abroad. Due to Immigration criteria, I needed to work so I undertook various roles within community development and in a nursery where I promoted play in the home, mainly with Bangladeshi families due to my language skills.

At the age of 21, I had my first child and have since had two more children. I always bought new books and encouraged any form of learn-ing within the home. My hunger for learning was always within me, and when I was talking to a colleague about wanting to do a degree, she pro-vided me with the details of Pen Green. At the age of 45 I enrolled. My children and family have always been at the forefront, and my learning was on the back burner. It has taken me over 20 years to complete a degree.

Assignment extract

Introduction

This assignment explores the thoughts, attitudes and experiences of home learning within the Early Years in Bangladeshi families. I wanted to explore why some parents support their children's learning more than others, within the home environment and explore the structural barriers faced by families.

Literature review

The Department for Education (DfE, 2021) sets guidelines for the Early Years' Foundation Stages (EYFS) "in learning, development and care," while the Education Act 1996 stipulates education is compulsory over five years, but having worked as an Early Years' practitioner, I know it is important for children to expand and explore all aspects of learning prior to coming into an educational establishment. Home learning compliments the curriculum and provides children with a better start.

Learning through play is crucial for positive, healthy development, regardless of a child's situation but "cross cultural evidence" is needed to obtain a greater understanding of different cultures, indeed, I found little research into the thoughts, attitudes and experiences of home learning for young children from a Bangladeshi heritage.

Methodology

A qualitative methodology was applied. The process provided a useful ingress as it permitted valuable data to be obtained. Participants needed to be of Bangladeshi heritage with a child(ren) of pre-school age. A purposive sampling provided a "deliberate choice of a participant." A total of five interviews were carried out in family homes, lasting 60 to 90 minutes. Each was transcribed and themes identified.

Data were gathered through face-to-face, semi-structured interviews providing a chance to delve deeper. Ellis (2007:14) describes this as "back-and-forth movement between experiencing" and enabled me to see through "the lens" (Ravitch & Riggan, 2017) of the participants.

Ethics

Arnold (2015) suggests "anyone participating in research should understand, at the outset, what the research is about, what their involvement is likely to be." I spoke to participants and followed this up with an email outlining the aims and objectives of the research, giving them time to digest the information before committing. University ethics forms formalised their written consent.

Participants were made aware they had the right to skip any questions or withdraw from taking part at any time and their values and beliefs respected and their knowledge not overridden.

Findings and analysis

As an Early Year's Practitioner, I noticed children with parents who do not speak English as their first language (EAL) are disadvantaged when starting nursery, but that parents valued their child(ren)'s education, wanted better for their child(ren) and encouraged some level of home learning, regardless of their own childhood experiences.

All five participants agreed that home learning gave their children a head start and better prospects in life. Blanden (2006) and Harris and Goodall (2008) recognise the importance of parental interest in children's education and the positive difference this can make. All participants were depending on better outcomes for their child(ren) through their engagement with the home environment but three had no previous experience of learning through play. Comments included (home learning) "increases their prospects and gives them a better chance at life in general," "helps them in their understanding of the world" and "gives them a head start, be curious and give them the confidence." All participants were second- or third-generation Bangladeshi, born and educated in the United Kingdom. Three were educated to degree level and two had A-Levels. Blanden (2006:15) noted a link between parental education and their children's attainment. Interestingly, three participants stated they had no or very little support themselves as children. However, all participants wanted to ensure the environment and experiences their child(ren) had within the home were educational, including "Just playing with my child," "reading to them using Arabic and English."

What became apparent was how situational barriers contributed to physical barriers. These varied amongst participants and included work commitments, financial difficulties and tantrums. A couple commented they preferred learning to be done within school but agreed parents played a vital role and wanted to support their child(ren) through whatever means they had access to, irrespective of their limitations.

Conclusion and implication for practice

The research provided an opportunity to explore a small group of Bangladeshi families' views and experiences around home learning. It would be interesting to conduct further research to see if some of these values are inherited and interlinked, particularly with children whose parents are first generation migrants. The research demonstrated Bangladeshi parents' attitudes and values towards children's learning are shifting from those experienced by myself and the participants when we were young children.

Shafia's reflections on the assignment

I have always had an empathetic attitude, and the last two years has seen me apply the theories I have learnt whilst studying. My lived experience of being a child, mother and grandmother means I can personalise my practices. Looking back, I would have relied on "tick box" assessments, but the learning has provided me the opportunity to be more adaptable and creative. When engaging with a family, I have a deeper understanding of the issues faced and have a bigger picture of the situation.

I worked with a child recently who did not have a proper bedroom. I applied for funding to provide the practicalities. She mentioned she would love a library in her bedroom, and I would have done anything to get her plenty of books, just like I had wanted, and now knew were vital.

I think deep down I know I never really got to fulfil my educational curiosities, hence the hunger for learning within me. I have always enrolled on training courses or taken opportunities for extra learning but desperately wanted to complete a degree of my own. I have totally enjoyed the degree. I have not always had the highest marks, but the journey is what I have actually fully enjoyed. If I feel disappointed in myself, I do have to try and remind myself I am a mature person who came back into education, not having really studied for 24 years. I appreciate the learning, the papers read, the conversations had and the weeks being together. Studying keeps my brain ticking and maybe in some way I am going back to my childhood. I am not sure what I will do next but just love learning.

Tutor's comments on Shafia's work

This work is very personal and authentic. Shafia has capitalised on her own unique experiences to unpick the circumstances within which children are learning in her community. She recognises the value of the home learning environment and the significant role that parents play in nurturing and developing their children as learners. She highlights a lack of literature and guidance about working with multi-lingual learners (Parker, 2019). Research has consistently found children who speak more than one language tend to score lower in standardised testing but exhibit advantages on metalinguistic or non-verbal processing tasks compared to monolingual peers (Friesen & Bialystok, 2012). One of the most exciting aspects of reading students' work is when they problematise further. Shafia has critically explored research and practice and poses some interesting questions at the end for future research.

Bachelor's Top-up Degree Level 6 assignment extract

Lucy Sherman

Assignment brief

At Level 6 students are asked to conduct a child study to explore a child's emotional world. They need to demonstrate their understanding of how relationships in the Early Years impact children's learning and their social and emotional development. This includes exploring the child's close relationships at home, or within a setting, working collaboratively with parents, colleagues or professionals from other agencies.

Introducing Lucy

I am a Childminder and a mother to an amazing daughter. On leaving school I went straight to college to study the Level 3 Early Years Educator and realised my passion was working with the youngest children, I particularly enjoyed spending time in the baby rooms. Having worked in a range of Early Years settings and doing my own studies, I began to realise the best way to achieve this for me was to set up my own business as a Childminder. So just as the world started to return to work after Covid-19, I was anxiously waiting my Ofsted registration visit. Last year I celebrated one year in business, a first-class BA (Hons) and being asked to publish a summary of my work.

Assignment extract

Introduction

I have eight years' experience working with children and have recently taken on a new role as a Childminder, focusing on a home-from-home environment which supports the individual learning, care and emotional needs of all children.

Methodology

I completed a child study to gain a better understanding of the emotional world of a child attending my setting using an adaptation of the Bick method of observation (Bick, 1964). The observations show reoccurring themes; strong relationships within the setting and schematic play (Arnold, 2010).

Due to Covid-19 restrictions I was unable to collect face-to-face data outside of work, so I studied a child in my setting and ensured all dialogue with parents was conducted by email to limit face-to-face interactions.

Case study

The Bick (1964) method involves unobtrusive observation, taking no notes, videos or photos during the time of observation. I then wrote what I remembered, including emotions evoked. I completed six ten-minute video observations over a three-week period.

Ethical considerations

As a practitioner I ensure children are respected and have their voices heard. Mukherji and Albon (2015:53) state, "early childhood research raises particular ethical issues owing to the age and vulnerability of young children, but at the same time young children should be viewed as competent." Arnold (2015) talks about assent where a child can only give permission in the moment, during observations there were periods of time where Lesley (pseudonyms used throughout) displayed discomfort, so I listened to her wishes and stopped observing.

All work is anonymised, and confidentiality maintained. As I am a Childminder, my own child is mentioned throughout my work, so I gained permission from her father and ensured he fully understands "Daisy's" participation.

Context of child and family

Lesley joined my setting full time from September 2020 and is 16 months old at the time of study (November 2020). She lives with both her parents and four older siblings. Lesley's mother was a Childminder herself, so Lesley was used to being home and socialised with other children. I have regular conversations with Lesley's mother to discuss her play at home. Lesley enjoys covering babies with blankets and putting on adults' shoes. Lesley's mother believes she plays through an enveloping schema (Athey, 2007) at home, not just in the setting.

Summary of observations

Observation one - morning

Lesley imitated Daisy by laughing and copying facial expressions. She made attempts to join in with Daisy's play by dropping toys on the floor and following Daisy through the tunnel. Throughout the ten minutes of observation, Lesley regularly checked back with me and looked for a reaction as she played. She returned to me for help, seeking reassurance as another child took a toy.

Observation two - afternoon

Lesley spent most of her time trying to gain my attention, she sat on my lap periodically, giving lots of eye contact, smiles and giggles. She used a scarf to cover her face as an attempt to play "peekaboo" and then began to seek my attention in more negative ways. She took a toy from Daisy to gain her attention, Daisy began to cry and she quickly returned the toy giving her a cuddle.

Observation three – morning

Lesley was independently exploring books, seeking lift the flap books. She would frequently check back with me by bringing a book and placing it in my lap. Lesley realised I was not going to interact, so she took the book over to Daisy who looked at the pictures with her. Daisy soon shifted her attention away from Lesley, causing Lesley to seek my attention by emptying the paper bin.

Lesley was confident and displayed a good relationship with Daisy. Lesley would often use her sleeve to cover her hands during the times where she struggled to gain any attention.

Observation four - afternoon

Lesley played with a variety of toys on offer, which Daisy tried to take away from her, she followed Daisy but did not attempt to take the toys back, so I stepped in to help. I found it hard to just sit back and allow Daisy to take toys from her friends.

Lesley continued to follow Daisy, joining in and copying her play. Daisy was very emotional and seemed uneasy about sharing. Lesley responded to this by offering cuddles to Daisy and calling her name. The lack of positive interaction with Daisy led Lesley to initiate play with me, and at this point I stopped the observation to ensure she did not become unhappy.

Observation five - afternoon

Lesley noticed two children playing together with the work bench and approached them to join in. She struggled to join in as they were busy together, so moved onto exploring the musical instruments. During this time, Lesley looked to me for interaction, smiling and playing peekaboo behind the play shop. She quickly noticed when Daisy was playing alone so joined in and sat with her.

Lesley spent the majority of this ten minutes playing independently although regularly checking back to me for reassurance. She tried to climb the sofa but struggled and turned to me for help. When I did not respond to her, she then pointed to Daisy who helped Lesley to get onto the sofa.

Observation six – morning

Lesley was alone for a short period of time during this observation. She looked to me to share experiences which meant it was difficult for me to remain unobtrusive. Lesley was really playful and interacted using a lot of positive facial expressions. Once Daisy returned, Lesley went to help her to build a tower with the tree blocks. They balanced the blocks one at a time until Lesley knocked them down.

Key themes

I identified three themes; Lesley "checks in" with me throughout all six observations. She looks back for reassurance when joining a new activity and often comes over to sit on my lap. Lesley also attempts to gain my attention in a variety of ways, beginning with positive interactions before moving onto negative ones, which she knows I will respond to.

The second key theme is that Lesley seems to have a strong, playful relationship with Daisy which is shown across all six observations. She seeks Daisy to join in with her play, copies her actions and seems lost when Daisy leaves the room.

The third theme which runs throughout three of the six observations is that Lesley explores through an enveloping schema (Arnold, 2003). She covers toys and uses blankets to cover her face. I noticed that the schema is only present in the observations taken in the morning.

Literature and analysis

I considered literature which supports my findings. Companionship (Trevarthen, 2001) discusses the importance of social interaction for children's learning and children's need to form trusting and fun relationships with adults and other children. Vygotsky (1986) expressed that children need social interaction from a community of people to support their cognitive development, and that children are able to learn their own values and beliefs by collaborating. Roberts (2011) has since developed "companionable learning" principles.

First key theme – relationship with me

Throughout all observations, Lesley used strategies to try to encourage me to interact and play. She would initiate games of "peekaboo," sit on my lap and pass me books and toys to play. Trevarthen (2001) states, "education of the young that fosters enthusiastic learning will be collaborative. . . it should grow in consistent relationships of trust and liking." I believe Trevarthen (2001) is expressing the importance of a trusting relationship and positive social interactions on a child's learning. Lesley always seemed settled and eager to explore the environment; maybe this is due to having multiple companionable relationships within the setting. Although Lesley was happy to explore the setting independently or with peers, she would regularly look back for reassurance.

Second key theme – relationship with Daisy

When observing Lesley's interactions with Daisy, I felt they too were displaying a companionable relationship (Trevarthen, 2001). Lesley would seek Daisy to share activities or experiences when I was occupied with the observations. Lesley was actively seeking Daisy to observe and join in with her play, she would follow the interests of Daisy and display enjoyment in socialising.

Trevarthen (2001) discusses the importance of children needing a community of people with a range of ages to meet their social needs. Lesley was able to seek a companionable relationship with me, however, when I was unavailable, she was happy to seek that relationship elsewhere. Roberts (2011) expresses the importance of children playing together and explains that it gives children an opportunity to discover a sense of themselves.

Third key theme – schemas and emotion

Observing Lesley sparked an interest as I was able to see her play and explore through an enveloping schema (Arnold, 2010), which involves children covering up themselves or objects. As I pulled together the key themes, I noticed her schema was only present during the morning, following being dropped off. Often Lesley would find a blanket and cover her face or would select a lift-the-flap book and repeatedly open and close them. In addition, Lesley played peekaboo and hid toys behind her back frequently; I wonder if this is Lesley's way of processing how her parents go but will return. I also noticed in some observations, during times where Lesley struggled to find social interaction, she would use her sleeve to cover her hands; this could also be a link to enveloping (Arnold, 2010) and processing her emotions.

Reflection and implications for practice

Reflecting on the observation and the emotional world of Lesley, I have found the process highly interesting. Lesley seems to have strong, companionable relationships (Trevarthen, 2001; Roberts, 2011) which could be helping her to settle quickly and explore her emotions through schematic play (Arnold, 2010). Reflecting on my own emotions, I realised this offered me reassurance as I felt relaxed knowing she felt comfortable with me.

Although I found the Bick (1964) method useful, I found it challenging as a lone worker. I struggled being fully unobtrusive as children needed me during the observations. I found it hard not to interact and felt necessary to do so on some occasions. Following this study, I am hoping to complete an observation on each child attending my setting, so I can gain a better understanding on their emotional world. I am hoping to use my knowledge to ensure I am planning and providing activities and resources that encourage children to explore their emotions.

Lucy's reflections on the assignment

I was really surprised by how much I took in from this assignment and how much detail I could recall from the observations. My understanding about the relationships that were emerging and the children's responses to each other was so thought provoking. I was able to really understand the complexity of the relationships that were developing, which in turn supported me to know how best to respond to the children. I still use the techniques we used during this assignment, especially when new children join us, as it enables me to watch and allows me a little insight into their emotional worlds. The challenge of being a lone worker still exists, although as I have got better at using the Bick method, I find it easier to manage.

Tutor's comments on the assignment

Lucy has written a very accessible narrative about her practice; she does not shy away from the closeness of her relationships with the child in the study and is humble in her ideas for future development. She demonstrates a commitment to equal rights and her ethical considerations are clearly guided by appropriate reading, particularly around child assent. This research illustrates how naturalistic observations of children can illuminate the luxury of learning and offer an insight into a child's emotional world, rather than being directed by learning outcomes, or cutting across play. Lucy is able to demonstrate how she uses the literature to support her understanding and is able to show a deep appreciation of the texts used. She has finished with further lines of possible inquiry which reflect the depth of her emerging understanding.

Master's Degree (Level 7) assignment extract

Katherine Clark

Assignment brief

At Level 7 the first assignment expects students to develop a deep understanding of early development and learning, considering their own unique context and then making links to ideas from pioneers in early childhood, current research, curricula and national policy.

Introducing Kat

I completed the Level 2, Level 3, Foundation Degree, BA (hons) and Master's with Pen Green. I had wanted to widen my experiences and study with a different organisation for my Master's, but after exploring various courses across the country and online found none offered the balance of support and experiential learning I had grown to enjoy at Pen Green. When I started the Master's, I had just begun working full time as an Early Years Tutor. I studied during Covid-19, meaning year one started face to face then moved online, year two was fully online, and the dissertation days were blended between both teaching methods. I leant heavily on my husband, mum, and older sister for support. I was determined to relax into learning and enjoy the journey. I worked hard to push aside concerns about being good enough or getting high grades and "trusted the process." This assignment was by far my favourite, because it meant I had the wonderful opportunity to celebrate a person I love deeply.

Assignment extract

Introduction

This research explored how parents careful tending of their child influenced learning and development. I created a child study using observations of my nephew George, alongside his parent's reflections and my own. George and his parents, Emma and Craig, were considered collaborators in the research, rather than participants. I teased out my values and beliefs, presenting my understanding of "true" learning. I worked closely with Emma and Craig because of their ability to understand the significance of the seemingly little moments and how these were telling the story of his childhood experiences.

Values and beliefs

I believe there are two key influences on children's learning and development, early relationships and parental involvement. Winnicott (1964) suggested infants cannot be considered in isolation. He pointed to the "gradual building up of the self" (1964:181), as the physical and emotional dependence infants had on carers to survive. Stern (2003) also considered links between mother-infant attachment dyads and developmental progression. He summarised a child's sense of self is constructed through internalising external experiences and, that early relationships are key to this lifelong process. These ideas became the foundation of this research, and my findings.

Ethics

I felt honoured to understand more about George's internal world, learning and development. To ensure this was evident throughout my work, I went about research with care, respect and gratefulness. I have shared information authentically and held onto Palaiologou's (2014) consideration of layers of ethical praxis to avoid tokenistic participation, following her advice to seek out methods that truly reflect young collaborators. The principles of this praxis and fluidity of ethical layers were evident throughout my study and remained at the forefront of my mind.

The firm marriage between ethics and methodology was central to my actions. I was deeply committed to ensuring I enabled collaborators the dignity, respect and autonomy owed to them. I was aware this research created potential shifts for those involved and, while ever mindful of "doing no harm" (Arnold, 2012:3), I attempted to do some good. George and his parents were keen to engage in this study and saw an exciting opportunity to understand him.

Methodology and methods

My ethical stance, professional heritage, George's context and our relationship guided my methodology. The research took a naturalistic approach (Isaacs, 1933) conveying experiences authentically was crucial to me and his parents.

An outline of methods used were:

- Journal notes (Arnold, 2007) to record time spent with George and reflective dialogues between me and his parents
- Tavistock Observation Method (Bick 1964) to gather a sense of his emotional development and personal curiosities
- Video observations (Arnold, 2015) to understand more about George's actions and motivations
- Narrative observations (Isaacs, 1930) to record detailed accounts of his explorations.

All data were collected over ten days, to ensure this was a "snapshot" of his world and represented a moment in time. The findings were presented in chronological order. Stake (2000) refers to intrinsic case studies as research that may not influence theory or give light to abstract constructs but is interesting for its own merit. My research may lack objectivity but was rich with partnership and deeply worthy in its own right. This process created a distinction between belief or opinion of George's learning and of the systematic process for understanding it.

George

George is five years old. He was born early at 31 weeks and four days, weighing three pounds. Tiny and fragile, he spent his first Christmas in the special care baby unit. Our whole family held its breath while waiting for him to grow strong. As George grew stronger, we had a collective slow exhale, he is now a bouncy little boy. He is wilful, funny and full of energy, and I love being with him.

Analysis

Two themes emerged; George was invested in relationships with others, and had a strong interest in mathematics, manifesting through schematic enquiries (Arnold, 2010). Piaget (1956) identified schemas as a cognitive process whereby repeating patterns within play formulates learning. George appeared driven to explore a cluster of schemas – connection, disconnection and trajectory lines (Arnold, 2010). Emma was keen to know "what he is really like in school" and Craig was interested in George's learning. The correlation between George's curiosities about relationships and schematic play appeared to mirror each of his parent's interests. I was curious about layers of learning; how his internal self-construct was fundamental to the cognitive learning acquired through schematic explorations (Arnold, 2010).

Observation one

In observation one, George had made paperchains at school and carefully carried one home. In my journal I record "George was full of beans, bounced all the way home and chatted non-stop," it seemed he was in a good mood. This was the first indication to his schematic curiosities (Arnold, 2010).

At home he became involved in cutting strips and gluing them, trying to make hoops. But tears soon followed, frustration set in and filming was paused. Emma gently offered guidance; her calm, attentive reassurance gave him what he needed to carry on. Emma explained, "It's a fine balancing act between letting him work out problems and solutions for himself, but also stepping in." She gave meaning to his experiences and enabled reengagement with learning. At first, I considered processes of attunement (Stern, 2003) and containment (Bion, 1977), whereby an intersubjective dance occurred between the pair enabling George to manage his overwhelming feelings. After sorting through all the data, I shifted perspective and began to recognise how George needed others to make sense of experiences, not purely to manage overwhelming feelings. Meins et al (2003) refer to similar processes as "mind-mindedness," an adult's acknowledgement of a child's mental state. They suggest parents who are mind-minded raise children who learn skills in empathy and understand others' sooner than their peers.

Observation two

Observation two was completed at school using the Tavistock Observation Method (Bick, 1964) showed George managing conflict with a peer. He was trying to play with Link-cubes (his favourite activity) but another boy had them. I noticed feeling frustrated and deflated, it would be fair to suggest these were projections (Klein, 1946). I was interested in his behavioural shifts. At home frustration was overwhelming, he needed two minds (Tronick, 1998) to process experiences and continue learning. But in school he used strategies to work through frustrations. Within these strategies he seemed to negotiate elements of himself in an effort to connect with peers, first he "shoots" his peer, then attempts flattery by smiling and calling his name; on failure George turned to the Link-cubes, making the first letter of the boy's name.

I wondered if this object gave him the familiarity he needed to regulate feelings and process thoughts. Isaacs (1930:102) considered free play as a means for children to "work out their inner conflict in an external world." This was reflected in George shooting his peer, a playful expression that enabled the conflict to be safely managed. Following this George experienced a sense of guilt from his fantasy; he tried to connect with his peer when this failed, he returned to something concrete, his schematic interests of connection, disconnection and trajectory lines (Arnold, 2010). It seemed reconfiguring the Link-cubes combined George's mathematical, cognitive interests of schema (Arnold, 2010) with learning about the connection, disconnection and trajectory of relationships. This appeared to be a relational equation, where he was giving up elements of himself, the desire for the blocks, to engage in play and create a shared experience.

Observation three

In observation three, George was junk modelling with his older cousin. His parents were away for the weekend. I recorded his play and watched it back with George.

George explained, "we made that, together, she was very, very good!" In my journal I wrote, "He looked at her keenly, following her instructions. He shifted his agenda to appease hers." Throughout the observations he had opportunities to explore schematic interests (Arnold, 2010), I was struck by how keen he was to remain connected to his cousin; physical closeness, negotiations to maintain play, practical actions of connecting and building alongside his reflective comments evidenced my ideas. Perhaps he was processing distance between himself and parents. I wondered if reconfiguring items out of junk was another representation of relational equation.

Symbolism refers to the simple process of one item representing another, observed in play it enables children to make sense of abstract thought through objects. The roots of symbolism stemmed from the pioneers of child development. Piaget (1950) considered it a medium for organising experiences. Vygotsky (1978) saw this as a way to construct knowledge; where children could gather past, present and future experiences and internalise learning. Vygotsky suggested, "All that matters is that the objects admit the appropriate gesture and can function as points of application" (:107). This gave rise to my curiosities; the function of the objects for George was for them to come together, creating something new and strong. Arguably these are the foundations for relationships, strong yet open to reconfiguration. When discussing symbolic play Kelly and Hammond (2011) acknowledge this as a developmental process, becoming more abstract as children's executive functioning strengthens. Carlson (2009) considers executive functioning as a skill learnt through mind-mindedness (Meins et al, 2003), enabling the management of emotions and the capacity to complete tasks. This supported the sense I was making regarding this layer of George's learning. Tentative connections can be made between George symbolising the complexities of relationships because of his strong executive functioning, visible in the completion of a self-chosen schematic (Arnold, 2010) task.

Later observations taken by Craig and Emma at home illuminated George's mathematical and schematic (Arnold, 2010) interests.

Observation eight

Observation eight was at home. George cuts up paper and writes numbers on each piece. Tall (2004) considers mathematical learning as a combination of three worlds;

- Embodied world, formulated through perceptions of physical and mental experiences.
- Perceptual world, where actions and symbols are needed to shift from "doing" maths into "thinking" mathematically.
- Formal world, whereby properties are reflected on to establish theory.

Tall (2004) considers these worlds through a Piagetian lens, highlighting the importance of physical exposure to arithmetic to ensure the worlds come together, formulating concrete procedural learning needed for life-long mathematical development. The notions of perceptions, actions and reflection (Tall, 2004) seemed strongly attuned to the pedagogic styles of Emma and Craig. Language and mind-mindedness (Meins et al, 2003) were used to consider perceptions through problem solving and persistence. George's actions were actively encouraged with a house full of junk modelling, and free play at school; his hands-on experiences of early mathematical concepts are wide and varied. Finally, reflection occurred both independently and through conversations, often stimulated through his natural curiosities.

George is at a disadvantage when it comes to mathematical development, being born early means that statistically he is less likely to achieve well academically due to delays in cognitive development (Nuffield Foundation, 2019). Wolke et al (2015) link this to neurological development and cognitive delays for very premature infants, proposing reduced academic abilities. Lower paid employment and poverty are all statistically more likely for babies born early. George's teacher and I discussed this research. She was interested but explained George's development is equal to his peers. She follows guidelines set out by National Centre for Excellence in the Teaching of Mathematics (NCETM, 2019), which outlines three areas for mathematical development: knowing, understanding and mastery. Her teaching methods appeared to put into action the hands-on exploration needed for the procedural learning Tall (2004) referred to. She explained her experience of teaching a range of children enables her to value what happens now, understanding self-motivated play as a driver in cognitive learning. George and his teacher love maths, his personal enquiries are respected and encouraged.

Conclusions and implications

The sensitive pedagogy offered appears to support George's developing sense of self (Stern, 2003) enabling him to create strategies for engagement in learning and enrich future cognitive development. Elements of this study appeared to be about managing "hostile" environments such as school, separation from his parents and negotiating in play. At these times schematic enquiries were pertinent (Arnold, 2010). Links were illustrated between George's internal world and cognitive development. Acknowledgement was given to the impact of parental engagement, and tentative considerations are made of babies who are born prematurely. The implications of the study for George's family have been an acknowledgement of their careful tending of their son, reassurance regarding his cognitive development and a continued commitment to future learning.

Kat's reflections on the assignment

Parts of this study shared my personal thoughts; other parts featured the family's considerations, and so striking a balance between presenting this academically and authentically was a constant challenge that warranted careful consideration. I aimed to carry out this research with integrity and transparency, and was afforded a unique perspective due to the existing relationships I held with Emma, Craig and George. This ensured new perspectives were considered collectively and dialogues were held without intimidation. I was able to understand a little person that I love and am still interested in the ideas I developed regarding emotional equations and would like to expand on this within future research.

Tutor's comments on Kat's work

Kat's study illustrates the mastery required to compile a child study at Level 7. She skilfully presents insights into George's relationships, curiosities and the context into which he was born. These are used to deepen the analysis whilst she weaves together theories about early childhood from differing fields with her own practice wisdom, and demonstrates her understanding of curricula expectations. Kat is thoughtful and generous throughout, working with her family to further understand how George learns through his interactions and his play. Despite knowing George so well, she had some genuinely authentic surprises which are shared in an engaging way.

Conclusion

The research conducted by educators within the course of their own studies can support a deeper understanding of the value and privilege of standing back and watching children, or in engaging in dialogical processes with their caregivers. Studying also enhances the analytical skills required to make robust links between theory and practice. Doing so strengthens educators' ideas about what could and *should* be for the children in their care. An informed and observant workforce is the very least young children deserve.

Some have pointed to the neglectful or apathetic attitudes that exist within the UK towards children (Cunningham, 1998; Aynsley-Green, 2019; Sissay, 2020). Play, the outdoors and relationships have consistently been highlighted as being fundamentally important in Early Years education, and for a while during Covid-19 it felt truly hopeful that a "new normal" would include changes to policies influencing family life and education that could reflect these inherent needs. Perhaps rethinking the balance in terms of how much time children get to spend in their family home, in the company of their parents, siblings and extended family. Perhaps noticing the reduction of organised / paid for / commercial activities was a good thing for young children in asserting their right to play. Perhaps appreciating the splendour of life outdoors, absorbed in a natural world that overloads the senses, to trust children to learn on their own terms and in their own time. Perhaps we do our nation's youngest citizens a disservice if we do not take time to reflect upon whether *getting back to normal* is what is best for children as learners.

Further reading ideas

Table 3.1 Further reading ideas

Early childhood policies	Child development	Emotion	Pedagogy/play	Research/ethics	Debates in education
Cunningham	Trevarthen	Music	Nutbrown	Cook	Robinson
Pascal	Donaldson	Douglas	Holton	Palaiologou	Apple
McMillan	Corsaro	Tait	Bruce	Burnam	Ball

References

Arnold, C. (2003) *Observing harry: child development and learning 0–5*. Maidenhead: Open University Press.

Arnold, C. (2015) *Doing your child observation case study. a step-by-step guide*. Maidenhead: Open University Press.

Arnold, C. & the Pen Green team. (2010) *Understanding schemas and emotion in early childhood*. London: Sage.

Athey, C. (2007) *Extending thought in young children: a parent - teacher partnership* (2nd edition). London: Paul Chapman Publishing.

Aynsley-Green, A. (2019) *The British betrayal of childhood*. Abingdon, Routledge.

BERA. (2018) Ethical guideline for educational research. https://www.bera.ac.uk/ researchers-resources/publications/ethical-guidelines-for-educational-research-2018.

Bertram, T., Formosinho, J., Gray, C., Pascal, C., & Whalley, M. (2016) EECERA ethical code for early childhood researchers. *European Early Childhood Education Research Journal, 24 (1)*, pp. iii-xiii. doi:10.1080/1350293x.2016.1120533

Bick, E. (1964) Notes on infant observation in psychoanalytic training. *International Journal of Psychoanalysis, 45*, pp. 558–566.

Blanden, J. (2006) Bucking the trend: What enables those who are disadvantaged in childhood to succeed later in life? https://dera.ioe.ac.uk/7729/1/WP31.pdf

Boakye, J. (2020) As a teacher during the pandemic, I've realised that a school is a genuine community. https://www.theguardian.com/commentisfree/2021/jan/01/as-a-teacher-pandemic-covid-school-community.

Bowlby, J. (2005) *A secure base.* New York: Routledge.

British Sociological Association [BSA]. (2017) Statement of Ethical Practice. [Online]. Durham: BSA. https://www.britsoc.co.uk/media/24310/bsa_statement_of_ethical_practice.pdf

Bronfenbrenner, U. & Morris, P. A. (2006) The bioecological model of human development. In R. M. Lerner & W. Damon (Eds.), *Handbook of child psychology: Theoretical models of human development* (pp. 793–828) Hoboken, N.J.: John Wiley and Sons Inc.

Carr, M. (2001) *Assessment in early childhood settings: learning stories.* SAGE Publications.

Carr, M., May, H., Podmore, V. N., Cubey, P., Hatherly, A. & Macartney, B. (2002) Learning and teaching stories: Action research on evaluation in early childhood in Aotearoa-New Zealand. *European Early Childhood Education Research Journal, 10* (*2*), pp. 115–125.

Childcare Act (2006) https://www.legislation.gov.uk/ukpga/2006/21/contents

Child Poverty Action Group (2020) Poverty in the pandemic: the impact of coronavirus on low-income families and children. https://cpag.org.uk/sites/default/files/files/policy-post/Poverty-in-the-pandemic.pdf.

Children in Wales (2020) COVID-19 and the impact on low income and disadvantaged families. file:///N:/COVID-and-Families-English-Report-Final.pdf

Children's Commissioner (2020) *We don't need no education? The thorny issue of whether children should go back to school.* London: Children's Commissioner.

Cho, J. & Trent, A. (2006) Validity in qualitative research revisited. *Qualitative Research, 6* (*3*) pp. 319–340. London: SAGE Publications.

Clough, P. & Nutbrown, C. (2012) *A student's guide to methodology*, 3rd edition. London: Sage.

Coe, R., Weidmann, B., Coleman, R. & Kay, J. (2020) *Impact of school closures on the attainment gap: Rapid Evidence Assessment.* London: Education Endowment Foundation.

Cullinane, C. & Montacute, R. (2020) *COVID-19 and social mobility impact brief #1: School shutdown.* London: The Sutton Trust.

Cunningham, H. (1998) Histories of childhood. *The American Historical Review, 103* (*4*), pp. 1195–1208.

Data Protection Act (2018) c.2. https://www.legislation.gov.uk/ukpga/2018/12/contents/enacted

Delamont, S. (2009) *Handbook of qualitative research in education.* London: Edward Elgar Publishing Ltd.

Department for Education (DfE) (2021) *Statutory framework for the early years foundation stage: setting the standards for learning, development and care for children from birth to five.* London: Education Department. Statutory framework for the early years foundation stage (publishing.service.gov.uk)

Education Policy Institute (2020) Preventing the disadvantage gap from increasing during and after the Covid-19 pandemic. https://epi.org.uk/wp-content/uploads/2020/05/EPI-Policy-paper-Impact-of-Covid-19_docx.pdf.

Elfer, P., Goldschmied, E. & Selleck, E. Y. (2012) *Key persons in the early years: Building relationships for quality provision in early years settings and primary schools.* 2nd edition. Oxon: Routledge.

Ellis, C. (2007) *Telling secrets, revealing lives. relational ethics in research with intimate others.* Tampa: University of South Florida.

Emery, C. (2020) The SAGE Encyclopedia of Children and Childhood Studies. In Cook, D. (2020) *The SAGE Encyclopedia of Children and Childhood Studies. Thousand Oaks*: SAGE Publications.

Evans, C.E. L. & Harper, C. E. (2009) A history and review of school meal standards in the UK. *Journal of Human Nutrition and Dietetics, 22*, pp. 89–99.

Eyles, A., Gibbons, S. & Montebruno, P. (2020) *Covid-19 school shutdowns: What will they do to our children's education?* London: Centre for Economic Performance.

Farrimond, H. (2013) *Doing ethical research*. Hampshire, UK: Macmillan Publishers Limited.

Forrest, A. (2020) I don't mind going hungry if my kids can eat: Families reveal struggle to afford food during lockdown. https://www.independent.co.uk/news/uk/home-news/help-the-hungry-families-children-food-poverty-parents-lockdown-stories-a9544091.html.

Friesen, D. & Bialystok, E. (2012) Metalinguistic ability in bilingual children: the role of executive control. *Rivista di psicolinguistica applicata, 12*, pp. 47–56.

Froebel, F. (1968) *The education of man*. Bath: Chivers.

Fulwiler, T. (2000) *The personal connection: journal writing across the curriculum: Language connections: writing and reading across the curriculum*. Colorado: Landmark Publications.

Gallagher, T. & Arnold, C. (Eds.) (2017) *Working with children aged 0–3 and their families: The Pen Green approach* (1st ed.) Routledge. https://doi.org/10.4324/9781315562445

Galletta, A. (2013) Mastering the semi-structured interview and beyond: from research design to analysis and publication. New York: New York University Press.

Goleman, D. (1996) *Emotional intelligence: why it can matter more than IQ*. London: Bloomsbury.

Harris, A. & Goodall, J. (2008) Do parents know they matter? Engaging all parents in learning. *Educational Research, 50 (3)*, pp. 277–289. https://doi.org/10.1080/00131880802309424

Hayes, N., O'Toole, L. & Halpenny, A. (2017) *Introducing Bronfenbrenner: A guide for practitioners and students in early years education*. Oxfordshire: Taylor & Francis Group.

Isaacs, S. & Isaacs, N. (1930) *The behaviour of young children. Vol. 1, Intellectual growth in young children*. London.

Janesick, V. J. (1999) A journal about journal writing as a qualitative research technique: history, issues, and reflections. *Qualitative Inquiry, 5 (4)*, pp. 505–524.

Laevers, F. (2000) Forward to basics! Deep-Level-Learning and the Experiential Approach, Early Years, 20 (2), pp. 20–29, DOI: 10.1080/0957514000200203

Laevers, F. (2011) Childcare - Early childhood education and care. *Experiential Education: Making care and Education More Effective Through Well-being and Involvement, 1 (1)*, pp. 52–55.

Lawrence, P. & Gallagher, T. (2015) Pedagogic Strategies; a conceptual framework for effective parent and practitioner strategies when working with children under five. *Early Child Development and Care, 185* (11–12) pp. 1978–1994.

Lego Foundation (2017) White paper learning through play: a review of the evidence. Denmark: Lego Group. https://cms.learningthroughplay.com/media/wmtlmbe0/learning-through-play_web.pdf

Locke, J., Yolton, J. W. & Yolton, J. S. (1989) *Some thoughts concerning education*. Oxford: Clarendon.

Major, L. E. & Machin, S. (2020) Covid-19 and social mobility. London: Centre for Economic Performance.

Maslow, A. H. (1943) A theory of human motivation. *Psychological Review, 50 (4)*, 370–396.

Mills, Z. (2020) Free school meals should be for all school holidays, not just for Christmas. https://policyinpractice.co.uk/free-school-meals-should-be-for-all-school-holidays-not-just-for-christmas/.

O'Connell, P. (2014) A simplified framework for 21st century leader development. *The Leadership Quarterly, 25*, pp. 183–203.

Ofsted (2020) COVID-19 series: briefing on schools, October 2020. https://assets.publishing.service.gov.uk/government/uploads/system/uploads/attachment_data/file/933490/COVID-19_series_briefing_on_schools_October_2020.pdf.

Owen, R. & Silver, H. (1969) *Robert Owen on education: selections edited*. London: Cambridge U.P.

Parameswaran, U. D., Ozawa-Kirk, J. L. & Latendress, G. (2019) To live (code) or not: A new method for coding in qualitative research. *Qualitative Social Work, 19 (4)*, pp. 630–644.

Pestalozzi, J. H., Green, J. A. & Collie, F. A. (1912) Pestalozzi's educational writings. London: Edward Arnold.

Prodger, A. & Devine, A. (2021) A celebratory approach to working with children with SEND. https://www.pengreen.org/2021/09/23/a-celebratory-approach-to-working-with-children-with-send/

Rashford, M. (2020) 19 October. https://twitter.com/MarcusRashford/status/1318092788471418882.

Ravitch, S. & Riggan, M. (2017) Reason & Rigor: How conceptual frameworks guide research. 2nd edition. London: SAGE. https://www.google.co.uk/books/edition/Reason_Rigor/lvBQCwAAQBAJ?hl=en&gbpv=1&dq=conceptual+framework&printsec=frontcover

Ringer, T. M. (2002) *Group action: the dynamics of groups in therapeutic, educational and corporate settings.* International Library of Group Analysis. London: Jessica Kingsley Publishers.

Robb, A. (2020) Researching the world in uncertain times: The role of bricolage. Covid-19, education and educational research. https://www.bera.ac.uk/blog/researching-the-world-in-uncertain-times-the-role-of-bricolage.

Roberts, R. (2011) Companionable Learning: a mechanism for holistic well-being development from birth. European Early Childhood Education, *19 (2)*, pp. 195–205.

Roberts-Holmes, G. (2014) *Doing your early years research project: a step-by-step guide.* California: Sage.

Rousseau, J. J. (1780) *Emile, ou de l'éducation: Par J.J. Rousseau, citoyen de Géneve.* A Londres.

Schon, D. A. (1982) *The reflective practitioner: how professionals think in action.* New York: Basic Books.

Schon, D. A. (1983) *The reflective practitioner: how professionals think in action.* Farnham: Ashgate.

Schon, D. A. (1994) *The reflective practitioner: how professionals think in action.* Oxford: Routledge.

Scott, D., Arney, F. & Vimpani, G. (2018) *Think child, think family, think community. Working with vulnerable families: a partnership approach.* pp. 6–23. United Kingdom: Cambridge University.

Shahnazarian, D., Hagemann, J., Aburto, M. & Rose, S. (2013) Informed Consent in Human Subjects Research. Office for the Protection of Research Subjects (OPRS) https://oprs.usc.edu/files/2017/04/Informed-Consent-Booklet-4.4.13.pdf.

Shteynberg, G. & Apfelbaum, E. P. (2013) The power of shared experience: simultaneous observation with similar others facilitates social learning. *Social Psychological and Personality Science, 4 (6)*, pp. 738–744.

Sissay, L. (2020) *My name is why.* Edinburgh: Canongate.

Singer, T. & Klimecki, O. M. (2014) Empathy and compassion. *Current Biology, 24 (18)* pp. 875–878.

Stake, R. (2010) *Qualitative research: Studying how things work.* New York: Guilford Publications.

Taylor, A. (2020) New food foundation survey: five million people living in households with children have experienced food insecurity since lockdown started. https://foodfoundation.org.uk/new-food-foundation-survey-five-million-people-living-in-households-with-children-have-experienced-food-insecurity-since-lockdown-started/.

Taylor, C., Wilkie, M. & Baser, J. (2006) *Doing action research: a guide for school support staff.* London: Paul Chapman Publishing.

The Children and Families Act (2014) https://www.legislation.gov.uk/ukpga/2014/6/contents

The Children's Society (2020) How local authorities can support the most vulnerable children and families during the Covid-19 outbreak. https://www.childrenssociety.org.uk/sites/default/files/cv-19-local-authorities-support-the-most-vulnerable-children-and-families-_0.pdf.

The Food Foundation (2020) *Free school meal holiday provision in England.* Parliamentary Facts and Figures Briefing. https://foodfoundation.org.uk/wp-content/uploads/2020/06/FSM_Briefing_1506_Final2.pdf.

Tinson, A. (2020) *Living in poverty was bad for your health before COVID-19.* London: The Health Foundation.

Trevarthen, C. (2001) Intrinsic motives for companionship in understanding: their origin, development, and significance for infant mental health. *Infant Mental Health Journal, 22* (1–2), pp. 95–131.

Vygotsky, L. (1978) *Mind in society: the development of higher psychological processes.* Cambridge, MA: Harvard University Press.

Vygotsky, L. (1986) Thought and language. The Massachusetts Institute of Technology, USA, Acorn Graphic Services.

Weale, S. (2020) England: 'shocking' decline in primary pupils' attainment after lockdown. https://www.theguardian.com/education/2020/nov/11/england-shocking-decline-in-primary-pupils-attainment-after-lockdown.

Whalley, M. (1994) *Learning to be strong.* London: Hodder and Stoughton.

Whalley, M. (2007) *Involving parents in their children's learning.* 2nd edition. Los Angeles: Paul Chapman.

Whalley, M. & Arnold, C. (1997) *Parental involvement in education: Summary of research findings.* London: Teacher Training Agency.

Whalley, M., Arnold, C., Orr, R. & Pen Green Team. (2013) *Working with Families in children's centres and early years settings.* London: Hodder Education.

Winnicott, D. W. (1964) *The child, the family, and the outside world.* London: Penguin Books.

Wood, V. (2020) Almost 2,500 children admitted to hospital with malnutrition this year as cases double in England. https://www.independent.co.uk/news/uk/home-news/food-poverty-hunger-child-malnutrition-hospital-layla-moran-coronavirus-a9615161.html.

4   Working with families

Sandra Clare

[In collaboration with Diana Morris, Fran Purdy, Debbie Moore and Lucy Krebs]

In this chapter you will find:

- Discussion of social policy and the impact this has on family life
- Exploration of why working with families matters
- Ideas from the Pen Green Centre about working with families
- Extracts from assignments illustrating different ways to research and reflect on practice with families in academic assignments.

Why working with families matters

The QAA (2022) encourage students to:

> recognise the historical, current and potential future social, environmental and economic distribution challenges facing children and families . . . taking a critical view of sustainability in local, systemic, national, environmental and global challenges and developments that impact on inclusion and equality among increasingly diverse societies.

"Parents" and "families" are not homogenous, and to support individual children, a keen interest in *their* parents and *their* family along with a critical understanding of the economic and political systems around them are vital. To fully appreciate the impact of socio-economic-politics on family life, consideration of what has come before is required. Every piece of legislation or policy is an expression of dominant social values of a particular time and culture. It is important to acknowledge how attitudes in the UK have developed and face uncomfortable truths about who is most affected by punitive policies and derisory rhetoric. Then, as now, gender, class, race, place and disability have the most significant influence and the intersectionality of factors further conflates how policy dictates family life.

In pre-industrial times vulnerable children were, by certain people, sometimes seen as "products of sin," born to repeat the mistakes of their parents and undeserving of care. Poor Laws from the 16th century stated, "Pauperism is in

DOI: 10.4324/9781003271727-4

the blood." Workhouses routinely separated children from their parents, making each work in return for their board and punishing attempts for members of the same family to speak to each other. Mothers were navigating life in a patriarchal society, marriage was a business arrangement rather than a loving relationship and the absence of a welfare state meant women and children needed to be under the care of a man for life. The option of raising a child as an unwed or widowed mother was largely unavailable.

The 18th century brought with it ideas that children are "gifts from heaven" needing to be saved from feckless families. For many being saved meant living in an institution; history has taught us far from being places of sanctuary they encountered systematic inhumanity. Poor Laws spanned multiple centuries, and by the turn of the 20th century pauperism was virtually a crime. Whilst some "deserving" (for example, those who could not work due to disability) would receive "outdoor relief" enabling them to remain in their own home, admittance to workhouses was a likely fate. The belief being that "the poor" would lose any desire to work and support themselves if they received aid.

The 1834 Poor Law Amendments removed the need for fathers to provide for infants they sired, yet treatment of single mothers was harsh. Victorians did not want to encourage sexual immorality, using the workhouse as a deterrent. Here illegitimate children were classed as orphans, separated from their primary caregiver and sent to work.

As child labour laws tightened in England, there became less use for young "orphans" so Victorian philanthropists and the State developed systems of child migration. Sending children to the colonies, mothers would be told their child had died and vice-versa. The belief being that children would have better life chances if separated from their "immoral" mothers, such practices continued even after the inception of the welfare state.

The Beveridge Report (1942) highlighted the five major problems preventing families bettering themselves: want, ignorance, squalor, idleness and disease. He recommended all five be addressed to enhance the post–war society. This led to the creation of the welfare state provision that was limited for parents who were not White or wed. As the century progressed, some began to question whether it was the financial and social problems faced by families that were more damaging to children than illegitimacy (for example see Wynn, 1964; Finer, 1974). It was not until 1987 that illegitimate children enjoyed the same legal rights as legitimate children (Family Law Reform Act, 1987), and for children born to unmarried mothers without a British Passport, parity was not enjoyed until 2021 (The British Nationality and Borders Act, 2021).

The 21st century began with a Prime Minister who promised the top three priorities to be "Education, Education, Education" (Labour Party Conference, 1 October 1996). The two decades since witnessed the development, and subsequent decimation, of policies that brought together schools, families, health and education. As a mother who benefitted from Sure Start

(Eisenstadt, 2011) and a practitioner who applauded Every Child Matters (Department for Education and Skills, 2003) I find it hard not to mourn the loss of services that felt philosophically family-centric. Much has been written about this period in other Pen Green books; further reading could include Working with Families (Whalley et al, 2013).

Parenting has become an ever increasingly private affair, wholly child-centred, emotionally involving and time-consuming (Hays, 1996). The neo-liberal focus on individualised success/care/blame pitches parents against society and each other. Feminist authors highlight how the normative parenting ideology is maintained through social policies which reward or punish based on gender, class, ability, race or marital status, and fail to recognise the transformed roles of mothers and fathers, or to reconcile the competing demands of unpaid domestic work, the education of children and paid employment (Borda, 2021; Brearley, 2021; David, 1984). Covid-19 illuminated the stubbornly pernicious way structural inequalities intersect to compound difficulty (Marmot, 2020).

So far I have briefly discussed parts of history to illustrate the impact of social policy on family life and to stimulate thoughts about this. For further reading see *The Invention of Childhood* by Hugh Cunningham, *Parents, Poverty and The State* by Naomi Eisenstadt and Carey Oppenheim or *The British Betrayal of Childhood* by Al Aynsley-Green. I have highlighted significant examples to remind you that some families are simply stripped of choice and dignity while society legitimises their condemnation and control. How systems of morality, economy and law restrict the body, the home, the experience of the child and even what each imagines to be possible. And that working *with* families is an essential endeavour. We know that families matter, and that most of all they matter to children.

At present in England, statutory guidance demands professionals actively seek relationships with children's families (EYFS, DfE, 2021). To work with vulnerable parents and children to ensure the safeguarding of both (Working Together to Safeguard Children, DfE, 2018). And to include families in decisions about children with disabilities (Children and Families Act, 2014). It is worth reflecting how historical ideas and contemporary expectations continue to shape family life in 2022 – who are the deserving and undeserving?

Why working with families matters at Pen Green

Longitudinal studies, including research drawing on British Birth Cohort studies, recognise parents as children's most enduring educators, noting the home learning environment and what parents *do* have a more profound impact on children's educational opportunities and outcomes than socio-economic status (Douglas, 1964; Feinstein, 2003; Fogelman, 1983; Sylva et al, 2004; Easen et al, 1992; Blanden, 2006; Desforges & Abouchaars, 2003). It is from this evidence base that contemporary social policy and Early Years practice has been crafted.

Staff at Pen Green were inspired by the work of the McMillan sisters (McMillan, 1919). Around the turn of the 20th century, they established nursery schools in some of the most deprived communities in the UK, challenging popular assumptions of the time about working with children and their families. They highlighted that parents are children's first and most important educators, and that parental involvement was pivotal to educational outcomes. At a time when social policy involved very few rights for mothers, and possibly even less reverence, Rachel and Margaret McMillan sought to involve them in the life of "the Nursery School." They felt teachers needed to get to know parents and draw on the talents from within the community, illuminating the understanding of all regarding child development.

Pushor (2007) differentiated between parental *involvement* and parental *engagement* and Crozier and Davies (2007) researching Bangladeshi and Pakistani heritage families noted rather than parents being "hard to reach," schools themselves inhibit accessibility. Both authors encourage the problematising of power differentials between schools and families, as discussed in Chapter 3 (see the "Pen Green Loop"). The Pen Green Loop was conceptualised to illustrate a dialogical partnership with parents. Ideas from critical pedagogues, including Paulo Freire and bell hooks, have shaped the collaborative nature of relationships at Pen Green.

The case for working with families is well covered within literature and research but less is written about how successful relationships with families are sought, built and maintained. Further inspiration for Pen Green staff was drawn from authors writing with The Children's Society about family and community services in 1983 (Adamson & Warren; Phelan; Holman) who describe the importance of humility, authenticity and consistency. Theories that could support adult learners understanding of working with families can be borrowed from different disciplines:

- Psychology – Containment (Bion), Holding (Winnicott)
- Education – Andragogy (Knowles), Social Learning (Bandura)
- Leadership – Pedagogical Isomorphism (Formosinho),
- Psychiatry – Transactional Analysis (Berne), Drama Triangle (Karpman)
- Sociology – Contact Theory (Allport), Bioecological Systems (Bronfenbrenner)
- Community – Development (Ledwith), Resourceful Friends (Holman).

Researching working with families

Case study is a unique way of analysing practice leading to new ideas to inform ongoing practice, it does not matter that the research cannot be reproduced, it is anticipated that "in all its particularity *and* ordinariness" (Stake, 2000:437) the case will be interesting. Strauss and Corbin (1990:42) noticed "experience can block you from seeing things that have become routine or 'obvious'" so time spent looking at practice will strengthen future responses and ensure students can articulate their praxis (Pascal & Bertram, 2012).

Case study assignments at Pen Green require the involvement of participants. Freire (1972:61) points out "no-one can say a true word alone – nor can he say it *for* another, in a prescriptive act which robs others of their words" and Holman (1987) pointed out "objects of research, are placed in the inferior position in which they are expected to supply information but not to obtain any." As such adult learners are expected to demonstrate sound consideration of what the family are being asked to do and why. It is the hallmark of an excellent assignment if it has been written with and proofread by the family involved.

Ethical considerations are broad and deep. Attention to details such as confidentiality, the right to withdraw, power differentials and anonymity form part of the overall undertaking to do no harm. It can be tempting to get caught up in telling the grizzly details of familial context, a form of "poverty pornography" where the family are "othered" with a level of detail that far outweighs academic relevance. Whalley (2013:67) highlighted "too often families become known because of their tragedies or their vulnerabilities." When the family are involved in the development of the assignment, this can be avoided. They can choose how their story is represented and can support students to unpick their professional role within their familial context.

> Whilst it is important to not make the *context* the story it is important to demonstrate understanding of socio-economic, cultural, and geographical factors that influence family life. The ability to critically rationalise the impact of vulnerabilities, injustices, and politics shows a comprehensive understanding of the context within which a family exists. This then needs to be complimented with consideration of theories that informed the students responses, strong pieces of writing tend to be humble, rejecting fears of being displaced and getting in touch with their need for others. It is robustly articulated praxis (Pascal & Bertram, 2012) rather than the ability to "work with," "deliver to" or "use" a family that will be academically credible.

Foundation Degree (year one) Level 4 assignment extract

Diana Morris

Assignment brief

The Working with Parents as Partners assignment requires adult learners to conduct a semi-structured interview with parents regarding their involvement in their children's learning. This refines the skills of working collaboratively with families in an ethical way, to recognise and extend children's interests and learning.

Adult learners will consider the importance of trust and authenticity in relationships with parents. Strong assignments will demonstrate an awareness of sharing theory with families and truly consider the parents' voice as we all as how this will be used in future practice.

Introduction to Diana

I became an Early Years practitioner following the birth of my own children after a career in banking and never considered myself to be academic! It had been 15 years since I completed any studying and had never written "proper assignments." The Working with Parents assignment was the turning point in my learning journey. This was when I really wanted to make a difference rather than just fulfil a criteria or get a mark. It taught me being passionate can be just as good as writing well, or maybe it is just the same thing with a little planning for good luck!

Assignment extract

Introduction

I conducted a semi-structured interview with a family of two parents and two children. I selected this family as they had experienced some unrecognised behaviours from their eldest child. I aimed to understand any learning the parents had and how I can use this with other families in the future.

Ethics

Ethical considerations are less about the child and more about the feelings and the emotions of the parents. I have ensured identities and personal information are protected using pseudonyms. The parents, Sarah and Peter, and I agreed on meeting times and methods used. Member checking (Stake, 2010) involved them reading and agreeing to what was included.

Methodology

Whilst considering the questions I wanted to use for the interview, I noticed I centred on the parents feelings and how these impacted their daily lives. Galletta (2013:2) states the importance of semi-structured interviews as "sufficiently structured to address specific dimensions . . . while also leaving space for study participants to offer new meanings."

I decided to use open broad questions to help Sarah and Peter to steer the interview and follow up questions to gain specific details. I also wanted to ensure my questions were not based on assumptions. For example, "what did you learn?" assumes they have learnt something, placing me as a teacher, whereas I wanted this to be an equal partnership.

The interview was recorded to enable me to listen back, transcribe it and more thoroughly analyse and code the data. Gibbs (2007) describes the transcription process as valuable to understand the subjects' thoughts and how repeated themes indicate the importance to them.

Interview

The interview was carried out solely with Sarah because Peter was unable to attend. The first theme I identified was schemas. Sarah described that she just thought Charlene was playing and had not really noticed any change because her play patterns were the same as they had always been. When Sarah and Peter read my previous assignment, they said, "it's hard to believe just how much education can come from her schemas." By linking Charlene's schemas (Athey, 2007) to areas of learning, Sarah had a better understanding of why these patterns were such an important part in Charlene's development. Sarah frequently referred to Charlene's trajectory schema and gave examples of how she has been able to identify the play patterns as they are happening and support Charlene in exploring them. Sarah said, "She really enjoyed walking down the line selecting food, *and all I could think was that it was her trajectory schema again.*" Nutbrown (2011) identifies the importance of adults understanding and facilitating children's schemas and how this can further extend their learning.

Reflection

After meeting with Sarah, I felt a little disappointed that the impact of the study seemed small. However, after reflecting and studying the differences in language used by Sarah from our very first meeting to the interview, I noted there was new understanding about the importance of Charlene's play and how Sarah supports this.

I reflected I could have supported Sarah more by providing her with the interview questions a few days before completing the interview.

Almost immediately after the interview with Sarah, two children had been drawing all over themselves with felt tip pens. When their parents had collected them, I explained to one that the child had shown signs of an enveloping schema (Athey, 2007). The parent looked concerned. When I explained that a schema is a repeated pattern of play and that it assists their thinking and development, the parent softened and wanted to learn more. This, along with the reflections of the meeting with Sarah, made me realise that whilst I talk to parents every day, I need to share more information to support their knowledge. As a result of this, as a setting we have shared a leaflet and plan to hold parent workshops on theoretical concepts, allowing us another way of further building relationships with them. I believe that having parents as partners, supported by these theories, is fundamental to achieve the best child centred practice and outcomes.

Diana's reflections on the assignment

I felt sure I needed to massively impact the family and alter the parents' perspective, I felt this would mean I had best supported them. During the assignment I could see by sharing information in a two-way exchange, the child benefitted. By the end I was an advocate for collaborative working and now believe it is fundamental. By really understanding each part of the assignment and the underpinning theory, I felt confident to open myself up to the possibility of working in a new way. This experience continues to positively impact me day to day.

Tutor comments on Diana's assignment

In her assignment, Diana discusses how she shared key concepts and the impact this had. She is deeply reflective about how she conducted the research and how to further improve relationships with parents in her setting. Diana's work is concise and makes firm links to theory, and she offers an excellent balance of description, analysis and reflection. She speaks of the family in a very respectful way, highlighting her ethical approach. There is a good balance between consideration of the methodology and reporting what happened. Diana's reflections on the process are sensitive and honest, and she is clear about the impact on her ongoing practice.

Foundation Degree (year two) Level 5 assignment extract

Fran Purdy

Assignment brief

Students work together with a family to produce a case study considering a period during which they worked together. They consider how their own attitudes, values and beliefs influence the way they work as well as demonstrating understanding of the complexities of family life in their local context. There is a strong emphasis on ethics and respect.

Introduction to Fran

When I was 18, I left my first semester of university studying Performance, and began an apprenticeship in Early Years. All I wanted to be whilst growing up was an actor and a mum. Since I was no longer acting, and I felt too young to be a mum, childcare was my next step; I soon realised it involved more than playing and cuddling babies! After qualifying with my NVQ Level 3 in childcare and working for a couple of years, I started my degree. I had never been academic and starting at the age of 23 made me wonder if I could write to the necessary standard. Pen Green was a turning point for me, both professionally and personally; I gained a love for writing, theory and research, I discovered my learning style, and I found my voice. This was all supported by my tutors, leading me to achieve a 1st class honours degree and a deeper understanding of working with children and families.

Assignment extract

Introduction

I am an Early Years Practitioner working in a nursery in the West of England. I have produced a case study alongside a family I worked with last year. This family consisted of baby, Ivy, her mother, Elizabeth, and father, Bob. Elizabeth had felt "patronised and judged" at baby groups she was taking Ivy to and was lacking in confidence. I carried out a semi-structured interview with Elizabeth to understand in greater depth how I supported her and her family.

Ethics

Ethical research is not just about collecting information but about "the dignity, rights, safety and well-being" of participants (Stuart & Barnes, 2005).

Throughout this assignment I "operate[d] within an ethic of respect" (BERA, 2011:5) involving the family fully by communicating with them regularly, answering questions and keeping them informed.

Pollard (2015:364) says the main principles of Relational Ethics are "mutual respect, engagement, embodied knowledge, environment, and uncertainty." I believe these principles matter when involving participants in research, being honest and open with families in order to create "mutual respect."

Values, attitudes, and beliefs about working with families

Working with families and creating strong relationships with them is essential to be able to support children effectively. The National Quality Improvement Network (NQIN; 2010) created ten principles for engaging with families stating "successful and sustained engagement with families is maintained when practitioners work alongside families in a valued working relationship" (NQIN, 2010:9).

Pallett (2017) wrote about the stigma of young parenthood. She found that 56% of the parents she interviewed between the ages of 16 and 25 had experienced stigma due to being pregnant or having had a child at a seemingly young age. Link and Phelan (2001:365) describe stigma as the labelling of differences, linked to "undesired characteristics" and "negative stereotypes" which separate "us" from "them" and lead to discrimination. Elizabeth explained she stopped attending groups because of the "*fear*" of being "*looked down upon.*" This could have potentially impacted on Ivy's development through not having social interactions with other people (Farrimond & Joffe, 2006).

Introduce the family and context

I cared for Ivy in nursery, Elizabeth told me she felt "*patronised*" when attending the breast-feeding clinic and shared with an "*older*" mother that she had recently moved to the area and was asked how she was "*getting on*" breast-feeding. Elizabeth said, "*Great!,*" and was told, "*Good for you!,*" whilst being tapped on the leg by the other mother. She felt reluctant to return to the clinic.

At another baby group, Elizabeth also felt "*judged and patronised*" when a group of mothers, who were "*older*" than her kept "*questioning*" how she cared for Ivy, suggesting she "*wind*" or "*feed*" her. Elizabeth felt these mothers commented "*because they were older [and] they thought they knew better.*"

These interactions were causing Elizabeth to avoid groups and "*doubting*" herself. I could see how this was affecting Elizabeth and could potentially affect Ivy and her development. I therefore supported Elizabeth in trying to gain confidence and empowerment as a young mother.

Consider how you supported the family and evaluate the impact of your support

I aim to build relationships with parents through embedding Braun et al's (2006) list of qualities such as respect, empathy and humility. I related this to Goldschmied and Selleck's (1996) "triangle of trust" (see Figure 4.1).

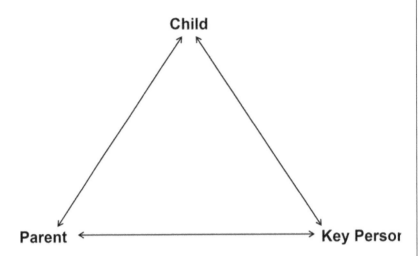

Figure 4.1 Triangle of Trust

The Triangle of trust illustrates the close relationship between a Key Person (Elfer et al, 2012), a child and their parents. Elizabeth said because I was "*open and honest*" with her about my own experiences, she felt she could be too. This created a trusting relationship where Elizabeth felt secure and supported. This led her to reach out to other people and services.

As I was pregnant at the time, I used social media forums for young mothers which I found empowering as a young mother myself. I thought sharing these forums with Elizabeth might help. Ammari and Schoenebeck (2015) found mothers communicating on social media can support one another, helping them feel confident and connected as parents. Ammari et al (2015) describe social media behaviours that connect to aspects of empowerment. Firstly the "intrapersonal component" is how people think about themselves. It involves reading families' stories, asking questions and developing the belief that parents are capable of caring for their children. Secondly the "interactional component" is about parents' awareness and their ability to work towards goals, learning about services and accessing them. Finally, the "behavioural component" is when parents act to achieve further outcomes. And the concept of "networked empowerment" explains how social media supports the process of empowerment through parents accessing services and one another. Elizabeth found the social media platforms "*helped [her] feel confident*" in talking to parents and asking them questions, giving her the "*confidence*" to share her own stories. Through "*relating*" with other mothers on the forum, Elizabeth felt "*in control*" when caring for Ivy and *"empowered as a young mum,"* giving her *"no reason to doubt [herself]."*

I believe social media can help create connections with others, but those connections are not as fulfilling as face-to-face relationships (Putman, 2000). I reached out to the local Children's Centre where I found a group for young mothers. I shared this with Elizabeth and she attended. Before she went to the group she felt "nervous" but eventually *"planned to meet with some of the other mums later that week."* Elizabeth said, *"once you make friends you feel more confident"* and finds now her and her *"mummy friends"* *"say that [they] feel like a community"* because they *"don't need the baby groups"* *"because [they] meet up on [their] own."* Elizabeth told me that if she *"had never met them then [she] would feel isolated."* Elizabeth said she was *"grateful"* for me *"finding the forums and the groups,"* telling me she felt these had *"made [her] a more confident mum."*

Supporting other families demonstrating the relevance of multi-agency working for families where complexity is evident

I realised from working with Elizabeth that words are highly effective, through making individuals feel things we may not realise or feel ourselves. Park (2010) highlights the importance of words having real consequences on how people identify and portray themselves to others. Elizabeth stated comments from other mothers such as *"you should [do this]"* and *"good for you"* were *"patronising"* and *"rude"* and made her *"lack confidence."* Reflecting on this, I realised even though I may ignore such comments, another person may feel differently. Therefore, I am now more aware of the words I use when speaking to families.

I also realised even though a family may need support, that does not mean a high level of involvement. Elizabeth accepted my offer of support and I pointed her *"in the right direction,"* but *"[she did not] feel pressured to do anything."* She took it upon herself to join the social media forums and attend the groups in her own time. I now advise and signpost families to services or groups, encouraging them to take the lead.

Conclusions and implications for practice

I realised there are a number of young parents in my setting and came to understand some may have experienced stigma. I will share this with the staff team, acknowledging intervention is not always required rather information sharing and signposting can be enough. I will begin offering information about other services, groups and activities openly throughout the setting, whilst continuing to work alongside the Children's Centre.

Speaking to Elizabeth and hearing how comments caused her to feel "*judged,*" I am more aware of how I communicate with families. I will also share this with the staff team alongside Elizabeth, as she would like to "*share*" her experience and "*support*" staff in understanding the impact of their words.

Fran's reflections on the assignment

This was the first time I had the freedom to explore supporting families. I was able to go deeper, finding other theorists relating to my study rather than just key theorists I had learnt about in the study week. I have taken this understanding and enjoyment with me into future assignments. I came to appreciate working with the entire family and creating strong relationships supports the children I care for more effectively.

Tutor comments on the assignment

Fran begins with a very clear introduction that sets the tone well. She ensures that the reader understands the expectations for the piece of work and the areas she intends to focus on. She has considered her own childhood experiences and how these have informed the development of her moral views, values and beliefs. She finishes the assignment with strong conclusions, bringing together her thoughts and learning. Throughout she makes strong connections with reading, considering the research of others, the participants, practice and the setting which made for a very interesting and thought-provoking piece of work.

Bachelor's Top-Up Degree Level 6 extract from dissertation

Debbie Moore

Assignment/dissertation brief

Adult learners design and conduct independent research to deepen their understanding of their chosen area of interest. They engage with others in the gathering and analysis of data. The adult learners delve deep into literature, become alert to gaps and think about how reading informs their own research questions. Successful studies are mindful of local context and result in changes that are reflective of what families need.

Introducing Debbie

I am a 44-year-old single mum to two children. Whilst completing my degree I worked full time as an Early Years practitioner in Reception class and year one, learned to play the drums and trained for several marathons. Completing the degree was originally a way to get a well-paid job, it has however been so much more. It has allowed me time to gain in-depth knowledge and understanding of my role, time to reflect on myself, my journey and my beliefs. The tutors have made me question myself, and this made me grow into a far better practitioner, a practitioner who knows what she believes in and is able to back this up with theory and research projects; a practitioner who will always put child and family needs first. I realised I am extremely passionate about learning through play and parental involvement, which is why I decided to do my dissertation on parental understanding of learning through play. The research went well, parents were extremely keen to help me, they say they have gained a lot from it and are looking forward to becoming more engaged in their child's play both in school and at home. This course is hard work but is absolutely worth all the hard work.

Assignment/dissertation extract

The following extract is part of Debbie's BA dissertation.

A research project to explore parents understanding of learning through play.

Introduction and context

I work in a Church of England School based in an inner-city area of the North of England. The school is predominantly attended by Muslim children, a high percentage are learning English as an additional language and many start Early Years unable to speak English.

I am curious how much understanding parents have of the benefits of learning through play. Before beginning Early Years training, I had no understanding of the value of play, I was reluctant to join in with my own children's play and certainly did not know how or why I should try and extend their play to develop learning. I remember having a discussion with the teacher who taught both my children about how I would have liked to have understood the importance of play, and she told me, "As a parent you should know." I did not and often wonder if other parents do. I wanted to be a practitioner who never made a parent feel how I felt when talking to the teacher.

Methodology

I used a questionnaire as they are quick, simple and can be shared online. However, I understand participants could choose not to answer a question. I used school "dojo" to ask for willing participants and then convened a small focus group (Gibbs, 2007).

Ethics

The British Educational Research Association's Code of Ethics (BERA, 2018) states research should respect the privacy, autonomy, diversity, values and dignity of individuals, groups and communities.

Due to Covid-19 restrictions, the focus group was online. I am not very confident in using Zoom and found it difficult to interact whilst online. I recorded the focus group and deleted the video once the final marks were awarded.

The parents were aware of the right to withdraw at any point, for any reason and that doing so would not affect how I teach their child or communicate with them. I agreed not to disclose any detail that identified participants and used pseudonyms.

Literature Review

"Play is like a reservoir full of water. The deeper the reservoir, the more water can be stored in it and used in time of draught" (Bruce, 1991).

What is play?

Lee (1969) believes "play is the main child's business in life, through play he learns the skills to survive and finds some pattern in the confusing world into which he was born." Goldstein (2012:7) defines play as "an activity freely chosen, intrinsically motivated and personally directed." Smidt (2010) agrees "all play is purposeful and can only be considered true play when the child has chosen what to do, where, and how to do it." Moyles (2005) says "for young children play and learning are inextricably linked, the one often leading to the other." Russ and Schafer (2006) and Howard et al (2006) agree play and learning dovetail. Learning happens naturally as children play; it occurs with no effort and appears seamless (Howard et al, 2006; Miller & Almon, 2009).

The benefits of play

Froebel (1968) believed "play is the highest expression of human development for it alone is the free expression of what is in the child's soul."

He explains that in play children build their understanding of the world. Nicolopoulou (2010) adds play helps children understand their culture, self-regulation and place in society. Duncan and Tarulli (2003) agree play helps children become contributing members of society.

Article 31 of the United Nations Convention on the Rights of the Child says, "Children have the right to relax and play (UNICEF, 2014). The Welsh Assembly Government Play Policy (2002) states: "Play is so critically important to all children in the development of their physical, social, mental, emotional, and creative skills that society should seek every opportunity to support it and create an environment that fosters it." The DfE (2017:9) agree "play is essential for children's development, building their confidence as they learn to explore, to think about problems and relate to others."

Many children are raised with busy lifestyles and not given opportunities to develop pretend play, which also allows them to express emotions. Kaugars and Russ (2009) say children who play are more imaginative and expressive. Children naturally copy adults around them, therefore it is important they witness adults being lively and creative. Hurwitz et al (2002) say "many parents view their children's activities as nothing more than mindless play."

Findings and analysis

Following the questionnaires and focus group (Gibbs, 2007), I held a validation group with critical friends (McNiff, 2016) where we used open coding.

I sent 30 questionnaires and received 16 responses. The voices of research participants are in italics. Nine of the sixteen agreed their child learnt and developed through play, however, only one said Early Years settings should teach through play only. Six would prefer a focus on formal lessons only with two preferring a combination.

The seven who said they did not value play would prefer settings to focus on formal teaching, preferring their child to concentrate on learning to read, write and count. This view of formal teaching is often brought into the home, where they fill their child's time with flash cards of text or numbers to stimulate learning.

When asked about whether they participated in play, or were played with as children, four said they regularly play with their child, four said they occasionally play and eight said they do not play. From the eight that engaged in play regularly or occasionally, six were played with as a child. All parents who did not play with their children had not played with their own parents either. Bruce (1991) states that "quite a number of adults have not experienced rich moments of play and may have engaged only fleetingly in play of superficial kinds in their own childhoods." Else (2009) adds, "individual views and opportunities are shaped and constrained by those people, cultures and governments around us" while Lillard (2014) states:

> Adults vary in their beliefs about what activities are important for children's development and whether play is a useful activity for children. These views go on to influence whether children are given time, space, and materials for play, as well as whether a parent plays with the child.

Else (2009) explains parents who focus on flash cards results in children who do not know how to play with their peers. Lillard (2014) explains in Euro-America, a child's most frequent play partner is a parent until they reach three or four where they will then begin to play with siblings and peers. In much of the world, parents are not viewed as appropriate play partners for young children. She feels differences in play partners could lead to differences between the quality of children's play across different cultures. Gaskin et al (2007) suggest "types of play in which children engage reflect the values of the parent's culture" and Hannikainen et al (2013) describe play as being an important tool for children to take part in cultural life, to learn how to live together, deal with authority, conflict, power, attitudes, abilities, knowledge and cultural values.

Five parents told me they believe playing helps children with gross motor skills. There were nine unable to explain the benefits of play, one did not think there was any benefit, with comments including: play *"allowed them to make tea," "it means I get some free time," "there is little benefit other than learning to clean up the mess they have made"* and *"it gives me the time to clean up."*

Whitebread et al (2012) point out "parents expect children to play and view it as useful to keep the children busy and out of the way, until they are old enough to be useful." Sutton-Smith (1986) feels strongly parents buy toys for their children that makes play very isolated in the home, they then expect schools to be the provider for child – child relationships.

Finding and analysis from the focus group

Four parents joined the focus group, I showed pictures of a girl blowing bubbles asking, "what is she learning?" Responses included *"Nothing, she is just blowing bubbles," "how to blow bubbles"* and *"she is learning new skills."* I then showed the same picture with headings; speech and language, gross motor development, fine motor development, math, science, oral motor development and social skills. One parent laughed and asked, *"how does blowing bubbles teach them maths?"* We focussed on individual areas of possible learning and discussed how they could help them develop through play. One parent sat quietly, listened to the suggestions and said, *"I'll be honest I've never thought about it like this."*

At the end of the focus group, I asked if they would help me with a follow up task. As it was half-term I asked if they would find a short period of time where they could play with their child and then send a message to let me know how it had been. All four did and were pleased their children enjoyed playing with them and liked they had started to seek them out to play. One said, *"I feel closer to my child now."* Another said, *"I want to play with my daughter now, I didn't before."*

Reflection on the process

I would have liked parents from both reception and nursery class. I was only able to ask reception class parents as another student had already asked for nursery parents' input and the class teacher did not feel it was appropriate for me to also ask for help with my studies. I was left wondering if I might have got different data from parents whose children have not yet started full-time education.

In the validation group a colleague pointed out I had possibly used language the parents may not understand and therefore this could have affected the responses. In the future I could do a sample questionnaire to a critical friend group in advance.

Implications and conclusions

I asked participants for feedback after the focus group. All felt they learnt a lot. Some said; *"I don't think lots of parents know how important play is, I didn't, and I've got two grown kids."* *"I wish I knew this before my child started school, I would have played with them more."*

Parents' feedback got me thinking about doing similar with parents of children that will be starting nursery and reception class. I spoke to the Headteacher and have restarted a "coffee morning" with focus on play that ran prior to Covid-19. Here we discuss possible areas of learning and help parents plan activities for children at home.

Debbie's reflections on the assignment/dissertation

As a parent of two children, I used play to allow me to clean my house, to teach my children routines and to have time to myself, rather than realising its intrinsic value. I was made to feel a poor parent by educational professionals who told me I should have known about the benefits of play. I realised some are bringing up children how they were brought up, others openly admit they saw it as just playing and had never had anyone explain to them what their child could be learning. I wanted to explore this further.

Tutor comments on Debbie's work

Debbie has drawn on personal experiences, sharing some of her misgivings or lack of understanding about play, to create and deliver a successful research project based within her own school community. She has an obvious passion for sharing professional knowledge in a way that is not patronising and is respectful of cultural differences. Solutions suggested are ways school could help rather than looking for perceived deficits in the parents which is refreshing in the modern context. Debbie has written in an accessible narrative that brings the reader along on the research journey with her and is honest about mistakes made along the way.

Master's Degree Level 7 assignment extract

Lucy Krebs

Assignment brief

Students are asked to undertake a case study about engaging with parents. Through this work they will be developing a theoretical framework, examining the key role parents play in their children's learning, deconstructing the concept of "partnership" and engaging with diversity and difference. Conclusions need to include a critical analysis of students' own behaviour and attitudes, and reflections on how their studies will develop their ongoing approach.

Introduction to Lucy

I was 17 when the birth of my eldest nephew prompted me to apply for CACHE Level 3 and subsequently trained as a nanny so I could work closely and individually with children and their families. In my first role caring for the child of two teachers, the family encouraged me to begin my distance learning degree. When my charge began school, employment ended but our relationship continues to this day, fostering the attachment formed in those early years.

I took a role as an Early Years Practitioner (EYP) in a free-flow nursery and my college encouraged me to lecture on their BA (Hons) and I love this role because, not only am I continuously developing my own knowledge but I get to share it with students.

Assignment extract

Engaging with Fathers on their Terms: A father's reflections on his role.

Introduction

It is evident in government policy, care provision and in popular culture that childcare is the primary responsibility of mothers while fathers fulfil a secondary role (Davies et al, 2017). However, in the present day, only 22% of families comprise of a full-time working father with a stay-at-home mother (Davies et al, 2017). Henwood and Procter (2003:343) suggest:

> [Fathers] are expected: to be **present** in the home and **involved** in their children's lives, to keep **contact** with and be **sensitive** to their child's needs . . . to value family time and generally be part of family life.

Lewis (2000) highlights a potential for an increase in stress and life dissatisfaction as fathers balance work with equal shares of childcare responsibilities.

While parent or family related legislation and provision focuses on the inclusion of "parents," there is more emphasis on the mother's role (Davies et al, 2017:11). However, Eisenstadt (2011:157) highlights initiatives such as Sure Start set targets to empower both parents, though it was evident in data collected fathers' attendance was low. Clapton (2017) notes Early Years' settings tend to focus primarily on mothers. The Early Years Foundation Stage (DfE, 2017) refers to "parents" where previously the terms "mothers and fathers" had been used. Clapton (2017:12) suggests "when fathers read the word parent . . . they assume it is intended for the mother." In popular culture, fathers are often cast in secondary roles or lacking parenting skills (Davies et al, 2017, p. 10). Internalising these feelings of "otherness" can discourage fathers from active involvement in Early Years settings as being labelled can become a "self-fulfilling prophecy" (McKinnon, 2014). Practitioners should work to overcome unconscious bias so fathers are not only involved but also meaningfully valued, by sensitive recognition of their autonomy (Whalley et al, 2013).

How a father views his own role is worthy of investigation. Using pseudonyms, this case study focuses on Nicholas; a married, full-time working father with two daughters, Helena (40 months) and Beatrice (13 months). He describes himself as a practicing Christian and hands-on father. His wife Dani is a stay-at-home mother, with Early Years and teaching qualifications. The family have been my close friends for nine years. Preceding this research, Nicholas and I have had many conversations regarding parenting. These conversations and our existing friendship are the inspiration for this case study. Recognising the self-concept and personal experiences of adults should be the starting point of professionals working with parents, because this can then be used to encourage motivation and recognition of what is needed to address perceived problems (Knowles et al, 1970).

Attachment is a consideration in regards to discipline (Music, 2011). Gottman et al (2001:7) highlight meta-emotion, "an organised set of feelings and concepts about emotion" will impact how parents respond to certain behaviour or emotional expression in their children. The stronger the attachment between child and parent, the more able a parent is to respond to emotions (Gottman et al, 2001; Bowlby, 1953). While Gottman et al (2001) suggest fathers are less likely to tune-in to the emotions of children, Music (2011) notes this may be cultural rather than biological. Trevarthen (2011) highlights the sharing of cultural expectations can also foster stronger relationships between parent and child, as well as develop the child's "social brain," thus attachment and boundary setting naturally develop together.

This case study aims to understand what influences Nicholas's role and parenting values from his perspective including the perceived strengths and challenges and to reflect upon his response to the Emotion Coaching Training he has undertaken as a result.

Methodology and ethics

I sought consent from Nicholas which outlined ethical considerations such as his right to withdraw and offered reassurance that withdrawal would not impact the friendship. To quote Ellis (2007:10), "A friend can be trusted to have your well-being at heart," and although it is the friendship that inspired the case study, (Stake, 2010) maintaining the friendship was my first priority. Providing clarity of method presented a challenge, because there needed to be flexibility in my approach to explore Nicholas's perspective and provide support. Taylor (2011) highlights the advantages of prior knowledge of participants when conducting research, however, suggests there are potential risks in assuming oneself as an insider. Although the participants are close friends, this does not mean our views and experiences are the same.

Interviews seemed to be the logical means of gathering data and these were shaped by "a personal history that pre-dates research engagement" (Taylor, 2011:8). A structured interview method could mean I was forcing the direction of the enquiry which gave Nicholas less autonomy (Albon & Mukherji, 2018) where to have it unstructured meant it may be possible to forget that it is an interview at all (Albon & Mukherji, 2018). Ellis (2007) notes in her research there were times when participants appeared to forget she was studying them, thus it seems evident it could happen in the case of a pre-existing friendship in a familiar setting. A semi-structured interview method provided a balance between ensuring focus and being able to get further information, if necessary (Albon & Mukherji, 2018), though this did not eliminate the idea that myself or Nicholas would keep the recording conscious at all times (Taylor, 2011).

Findings

Table 4.1 Findings from Interview 1

Roles and responsibilities	Perceptions of self	Influences and support
Own: • To provide for the family	**Strengths:** • Teamwork • Consistency regarding behaviour • Care responsibilities	**Influences:** • Religion • Wife's training • Own research • Extended family
Shared with Dani: • Hands on at home • Religious instruction • Consistent discipline • Teamwork • Bedtime • Care duties	**Challenges:** • Discipline and wilful behaviour	**Support:** • Wife • Church group • Friends **Comparisons:** • Extended family • Friends • Colleagues

Taylor (2011:15) highlights that it is hard to be objective with participants with whom we have friendships but equally I was conscious the data collected had not provided a fully representative picture of Nicholas. Thus, the second interview was based on what had been discussed in the first interview, summarised in Table 4.2.

Table 4.2 Findings from Interview 2

Topic	Discussion
Discipline	• The term discipline, responses to challenging behaviour • Emotional cause behaviour • How Nicholas feels when dealing with behaviour • Success or lack of in the current approach • Beatrice's difficulty in separating from Dani
Values	• Traits he would like his children to have • Helping them to value Bible teachings • Children listening to others • Making children a part of plans, involvement but are not always the focal point of trips and activities
Emotions/Feelings expressed:	• Anger • Frustration • Resignation/helplessness • Empathy/sympathy • Overwhelming

Discussion

Roles and responsibilities

Initially, Nicholas said his primary responsibilities were to provide for his family and raise his children in "the fear and instruction of the Lord" (Table 4.1). In the first answer Nicholas gave, he believes his roles are traditional paternal roles (Music, 2011). As Bowlby (1953) and Lewis (2000:12) highlight, fathers may judge their parenting abilities by comparing themselves with their partner, however, fathers may take a different role that complements but differs to mothers. For Nicholas and Dani, they work as a team to maintain consistency for both children. Music (2011:194) suggests in contemporary western societies it is more likely fathers will be a "nurturant/participant parent" and this not only strengthens the relationship between father and child but also between parents. Throughout, Nicholas emphasised how he valued Dani. They recognise they each have needs and respond accordingly, vital for paternal well-being and satisfaction (Lewis, 2000). Being emotionally supportive of each other also helps children to develop self-regulation and emotional resilience (Gottman, 2001).

Behaviour and emotions

Nicholas recognised his strengths in consistency regarding discipline, suggesting he was more firm than Dani, (Table 4.1) but also told me he thought Dani was more attuned to the children's emotions (Table 4.2).

However, biologically fathers are no less able to tune into the emotions of children than mothers (Music, 2011). When talking about the difficulty Beatrice had in separating from Dani, it is evident that Nicholas was recognising and responding to her emotional cues. Nicholas said, "I was resigned to it and at least I knew what the solution was . . . to give her to Dani" (Table 4.2). For both Helena and Beatrice, he noted feeling helpless, but for the former there appeared to be no solution where for the latter there did. Gottman (2001) noted when parents do not recognise their own emotions in responding to children's behaviour, this increases the likelihood of anger and helplessness which does not promote self-regulation. As Knowles et al (1970) suggest, this opportunity to reflect on things that had not worked in the past to identify a problem meant we could work together to find a relevant solution.

Moving forward

As highlighted by Eisenstadt (2011:157), "the real challenge is to share knowledge in ways that build confidence in both parents and children in what is possible for the future." It was integral to consider Nicholas's personal values and parenting skills when working with him to find a solution to the challenges he perceived (Norton et al, 2013). This meant sensitivity and consideration of his experiences and personal values to provide an engaging solution (Knowles et al, 1970; Pascal & Bertram, 2012). I had undertaken Emotion Coaching training which focuses on parents supporting children in recognising and managing their emotions rather than responding to the behaviour itself. I realised this would be relevant for Nicholas and Dani. The four stages of Emotion Coaching (Gottman et al, 1997) are:

1 Recognise and empathise
2 Validate and label
3 Setting limits (if needed)
4 Problem solving with the child.

Emotion Coaching also emphasises allowing children to calm before setting limits as when a child is distressed, their brain is in a state which prevents them from taking in new information. Knowles et al (1970) highlight providing information that is relevant to adults and seeks to provide a solution to a problem is integral to effective andragogy.

I used experiences of my own alongside ones relevant to Nicholas to outline the principles of Emotion Coaching (Knowles et al, 1970). The friendship I have with Nicholas was valuable here; on reflection I am not sure I would have shared my own personal experience with someone with whom I had a purely professional relationship. As discussions developed, Nicholas shared his experience of depression and how valuable he had found others acknowledging the strength of his feelings, even if he felt they were not wholly rational. Taylor (2011) highlights depth of discussion is valuable in research with friends. I felt this discussion was the turning point in Nicholas seeing the value of Emotion Coaching; recognising Helena may feel strongly about something, even if he did not. Due to the emphasis Nicholas placed on consistency and the value he places on Dani's training and expertise, I undertook the training with both Nicholas and Dani. Clapton (2017) notes fathers are more involved when mothers are supportive and encouraging, and working in partnership with both parents is a core principle of the EYFS (DfE, 2017). There were some challenges with regards the training, especially that of time. There was not time for a full debrief, the dialogue of which could have been really valuable for reflection and development (Tait & Prodger, 2017). We agreed to "check-in" with regards to whether they had found it successful, and this in the end took place through text message which somewhat limited the spontaneity of a face-to-face discussion (Albon & Mukherji, 2018).

Conclusion

This case study sought to understand Nicholas from his perspective and collaborate to address a perceived challenge. Though a case study of one family, it does demonstrate key considerations for practitioners engaging fathers. It is perhaps due to the labels to which he had been attributed that he did not at first acknowledge the complexity of his role (McKinnon, 2014), but he is actively engaged in family life and does not consider working full time to present a challenge due to the expertise of his wife Dani. Through discussion with Nicholas combined with the knowledge of the family, I was able to suggest an approach that would suit the family's needs and values. While friendship may not be attainable for all practitioners, opportunities to get to know families better can be afforded by parenting groups relevant to them. Nicholas says the experience has been valuable for him. In his response to the check-in message he said:

> Yes, I have had a chance to use it on a couple of occasions! Tried to take a breath and, instead of my natural instinct to tell Helena to man up, acknowledged that she was sad and try to find a way forward together – it's been helpful.

My primary responsibility was to ensure that as a friend I had Nicholas's well-being at heart, so in providing an adequate response to his needs I hope I have done this. However, it is worth recognising that meaningful collaboration was achieved through acknowledging his initial scepticism and responding to it with sensitivity and providing a relevant and engaging solution. What Nicholas demonstrates is that fathers also have their own views, and practitioners should value these highly to meaningfully engage both parents. As Whalley et al (2007:66) emphasise: "parents means fathers too."

Lucy's reflections on the assignment

This case study encouraged the development of my academic voice and to really consider the ethics of research with friends, which is important in Early Years when considering how close Early Years Professionals become to the families with whom they work.

Tutor comments on Lucy's work

Lucy chose to work with a friend, who was a father. She expertly teases out the ethical challenges this presented both in relation to their pre-existing relationships and gender.

Lucy sets the scene by reviewing the position of various writers then relates these to her explanation of the research she conducted. She has successfully woven considerations about the methodology and ethics together, and her demonstration of understanding and links to reading are outstanding. Rather than shy away from acknowledging her friendship with the participants, she raises it as a focal point to consider.

The materials are presented in a deeply respectful way with excellent links to a wide range of theory. Throughout there is an insightful understanding of the key concerns, and Lucy has also been bold in her critical appraisal of the relationship between theory and practice.

Conclusion

Adult learners often worry about articulating differences made to family life as a result of involvement, they do not have the luxury or resources of large-scale longitudinal studies, and even Smith et al (2018) noted most studies with families demonstrate the difficulties in relating outcomes to programmes of support. Developing the individual's capacity to be self-directing, offering people alternatives to their current pathway and encouraging them to reflect on who they wish to *be* would be an outstanding implication for practice. The confident articulation of whether involvement has led families to gain more control over their lives will demonstrate the impact support offered can have on children's learning and development, social mobility and family life.

Adult learners could conclude their work by discussing how they are promoting learning as a lifelong experience, pushing boundaries, and encouraging constructive discontent within their community. In sharing power, being aspirational and demonstrating advocacy, adult learners can highlight to families they have the power to change things for themselves. This demonstrates the learner's willingness to challenge orthodoxy and use existing theory with originality and flair, whilst remaining true to the demands of their professional context and community. Ideas like this are reflective of the aspirations of the QAA (2022) for a graduate workforce who can act as agents for change with a commitment to social justice.

Further reading ideas

Table 4.3 Further reading ideas

Social policy	Relationships	Andragogy	Community
Joseph Rowntree	Bion	Knowles	Bronfenbrenner
Aynsley-Green	Winnicott	Freire	Whalley
Oppenheim	Music	Gallagher & Lawrence	Ledwith
Eisenstadt	Liebermann	Mezirow	Holman
Friedman	Fraiburg	Easen	Gilchrist

References

Adamson, J. & Warren, C. (1983) *Welcome to St Gabriel's Family Centre!* London: The Children's Society.

Albon, D. & Mukherji, P. (2018) *Research methods in early childhood*, (3rd edition). London: SAGE Publications.

Ammari, T. & Schoenebeck, S. (2015) Networked empowerment on Facebook groups for parents of children with special needs. Presented at The 33rd Annual ACM Conference on Human Factors in Computing Systems. 18.4.2015. Seoul, Republic of Korea. CHI. https://dl.acm.org/citation.cfm?id=2702324.

Athey, C. (2007) *Extending thought in young children – A parent-teacher partnership*, 2nd edition. London: Sage.

BERA. (2018) Ethical guideline for educational research. https://www.bera.ac.uk/researchers-resources/publications/ethical-guidelines-for-educational-research-2018.

Beveridge, W. (1942) *Social insurance and allied services (The Beveridge Report)*. London: HMSO.

Blanden, J. (2006) *Bucking the trend: what enables those who are disadvantaged in childhood to succeed later in life? DWP Working Paper 31*. London: Department for Work and Pensions.

Borda (2021) Mothers, mothering, and COVID-19: Dispatches from the pandemic. In O'Reilly, A., & Green, F. J. (Eds.). (2021). Demeter Press. https://doi.org/10.2307/j.ctv1h45mcj.

Bowlby, J. (1953) *Childcare and the growth of love*. Harmondsworth: Penguin.

Braun, D., Davis, H. & Mansfield, P. (2006) *How helping works: Towards a shared model of process*. London: Parentline Plus, Centre for Parent and Child Support, One Plus One.

Brearley, J. (2021). *Pregnant then Screwed*. London: Simon & Schuster UK Ltd.

British Educational Research Association (BERA). (2011) *Ethical Guidelines for Educational Research*. https://www.bera.ac.uk/wp-content/uploads/2014/02/BERA-Ethical-Guidelines-2011.pdf.

British Nationality and Borders Act (2021) https://www.legislation.gov.uk/ukpga/2022/36/contents/enacted

Bronfenbrenner, U. (1979) *The ecology of human development*. Cambridge, MA: Harvard University Press.

Bruce, T. (1991) *Time to Play in early childhood education*. London: Hodder Education.

Children and Families Act (2014) https://www.legislation.gov.uk/ukpga/2014/6/contents/enacted.

Clapton, G. (2017), Good practice with fathers in children and family services. *Institute for Research and Innovation in Social Services* (IRISS), *38*, 1–16.

Crozier, G. & Davies, J. (2007) Hard to reach parents or hard to reach schools? A discussion of home–school relations, with particular reference to Bangladeshi and Pakistani parents. *British Educational Research Journal, 33* (*3*), 295–313, DOI:10.1080/01411920701243578.

David, M. E. (1984) Motherhood and social policy-a matter of education?, *Critical Social Policy, 4* (*12*), 28–43. doi:10.1177/026101838400401202.

Davies, J., Goldman, R. & Burgess, A. (2017). *Contemporary fathers in the UK series: Methodology. Marlborough*: Fatherhood Institute.

Department for Education (2017) *Statutory framework for the Early Years Foundation Stage: Setting the standards for learning, development and care for children from birth to five*. London: Education Department.

Department for Education (2018) *Working together to safeguard children*. https://www.gov.uk/government/publications/working-together-to-safeguard-children--2.

Department for Education (2021) *Statutory framework for the Early Years Foundation Stage: Setting the standards for learning, development and care for children from birth to five*. London: Education Department.

Department for Education and Skills (2003) *Every Child Matters*, London: DES Publications.

Desforges, C., & Abouchaar, A. (2003). *The impact of parental involvement, parental support and family education on pupil achievement and adjustment: a literature review*. London: Department of Education and Skills.

Douglas, J. W. B. (1964) *The Home and the School*. London: MacGibbon and Kee.

Duncan, R. & Tarulli, D. (2003). Play as the leading activity of the preschool period: Insights from Vygotsky, Leont'ev and Bakhtin. *Early Education and Development, 14* (*3*), 271–292. (tandfonline.com).

Easen, P., Kendall, P. & Shaw, J. (1992). *Parents and Educators: Dialogue and Development Through Partnership. Children and Society, 6* (*4*), 282–296.

Eisenstadt, N. (2011). *Providing a sure start*. Bristol: The Policy Press.

Elfer, P., Goldschmied, E. & Selleck, D.Y. (2012) *Key persons in the Early Years: Building relationships for quality provision in early years settings and primary schools*. Oxon: Routledge.

Ellis, C. (2007). Telling secrets, revealing lives: Relational ethics in research with intimate others. *Qualitative Inquiry, 13* (*1*), 3–29.

Else, P. (2009) *The value of play*. London: Bloomsbury Publishing. ProQuest Ebook Central – Reader.

Family Law Reform Act (1987) https://www.legislation.gov.uk/ukpga/1987/42.

Farrimond, H. R. & Joffe, H. (2006) Pollution, peril and poverty: A British study of the stigmatization of smokers. *Journal of Community and Applied Social Psychology, 16* (*6*), 481–491. http://onlinelibrary.wiley.com/doi/10.1002/casp.896/abstract.

Feinstein, L. (2003) Inequality in early cognitive development of British Children in the 1970 cohort. *Economica, 70,* 73–97.

Finer, M. (1974) (Ch.) *Report on the committee on one-parent families.* London: Her Majesty's Stationery Office, 1974, 2 Vols. The Government Book-shop, H.M.S.O., P.O. Box 569, London, SE1 9NH, England. https://api.parliament.uk/historic-hansard/written-answers/1974/jul/02/one-parent-families-finer-report.

Fogelman, K. R. (1983) *Growing up in Great Britain.* London: Macmillan.

Freire, P. (1972) *Pedagogy of the oppressed.* London: Penguin Books.

Froebel, F. (1968). *The education of man.* Bath: Chivers.

Galletta, A. (2013) *Mastering the semi-structured interview and beyond: From research design to analysis and publication.* New York: New York University Press.

Gaskin, S., Haight, W. & Lancy, D. (2007) The cultural construction of play. In Goncu, A. & Gaskins, S. (ed) *Play and development, evolutionary, sociocultural and functional perspectives.* London: Taylor & Francis Group, pp. 179–200.

Gibbs, G. (2007) *Analyzing qualitive data.* London: Sage.

Goldschmied, E. & Selleck, D. (1996) *Communication between babies in their first year.* London: NCB.

Goldstein, J. (2012) *Playing in children's development, health and well-being.* Brussels: Toy Industries of Europe. Play-in-children-s-development-health-and-well-being-feb-2012.pdf (ornes.nl).

Gottman, J. (2001). Meta-emotion, children's emotional intelligence, and buffering children from marital conflict. 10.1093/acprof:oso/9780195145410.003.0002.

Gottman, J., Katz, L. & Hooven, C. (1997) *Meta-Emotion – how families communicate emotionally.* New Jersey: Lawrence Erlbaum Associates.

Hannikainen, M., Singer, E. & Van Oers, B. (2013) Promoting play for a better future. *European Early Childhood Education Research Journal, 21* (2), 165–171.

Hays, S. (1996) *The cultural contradictions of motherhood.* New Haven, CT: Yale University.

Henwood, K., & Procter, J. (2003). The 'good father': Reading men's accounts of paternal involvement during the transition to first-time fatherhood. *British Journal of Social Psychology, 42* (3), 337–355. https://doi.org/10.1348/014466603322438198.

Holman, B. (1983). *Resourceful friends - Skills in community social work.* London: The Children's Society.

Holman, B. (1987). Research from the underside. *British Journal of Social Work, 17,* 669–683.

Howard, J., Jenvey, V. & Hill, C. (2006) Children's categorisation of play and learning based on social context. *Early Child Development and Care, 176* (3–4) 379–393.

Hurwitz, S. (2002) Childhood education. to be successful-let them play! *For Parents Particularly, 79* (2). Gale Academic OneFile.

Kaugars, A. S. & Russ, S. W. (2009) Assessing preschool children's pretend play: Preliminary validation of the affect in play scale-preschool version. *Early Education and Development, 20* (5), 733–755.

Knowles, M. S. (1970) The modern practice of adult education: From pedagogy to andragogy. In Tight, M. (1983) (ed) *Adult Learning and Education.* London: Groom Helen.

Lee, C. (1969) *The growth and development of children.* London: Longman.

Lewis, C. (2000) *A man's place: Fathers and families in the UK.* York: Joseph Rowntree Foundation.

Lillard, A. (2014) *Early development. The Development of Play, 2* (2) 425–460.

Link, B. G. & Phelan, J. C. (2001) Conceptualizing stigma. *Annual Review of Sociology, 27,* 363–385. https://campus.fsu.edu/bbcswebdav/institution/academic/social_sciences/sociology/Reading%20Lists/Mental%20Health%20Readings/Link-AnnualReview-2001.pdf.

Marmot, M., Allen, J., Goldblatt, P., Herd, E. & Morrison, J. (2020). *Build back fairer: the COVID-19 Marmot Review. The Pandemic, socioeconomic and health inequalities in England.* London: Institute of Health Equity.

McKinnon, E. (ed.) (2014) *Using evidence for advocacy and resistance in early years services.* London: Routledge.

McMillan, M. (1919) *The nursery school.* London: Dent and Sons.

McNiff, J. (2016) Action research for professional development. http://www.jeanmcniff.com/ar-booklet.asp.

Miller, E. & Almon, J. (2009). *Crisis in the kindergarten: Why children need to play in school.* College Park, MD: Alliance for Childhood. KindergartenReport_finalforpdf.indd (ed.gov).

Moyles, J. (2005) *The excellence of play.* London: Open University Press.

Music, G. (2011). *Nurturing natures: attachment and children's emotional, sociocultural, and brain development.* Hove, East Sussex: Psychology Press.

National Quality Improvement Network (NQIN). (2010) *Principles for engaging with families: A framework for local authorities and national organisations to evaluate and improve engagement with families.* London: NCB. http://www.socialserviceworkforce.org/system/files/resource/files/engaging_with_families_0.pdf.

Nicolopoulou, A. (2010). *The alarming disappearance of play from early childhood education. Human Development, 53,* 1–4. DOI: 10.1159/000268135. The Alarming Disappearance of Play from Early Childhood Education – CORE.

Norton, F., Woodhead, J., Gallagher, T., Benford, J. & Cole, C. (2013) Growing together for parents of children 0–3: so much more than stay and play. In Whalley, M., Arnold, C. & Orr, R. (2013) (Eds) *Working with families in children's centres and early years settings.* London: Hodder Education.

Nutbrown, C. (2011) *Threads of thinking; Schemas and young children's learning.* 4th edition. London: Sage.

Pallett, A. (2017) The stigma of young parenthood. Artefact. http://www.artefactmagazine.com/2017/02/20/stigma-young-parenthood/.

Park, E. (2010) *The affluent psyche.* PhD. London School of Economics and Political Science.

Pascal, C. & Bertram, T. (2012). Praxis, ethics and power: Developing praxeology as a participatory paradigm for early childhood research. *European Early Childhood Education Research Journal, 20 (10)* 1080/1350293X.2012.737236.

Phelan, J. (1983). *Family centres: a study.* London: The Children's Society.

Pollard, C. L. (2015) What is the right thing to do: use of a relational ethic framework to guide clinical decision-making. *International Journal of Caring Sciences, 8 (2),* 362–368. http://www.internationaljournalofcaringsciences.org/docs/13_pollard.pdf

Pushor, D. (2007). *Parent engagement: creating a shared world.*

Putman, R. D. (2000) *Bowling alone: The collapse and revival of American community.* New York: Simon & Schuster.

Quality Assurance Agency for Higher Education (QAA). (2022) *Subject benchmark statement for Early Childhood Studies.* Gloucester, UK: QAA. https://www.qaa.ac.uk/quality-code/subject-benchmark-statements/early-childhood-studies.

Russ, S. & Schafer, E. (2006) Affect in fantasy play, emotion in memories and divergent thinking. *Creativity Research Journal, 18 (3),* 347–354.

Smidt, S. (2010) *Playing to learn: the role of play in the early years.* London: Routledge. (vlebooks.com).

Smith, G., Sylva, K. Smith, T. Sammons, P. & Omonigho, A. (2018) STOP START Survival, decline or closure? Children's centres in England. The Sutton Trust. https://www.suttontrust.com/wp-content/uploads/2018/04/StopStart-FINAL.pdf.

Stake, R. (2000). *Qualitative research: Studying how things work*. New York: Guilford Publications.

Stake, R. (2010) *Qualitative research: Studying how things work*. New York: Guilford Press.

Strauss, A. & Corbin, J. M. (1990). *Basics of qualitative research: Grounded theory procedures and techniques*. USA: Sage Publications, Inc.

Stuart, J. & Barnes, J. (2005) *Conducting ethical research*. London: National Evaluation of Sure Start. http://www.ness.bbk.ac.uk/support/GuidanceReports/documents/165.pdf

Sutton-Smith, B. (1986) *Toys of culture*. New York, NY: Garden Press.

Svanberg, P. (2007) *Attachment in practice DVD and transcript*. Siren Film & Video Ltd.

Sylva, K., Melhuish, E., Sammons, P., Siraj-Blatchford, I. & Taggart, B. (2004) *The Effective Provision of Pre-School Education (EPPE) Project: Findings from pre-school to end of Key Stage 1*. Institute of Education. http://www.ioe.ac.uk/RB_Final_Report_3-7.pdf

Tait, C. & Prodger, A. (2017) *The Many Different Ways We Involve Families*. In Whalley, M. & Arnold, C. (ed) *Involving parents in their children's learning. acknowledge-sharing approach*. 3rd edition. London: SAGE Publishing.

Taylor, J. (2011) The intimate insider: negotiating the ethics of friendship when doing insider research. *Qualitative Research, 11 (1)*, 3–22. doi:10.1177/1468794110384447.

Trevarthen, C. (2011). The generation of human meaning: How shared experience grows in infancy. In A. Seemann (Ed.), *Joint attention: New developments in psychology, philosophy of mind, and social neuroscience* (pp. 73–113). MIT Press.

UNICEF (2014) Convention on the rights of the child. UN Convention on the Rights of the Child - UNICEF UK.

Welsh Assembly Government (2002) *Play policy*. Play Wales | Chwarae Cymru.

Whalley, M. (2017) *Involving parents in their children's learning. A knowledge-Sharing Approach*. London: SAGE.

Whalley, M., Arnold, C., Orr, R. & he Pen Green Centre Team (2013). *Working with families in children's centres and early years settings*. London: Hodder Education.

Whalley, M. & the Pen Green Centre Team (2001). *Involving parents in their children's learning*. London: Paul Chapman Publishing.

Whalley, M. & the Pen Green Centre Team (2007) *Involving parents in their children's learning*, 2nd edition. London: Sage.

Whitebread, D., Basilio, M., Kuvalja, M. & Verma, M. (2012) *The importance of play*. University of Cambridge. (cam.ac.uk)

Wynn, M. (1964) *Fatherless families: a study of families deprived of a father by death, divorce, separation or desertion before or after marriage*. London: Joseph.

5 Practitioner research

Why practitioner research has value

Dr Christine Parker with Laura Francis, Lisa Yung, Laura Stinson and Angela Dean

In this chapter you will find:

- How to start thinking about your research project
- A description of the research process
- What it means to have a strong ethical stance
- Extracts from assignments that demonstrate research methodology and methods that are suitable for research in early childhood.

"What is my concern?" (McNiff with Whitehead, 2002:72)

The idea of planning and implementing a research project as an undergraduate or postgraduate is daunting; when you are working full time in an Early Years' setting the practicalities can seem overwhelming. So why research? Why make studying so demanding? Over the last 30 years, many practitioners working in Early Years,' school, higher education and integrated settings have found the courage to research an aspect of their working life. A practitioner researcher (Arnold, 2012) has a different perspective to the research process than a university-based academic coming into a setting. This is a lived experience (Whitehead & McNiff, 2006) which has both advantages and disadvantages. The advantage is the wealth of knowledge and experience you have – your practice wisdom (Klein & Bloom, 1995; Goodfellow, 2003). The principal disadvantage is that you are so immersed in your workplace that it is a challenge to see clearly, find a way through and pinpoint what is worth researching. Whatever level your qualification is, the research process you implement follows the same route. This is helpful, as you strive for a higher qualification, your familiarisation and confidence with the research process will increase.

Repeatedly I take adult learners back to the questions McNiff with Whitehead (2002:72) pose":

> What is my concern?
> Why am I concerned?
> What do I think I can do about it?

DOI: 10.4324/9781003271727-5

What will I do about it?
How will I gather evidence?
How will I ensure my judgments are reasonably fair and adequate?
What will I do then?

You can check with a capable peer (Vygotsky, 1978:86) that they agree with the validity of your research proposal.

Your research project is an investigation into an aspect of your work that you feel passionate about, you have a genuine concern for, and you have the motivation to make a situation better. The four students contributing to this chapter illustrate this point very well: they are Laura F, Lisa, Laura S and Angela. It can be a deeply personal investigation as you will discover in Angela's writing where she reflects on her own learning journey, or it can be an investigation that has wider implications for your workplace, as demonstrated by Lisa, researching perceptions of play in the home. Laura F's research is a child study because she wants to understand a child and his learning within development (Dewsbery, 2020), enabling her to be responsive to him with her wisdom practice. Laura S exemplifies the value of deepening her understanding of a family she works with and their response to the impact of school closure during the national lockdowns (PHE, 2020).

How do I view the world?

Every practitioner researcher holds a personal worldview that influences the way they approach their research project. You need to think and reflect on your own worldview; your beliefs, values and principles and how they affect your personal and professional life. When you can articulate your concept of a worldview, you will be able to state the "paradigm" within which you intend to place your research. Personally, I have identified a belief in people that informs what I do as a researcher. Consequently, social justice is an underpinning principle to my actions. I integrate concepts of research to develop my political insights, including a consideration of heritage, my own as well as those of all who are research participants. I see the value in engagement in emerging and developing partnerships and finally striving for emancipation in terms of research benefiting all participants and especially with children at the centre.

I hope by stating the paradigm of social justice I achieve some clarity in defining what your research paradigm might be. Fletcher (2014:xi) usefully defines paradigm to mean "a model for expressing truths, a way of doing so that is whole, distinct and different." He goes on to present a view of the Pen Green paradigm that identifies the notions of "Involvement" and "Insights" as the key ideas that are embraced and developed at the Pen Green Centre. Once you are confident with your belief system, you are ready to consider defined research paradigms. McNiff with Whitehead (2002:27–38) write an excellent chapter on research typologies. Engaging in their writing will help you to consider whether, for example, you are either interpretivist (McNiff with Whitehead, 2002:58) or positivist (Moss, 2019:32).

So, what am I going to do about my concern?

By addressing "my concerns" and with the support of your tutor, you will arrive at your research question(s). Research methodology is the overarching means by which you intend to carry out your research project and find some solutions to what is troubling you. Whether that be either child study (Arnold, 2015; 2021) or case study (McKinnon, 2014) or either quantitative or qualitative, (Cohen et al, 2011) or either autoethnographic (Denzin & Lincoln, 1998) or action research (McNiff with Whitehead, 2002; Marshall et al, 2011). These are choices you need to make. Your research methodology steers your research course and helps you to choose the research methods and techniques you will apply. So, for a child study, observations are the ideal research technique. For a case study you can apply a multimethod approach including observations, semi-focussed interviews and questionnaires. An autoethnographic approach lends itself to journaling and storytelling. Narrative approaches have become increasingly popular within qualitative research; creating safe spaces for researchers and research participants to relate their stories as their truth.

How do I articulate my ethical stance?

Consideration of your ethical stance comes alongside deciding on research methodology, methods and techniques, and is an essential part of any research process. It is not unusual to see an adult learner's ethical stance strengthen assignment by assignment. This appears to happen when you have a powerful sense of your research paradigm, especially if that is connected to notions of equality, equity, social justice and understanding children deeply. And it is obvious when it does not. Ethics are not for just for assignments, and are very much aligned to your worldview, your research paradigm. You know you have a strong ethical stance when you apply your understanding of ethics in your everyday working life.

To be ethical in your research, you need to be deeply respectful of everyone who is engaged alongside you in the research process. You must protect all the research participants and consider how you will gain signed consent, retain confidentiality and anonymise participants' names (Arnold, 2015; McKinnon, 2014). You need to demonstrate that you adhere to accepted ethical guidance, such as BERA (2018) and EECERA (European Early Childhood Education Research Association) (Bertram et al, 2018). It is important to consider how you intend to protect yourself. Research has an emotional component, and it is difficult to judge which aspects of your research will touch you deeply and trigger an overwhelming emotional response. Reading other authors' ethical considerations is time well spent and helps you to articulate and substantiate your view and thus your approach (O'Reilly & Kiyimba, 2015; Robson, 2011; File et al, 2017).

Oh, so this is research!

Once you have a clear implementation plan, a direction of travel and it has been approved by your tutor, you are ready to get started. Try to be systematic in your approach and stick to your timeline. If or when your plan seems to be going awry, seek help straight away. Keeping a research diary or journal can help you to see what you are achieving step-by-step; it is also another source of research data. The challenges of research can be dispiriting but on reflection this is where you will learn the most.

What do I do with all this stuff?

Your research data is all the "stuff" that is created from your research implementation; e.g., observations, journals, completed questionnaires, focus conversation scripts, semi-structured interview scripts. It can feel "messy" at this stage because of the quantity of data that have emerged, equally you can feel disequilibrated because you feel you have insufficient material to analyse. Your data could include some numerical evidence, such as, the number of participants or the collation of quantitative data from a questionnaire. Within the context of early childhood, it is likely that most of your data will be qualitative and in the form of words or narrative; e.g., journals, scribed observations, interviews and focus group (File et al, 2017:65) transcripts. At this stage of your research cycle it is useful to check-in with your tutor to help you decide how you intend to analyse and interpret your research data and outcomes.

At Pen Green there are specific theoretical frameworks that are used daily to support dialogue and deepen understanding about children, their actions, their learning within development (Dewsbery, 2020), the emotional aspects of nursery life and possible lines of direction (PLODS) (Whalley et al, 2017:171–172). These are:

- Well-being and involvement (Laevers, 2011)
- Schemas (Athey, 2007; Bruce, 2015; Nutbrown, 2011; Arnold et al, 2022) and
- The Adult Pedagogic Strategies (Whalley & Arnold, 1997; Lawrence & Gallagher, 2015).

Find the theory or theories that resonate with you and are reflective of your world view. Be critical of where that concept or theory came from and how it is reflective of what you think. Your theoretical framework is informed by the theorists you present in the literature review and is reflective of your worldview.

Findings

Choose the most appropriate and efficient way to present your findings. Your presentation of findings may include analytical components, so for example, in Laura F's assignment you will see how her learning stories (Carr, 2001) demonstrate and clarify her observation analysis. Lisa presents extracts from her focus group discussion script in italics to make those examples stand out. Her data analysis surrounds these extracts and exemplify her thought processes in trying to understand her thinking and colleagues' statements. She uses the extracts to argue her points.

Laura S, similarly, to Lisa, uses script in italics to ensure her findings, Rachel's story, stand out, she honours Rachel's dialogue. There is clarity in the way she presents their shared analysis and the extracted themes. The use of the knitting metaphor supports the structure of Angela's work, and the reader is signposted through the research process and analysis.

How can I reflect on the research process?

Patrick Whitaker[1] (1993) would always ask the evaluative questions:

> What went well?
> What didn't go so well?
> Even better if . . .

This evaluation framework continues to be relevant and useful today. Consider the aspects of your research project that were successful in terms of data generation, theoretical frameworks that supported your analysis and the responses of participants that supported and challenged your thinking. Be honest about what did not go so well. This is where the learning lies.

What have I learnt about my research concerns/questions?

Ensure that in your concluding statements you return to your research question(s) and aim. It is all too easy to be distracted and go off in other directions. As previously stated, it is helpful to share with a capable peer (Vygotsky, 1978) to articulate what you consider your research outcomes to be, including what you have learnt. These can be the hardest questions to answer. What have you unravelled that you did not know before? What do you understand that you did not understand before the research study was implemented? What do you feel that is different? Seldom does a practitioner researcher identify that they did not learn, but if that is the case, you must ask yourself, was this research? So what?

What do I recommend for future practice at work and beyond?

Your conclusion should support you to identify the implications for your practice in the future as well as the relevance to your study beyond your workplace. There are elements of practitioner research at every level of study at Pen Green as well as research being an important part of practice within the centre's work with young children and their families. Having outlined the research process, the students' assignment extracts enrich my description and bring practitioner research to life beginning with Laura F's child study, followed by Lisa's focus group investigation into play in the community. Laura S's research assignment illustrates the power of a story that needs to be told and disseminated to help understanding of the impact of the national lockdowns on families living in disadvantaged communities. Finally, Angela's MA dissertation knits a learning journey of vibrant colours, different patterns and sometimes some unpicking along the way.

Foundation Degree (year 1) Level 4 assignment extract

Laura Francis

Assignment brief

The Level 4 assignment expects students to conduct a child study. Students are required to know and understand a range of observational techniques. They are expected to apply theory to observations and understand the connection between observation, assessment and planning. Students reflect on their own practice and identify strengths and areas for development.

Introducing Laura

I am a proud mum of two boys and I work as an Early Years Assistant at Pen Green. I am passionate about supporting children's learning and development and working with children and their families. I studied for my Level 3 Early Years Diploma at Pen Green. After successfully completing my diploma, I made the decision to continue my professional development and study for my foundation degree. I chose to study at Pen Green, knowing I would learn so much due to the knowledge and expertise of the tutors.

Assignment extract

Methodology

I gained permission to carry out a child study from the child's mother. I observed him engaged in three experiences of interest to him, over a three-week period. In my setting, I use a range of observation techniques, including:

> Narrative – A detailed observation, which can be focussed on one area of development (Brodie, 2013).
> Video – This technique enabled me to revisit the experience, identifying the learning taking place and observe the child's body language and facial expressions (Brodie, 2013).

I have used my observations to write learning stories (Carr, 2001). Carr developed learning stories, describing them as an "alternative method of observation" and states that they are "written vignettes of individual children" (:90).

Ethics

The Ethical Code for Early Childhood Researchers states that "participation in research is on the basis of voluntary, informed consent" (Bertram et al, 2015:6). I provided the child's mother with authentic information about the study, gaining permission on his behalf for him to participate.

I have ensured anonymity by using the pseudonym "Ben" for the child. Arnold (2015:35) discusses that for young children we seek "assent" by relying "on our powers of observation" and not allowing the research to "take precedence over their general well-being as observed in the moment." I showed Ben the camera and gauged from his relaxed body language that he was happy to be filmed. If at any point he was not happy, I would immediately have stopped filming.

I respected Ben's right to confidentiality by only showing the videos to his mother. If any safeguarding issues had arisen, I would have followed the correct procedures, acting in Ben's best interests. Arnold (2015:36) explains how participants "need to be reassured that if they withdraw or complain, there will be no impact on the service they or their child receive." I explained this to Ben's mother.

Child's context

Ben is aged two years four months. He lives with his mother, father and younger brother. He has an interest in vehicles. He often seeks these resources out to explore at nursery. Ben's mother tells me he enjoys playing with vehicles at home too. I have known Ben for eight months and I have been his key person (Elfer et al, 2011) for two months.

Analysis of observations

I applied a "Schematic Framework" (Arnold, 2015:105) to analyse my observations. Piaget (1953:384) explained that children learn by "assimilating material, ideas, and situations in the world into inner schemas and concepts."

Athey (1990) was a constructivist teacher who built on Piaget's work. She explains that "Constructivists are child-centred teachers who are trying to become more conscious and more theoretically aware of what is involved in the process of coming to know" (:30). Athey described schemas as "a pattern of repeatable behaviour into which experiences are assimilated and that are gradually co-ordinated. Co-ordinations lead to higher-level and more powerful schemas" (:37).

Arnold (2015:105), identifies some of the main schemas as:

- Trajectory – moving in straight lines, arcs, or curves.
- Connecting – children become interested in connecting themselves to objects or other people and objects to one another.
- Lines – representing lines by lining up objects or by making marks.

In the style of New Zealand learning stories (Carr, 2001), I discuss what I recognised from observing Ben, and the schemas I observed Ben engaging in throughout his play.

Learning Story

Ben Exploring the Trains

Ben, I noticed your interest in joining the trains together, using their magnets. You show such curiosity in the magnets and how they

Figure 5.1 Ben playing with trains (1)

connected the trains, testing their function by pulling them apart and reconnecting them (Figure 5.1).

You demonstrated an understanding of "functional dependency" Athey (1990:70), whereby you understood that the magnets needed to be connected for the trains to remain together. Ben, I recognised from your play, you were engaging in a "Connecting Schema" (Arnold, 1997), whereby you show an interest in connecting the trains to one another. You pushed the trains over to the track, moving them around the track, checking to see if they remained connected (Figure 5.2).

Figure 5.2 Ben playing with trains (2)

Ben, when the track disconnected, you attempted to reconnect it, showing an understanding of how to fix it (Figure 5.3). When it proved to be difficult, you persevered with it, showing determination in reaching your goal. By doing this you demonstrated the "active learning" characteristic of effective learning (DfE, 2021a:13).

Ben, you pushed the trains over to the mat, where you connected more trains together (Figure 5.4). You pointed to each carriage as you called out the corresponding number, known as the one-to-one principle (Gelman & Gallistel, 1978).

You were also engaging in a "Lines Schema" (Arnold, 2015:105), whereby you lined up the trains. Engaging in more than one schema is known as a cluster (Athey, 2003).

Figure 5.3 Ben playing with trains (3)

Figure 5.4 Ben playing with trains (4)

Bruce (2011:78) explains: "Schemas are not isolated: they develop in clusters and are part of whole networks in the brain."

Ben, you connected more trains, watching as the line grew in length, with each added train. You are beginning to develop a mathematical concept that the more trains connected, the longer the line becomes. Prodger (2013:62) explains how creating lines and connecting could be an early example of experimenting with length and amount. I supported your mathematical development and your communication and language development by using language of size (DfE, 2021b). I said, "It is getting longer," and you continued to push the trains, showing such enjoyment in your play.

After observing Ben lining up the cars and moving them, I positioned the cars by the slide, to respond to his "Trajectory" and "lines' schema" (Arnold, 2015:105). Ben chose to line the cars up and count them. I supported his understanding by offering language such as "next to" and "longer." I have planned to support Ben's interests in the lines and connecting schemas (Arnold, 2015), using the outdoor vehicles, along with resources to connect them with, such as string, as well as number tiles.

Implications for practice

After applying the theory of schema (Arnold, 2015) to my observations, I have learnt that identifying schemas enables me to plan activities that interest children and extend their learning. I intend on using video observations more frequently and continuing to involve parents in their children's learning. This will encourage partnership working (DfE, 2021a:5), between parents and practitioners, enabling parents to identify the similarities between what their child does at nursery and at home.

Laura's reflections on the assignment

I particularly enjoyed writing this assignment, as it gave me a thorough insight into Ben's interests, enabling me to plan to support his future learning and development. I made the decision to write "to Ben" within the analysis section of my assignment, as I believe it made the narrative more meaningful, for sharing it with him.

Tutor's comments on Laura's work

Laura's methodology section informs how she intends to observe Ben, and then through the process of creating learning stories (Carr, 2001) analyse these observations. She demonstrates the importance of articulating ethical concerns as a researcher. The learning stories demonstrate an effective analysis of Ben's actions and learning. Laura has thought deeply about these observations and made links to schema theory.

Foundation Degree (year 2) Level 5 assignment extract

Lisa Yung

Assignment brief

The purpose of the Level 5 assignment is for the student to engage in practitioner research and consider its potential for improving practice. Students need to be able to carry out their research project and apply methods for collecting and analysing data. They need to evidence their knowledge of the theory and concepts relating to their inquiry focus. They must be able to consider the ethical aspects of their research project.

Introducing Lisa

I am based in the North of England and work as a language development worker. I am a regional Makaton tutor (2022), and an I CAN trainer (2022). I work as a member of a large team delivering an intervention programme of support to children and families in three ethnically diverse inner-city areas, located in the 10% most deprived areas in England. The programme is implemented in the home environment for one hour a week over six weeks. Each week, the programme focuses on a different foundation of speech and language development, including communication, play, attention and listening, turn-taking and encouragement.

Assignment extract

Through practitioner research (Walker & Solvason, 2014) I investigate the importance of supporting parents in their child's play. Walker and Solvason explain that practitioner research enables us to learn more about our professional practice and make changes to improve outcomes. I believe a focus group (File et al, 2017:65) is appropriate for this assignment. It involves an element of discussion and interaction and will allow me to collect relevant data whilst participants explore the subject from different angles (Walliman, 2018). Eight work colleagues were invited, and eight participants accepted my invitation (Morgan, 1998). I devised a set of questions that I would use as a guide to generate a discussion. Before the focus group I piloted the questions with a small group of co-workers to assess if the questions would allow me to collect the relevant data (Teijlingen & Hundley, 2001).

Ethics

I gained informed consent from all research participants, explaining how the data would be used and that their participation was voluntary (Connelly, 2014). The British Educational Research Association (BERA, 2018) explains that it is essential that research participants are respected and make decisions independently regarding their participation. I shared the purpose of the research with each participant individually and informed them that they had the right to withdraw at any time without repercussions (BERA, 2018).

I needed to inform participants that their contributions would be shared with others and advise that these discussions would be kept confidential (Clough & Nutbrown, 2012:83). Barnes (1979) states that research data should be presented so that respondents can recognise themselves; however, the reader should not be able to identify them.

Sample from analysis

To reflect on what was discussed and ensure the participants' voices are heard, their own words are included (Clough & Nutbrown, 2012). I have summarised the data using open coding (Corbin & Strauss, 1990) allowing me to summarise and identify and key themes and link relevant theory concerning those themes. I identified two main themes: parents' interaction and cultural influences.

Opening the focus group discussion, I asked participants, "Do all parents you visit engage in play and interact with their child?"

Richard responded, "*Each parent is different. Some engage in play and interact, some parents need encouragement.*"

I asked why this might be and Lucy added, "*I think a lot of the time, parents' culture has a lot to do with their involvement during play, South Asian and Eastern European families seem to need more encouragement.*"

Sarah agreed with Lucy and Richard and shared feedback from parents, "*Some parents have told me they do not sit down and play with their children often because they play with their siblings instead.*"

Although it takes different forms, play is a central activity in all cultures for all children. Parents across cultures have different ideas about development, parent-child interaction and play (Goldstein, 2005). Cannella and Viruru (1997) describe how beliefs about the value of play in children's development and learning can differ from one culture to another. Universally families want the best for their children, learning may be viewed as something that happens within a setting, not in the home environment (Harris & Goodall, 2008). Wheeler and Connor (2009) describe how acknowledging and supporting the importance of the home environment for children's learning and development helps the family in their role as educators for their children.

The discussion continued with Julie sharing her thoughts and experiences, "*Some families seem more focused on their child knowing their colours, numbers and shapes rather than playing.*"

Anna agreed and explained how she had similar experiences, "*Yes, I agree. Parents will repeatedly ask their child, What colour is this? What shape is this? Rather than focusing on the play.*"

Luanne contributed to the discussion and shared her experiences: "*Some parents tell me that their child does not play with them. When I observe them, the parents put pressure on their children to play their way, the child then gets upset or leaves the activity.*"

Tomasello and Farrar (1986) suggest that if parents modify their interaction style, communication between parent and child is promoted. However, this approach is based on western interactions. In some cultures, parents may be dominating and use a more direct approach in their interaction style.

Akhtar et al (1991) state how when a parent jointly focuses on their child's interests and follows their child's lead, this benefits the child's development. Girolametto and Weitzman (2002) agree and describe how the quality of the adult's interactions influences opportunities for the child and promotes speech and language development. Bercow (2018) explains how speech, language and communication skills are essential for brain development and attachment (Bowlby, 1988) in the Early Years, for thinking, expressing ourselves, understanding others, emotional well-being and social interaction.

Conclusion and implications for practice

Through my research project I have developed my understanding of cultural influences on parent-child interactions and how they influence interactions between parents and their children during play. Through a focused conversation (Clough & Nutbrown, 2012:72), I have been able to gain knowledge of my colleagues' challenges and experiences of supporting parents during play. I found it interesting that they had similar experiences.

The families I visit are from diverse cultural backgrounds; they have different values, beliefs, and life experiences. Play can take different forms, depending on the child's environment and parents' beliefs about children's learning and development. In this assignment I have identified that cultural values and beliefs may impact on parents' ideas of children's learning and development and that the home may not be identified as a learning environment. I believe the values and beliefs of all families should be respected and considered. I will ensure the families I work with feel that their opinions, feelings and diversity are valued (Draper & Duffy, 2010). I will introduce a discussion into the programme with parents where they can share their unique ideas about play and what play means to them as a family. Athey (2007) states that parents and professionals can benefit by together identifying the family's individual needs and developing strategies to build positive relationships. Acknowledging the home environment's vital importance is essential and supports parents in their role as educators for their children (Wheeler & Connor, 2009).

During the focus group discussion participants discussed how some parents explained how they do not play with their children as they play with their siblings. I want to discuss this with my line manager and amend the programme we deliver to parents. It should include theory and information regarding the importance of the home environment for children's learning and development, that parents are the child's first and most crucial educator (Ball, 1994).

A family's cultural identity is likely to influence interactions between parent and child. Professional educators need to be aware of the diversity across and within cultures regarding adult-child interaction. There is no right way to play. As a professional I should be open to other approaches. I intend to source specific training for myself and colleagues to develop our knowledge and confidence in this aspect of our work. I look forward to an opportunity to share my research in a team meeting. The team would be able to consider how they might further develop their partnership working with parents (Easen et al, 1992).

Reflection

Lather (1991:52) states, "Research should empower individuals to change as well as understand." As a practitioner researcher (Walker & Solvason, 2014), I gathered and interpreted qualitative data (Richards, 2015). The focus group discussion (Clough & Nutbrown, 2012) gave me an insight into my colleagues' first-hand experiences of supporting families and the challenges they may encounter. Engagement in this research project has enabled me to develop a deeper understanding that western theories do not necessarily apply to all children and families. When supporting families, assumptions should not be made. A family's cultural beliefs and values may influence the parent-child interaction style (Goldstein, 2005).

Lisa's reflections on the assignment

As I work in a culturally diverse area and most of my work is based around working with parents and supporting their interactions with their children during play, I felt it was important to consider how play is thought about across cultures. I wanted to develop my understanding of cultural influences on parent-child interactions and how they influence interactions between parents and their children during play. I enjoyed carrying out the research for this assignment, exploring the literature and different perspectives of what play means within diverse cultures.

Tutor's comments on Lisa's work

Lisa considers how parents value their children's play and problematises what it means when some parents appear not to be so ready to be play partners with their child. In her conclusion she recognises that all families are unique and are not necessarily to be viewed solely as a member of a particular culture/community. This thinking is in line with the guidance given in the "Help for Early Years Providers" (DfE, 2021c). Consequently, her implication for practice is to create the opportunity, early in the programme, to have an open dialogue about attitudes to play and what that looks like for the family. She considers the universality of western theories and questions their relevance to families from other global cultures and communities.

Bachelor's Top-up Degree Level 6 extract from research dissertation

Laura Stinson

Assignment brief

For the BA dissertation, students are expected to carry out an independent research study. The aim is for the student to deepen their understanding of their chosen area of interest in the context of their workplace. Students need to demonstrate that they have a systematic understanding of practitioner research in the field of Early Years. They must demonstrate their knowledge and understanding of research methodology, methods and techniques and their effectiveness. Students are expected to describe the research process, how they have generated data, present their findings and how they have approached their analysis. The consideration of a range of perspectives and developing their critical writing are other vital components.

Laura's dissertation offers an insight into life inside a disadvantaged community when schools were closed during the Covid-19 pandemic

(PHE, 2020). Shared through the method of storytelling, a mother's lived experiences are revealed, bringing to light her triumphs, challenges and losses during unprecedented times. Applying an ethnographic approach (McKinnon, 2014) and online platforms for data collection, Rachel's story was revealed and developed collaboratively. The focus of this extract is on Rachels' story and on one aspect of Laura and Rachel's findings and analysis.

Introducing Laura S.

For the past ten years I have worked in a primary school within my home community and have dedicated time and effort to securing the necessary qualifications, skills and knowledge to improve my own outcomes and those of the children and families. Over this time, I have progressed from an unqualified Apprentice Teaching Assistant to one with Bachelor of Arts Degree status. I have learnt so much about myself as a practitioner, my beliefs and values and what truly matters when shaping and supporting the lives of children and families. I have developed a passion for understanding families on a holistic level and the importance of taking time to understand their day-to-day lives, successes and struggles to provide support that is genuine, required and offered from a place of absolute trust and care. I have gained a greater appreciation for the fundamental role of the family and how vital human connection is both within the home and the community. Recognising this and working in line with these values not only has my professional practice strengthened but my personal practice as a mother of two (soon to be three) young children too.

Assignment extract

A story of school closures within a disadvantaged community.
"Once upon a tower block. . ."
Rachel's story:

> School closing again just worsened my loneliness and the tower block got even quieter. I think many of the children in the block were offered a place in school under the criteria of vulnerable and I felt envious, annoyed in some ways because I longed for a place for Lucy too. To be truly honest, I think I longed for the place for myself, as selfish as that sounds, because Lucy's been fine at home and we have had so many brilliant experiences together. Over the past few weeks we have been shopping thanks to the food vouchers from school, and Lucy has loved becoming the list lady. We have cooked new

foods together and ate them cuddled up on the sofa, made potions out of the washing supplies school sent over and so many imaginary games have been created from spoons becoming princesses, boxes becoming skyscrapers and sofas becoming a hideout from dragons. I don't know much about maths and English but I do know how to make her happy and I take gratitude in that. I wouldn't even ask for a place for her anyway, as much as I want it, because I would never let anyone think I couldn't cope. I'm judged enough and I don't want to tarnish the view you all have on me, even though you would understand, because right now you are the only people who look beyond my appearance, the décor of my home and the fact Lucy's uniform was provided by yourselves six months ago.

I spoke to Lucy yesterday about what she missed about school and she thought for a while, tongue licking her lips and cuddled herself. She revealed she missed the jam on toast the most, Miss Lawson's fleece and the shiny star stickers she gets at the end of each day for being amazing. She pointed to a blanket drying over the door and compared the texture to the fleece, rubbing it so softly on her face. If I had the money, I'd buy the fleece myself just to wear it and make her feel better but I don't think it's the fleece itself she wants, it's the teacher, or is it? I don't know! Anyway, I went with the cheapest option and bought a jar of jam instead and she enjoyed it but said it wasn't the same. We put some teddy bears around the table as though it was snack time and hey presto it felt a little better. This made me so close to calling the school and asking for a place but quick as a flash she was happy playing elsewhere, the moment forgotten, in her mind at least. I watched her playing and thought about the things I miss about the school and frankly it didn't require much thought. I missed the staff members who call me over for a chat each morning, the jokes the caretaker tells me at the gate, the mums and dads outside moaning about the weather and the food bank in the hall – that was a lifesaver! It's outside now but I feel ashamed standing outside the school for everyone to see me bagging up much needed shopping. Food is so expensive now with Lucy at home all day and the shops have limited food available thanks to stockpiling. The school for me isn't just a place I drop Lucy off to learn at you see, it's a place I feel a part of, a place where I am known and a place I can count on to put a smile on my face each day. Without it, I suppose I just feel like a nobody and I know your staff are professionals but you make me feel like I'm a somebody. I cannot wait to spend time with you all again during play days and coffee mornings – especially if you have the posh coffee!

Remember last week you called to check up on Lucy and we ended up talking for half an hour about life in general, well that chat meant the world to me. You didn't hang up the call after I'd told you how Lucy was doing but stayed on instead and we had a good laugh. Much needed normality. I loved the ideas you gave me for helping Lucy learn at home especially the way they were so manageable. The first-time school closed, I was being sent work that honestly I would need a thousand pounds to support. I mean sand, paint, coloured card, puppets, flash cards – the list was endless, it was so daunting. I felt out of my depth, such a failure and sorry but I avoided school phone calls that week in case I was asked how Lucy got on with it all. However, this time, the learning support was great, very much about quality time together and learning through communication, bonding and simple things like listening to the sounds of outside, singing rhymes and learning to dress yourself. For a three-year-old this was perfect and for a mum on a tight budget it was superb. You know them days that go on and on and you realise you've spent most of it talking to a child or staring at the wall, well going outside to simply listen to the sounds was moving. Who'd have thought you could get so much from standing against a fence and listening to the world go by. Just me and Lucy together, listening to the birds it was blissful.

So overall, I'd say school closures have been confusing. Lonely, quiet, mundane and worrisome with everything made more expensive and the pressure to perform like those who have money to spare. Yet at the same time, it's been sentimental, comforting and I have overcome so many difficulties by myself, so yes quite uplifting. Nevertheless, I cannot wait for it to open again so I can speak to people, see familiar faces and get out this tiny flat for a while. Lucy will be so pleased too and as a mum I cannot wait for her to have her jam on toast again surrounded by friends, to snuggle up by Miss Lawson's fleece and to run out the gates with her sticker feeling like the best, most special girl in the world. That will just be brilliant!

Analysis

Rachel and I agreed the themes most evident throughout were "living in disadvantage," "social connections" and "the role of school." Rachel felt these represented her experiences accurately. It was important she had full involvement as often adults living in disadvantage can lack voice and feel powerless in circumstances surrounding their lives (Ridge, 2009).

There was no escape from the shadow of disadvantage which lingered throughout Rachel's story. She exposed how disadvantage impacts families on a scale much wider than income alone, they are multidimensional (McKnight et al, 2017). Although income was indeed an issue, components such as lone parent status, financial stress, food insecurity, lack of social and cultural capital and control over decisions that affect life outcomes were also present. Feinstein et al (2004:6) regard these as "distal factors" representing "the more global or descriptive aspects that characterise the environment and provide an index of a family's demographic or socio-economic situation." He explains how distal factors impact directly on "proximal family processes" representing the interactions between parent and child and upon "characteristics of the home" (Feinstein, 2004:6) being the physical features of the place where a child grows up. Feinstein (2004) explains how these factors are potential risks to children's development. Rachel's story suggested all three risk factors did interplay. I could not help but respect Rachel for her parenting within these factors. I felt she provided Lucy with an upbringing rich in love, warmth, imagination, nurture and time. Rachel and I acknowledged Lucy may benefit from greater nutrition, more material resources and more widening experiences obtained through a greater income but agreed with Masten and Sesma (1999) that counting risks does not always indicate the threats children face. To understand influences on development realistically, more time should be taken to understand the family and "respect the nurturing and supportive experiences that happen day to day within the home" (National Quality Improvement Network, 2010:15).

One aspect of Rachel's story I felt captured the reality of disadvantage was her desire to buy a fleece like that of Lucy's practitioner but with limited finances and little choice, settled for a jar of jam. Rachel discussed how Lucy was her main priority and reinforced how parents, particularly mothers, will go without to provide more resources for their children (Middleton et al, 1997; Goode et al, 1998). She explained how the fleece or jam were more important than her own needs. Rachel described the happiness she felt when interacting with Lucy over jam on toast and teddy bears which captured Sylva et al's (2004:5) suggestion that "what parents do with their children is more important than who they are." Smith and Barron (2020:11) suggest "a life without choice suffocates the imagination" and this did appear true in aspects of Rachel's life. Her actions proved she could tap into her imagination and she worked tirelessly within her circumstances to keep it alive. We agreed that purchasing the fleece or jam would have had the same impact on Lucy, in that it provided a sense of school comfort, but concluded how Rachel provided Lucy with something school could not – a mother who loves unconditionally and holds her daughter in mind every day.

Rachel's story implied education within schools was not the most important provision for disadvantaged families. She regarded it "*an added bonus.*" The beauty in Lucy's words encapsulated this perfectly; "*jam on toast, Miss Lawson's fleece, stickers at home time.*" It was not the teaching she recalled but the feelings she got at school that had imprinted upon her heart and mind. She felt recognised at school, comforted, loved and full; the same feelings Rachel vocalised she appreciated most and longed for too. She captured the true work of schools and practitioners, stating *"people don't realise what actually goes on behind the school doors, they think practitioners only teach children."* Bringing to light McInerney's (2020) statement that "education was never the sole focus of schools, and it's a shame it has taken a pandemic to prove it."

Laura's reflections on her dissertation

Authoring my dissertation was a roller-coaster ride; full of ups, downs, twists and turns. However, once I got rolling with it, the ups most definitely outweighed the downs! I think the key to it becoming such a positive experience was choosing a topic which resonated with me and one I was actively interested in. Although, the pressure of planning and writing a dissertation was at times intense, especially with a young family to support and a full-time job, I gained great enjoyment and satisfaction observing my research develop and the relationships with participants from my own community strengthen. I did take a risk with my dissertation and stepped away from the methods I was accustomed to using. I feel in remaining true to myself and writing in the way I enjoy; the entire process became a lot easier.

Tutor's comments on Laura's work

The strength of Laura's work lies in how she created a collaborative partnership with Rachel, her co-researcher. Laura shows beautifully how storytelling works as a valid and authentic practitioner research method, capturing Rachel's story about her experience of school closure with her three-year-old daughter, Lucy. She had the courage to co-construct (Stern, 1998) relevant literature. This is an original research study, with impact.

Master's Degree (Level 7) extract from research dissertation

Angela Dean

Assignment brief

A research study at MA level should have a well-developed and logical structure. The literature review must demonstrate critical writing where a range of perspectives are presented as well as the literature's relevance to the student's work context. Thinking more deeply about beliefs and values is expected and a consideration of research paradigms. Justification of research methodology, methods and techniques needs to be well referenced and considered. To achieve a high mark, readers will look for originality and creativity, both of which are clearly demonstrated here in Angela's assignment extract.

Angela's Master's dissertation demonstrates the use of metaphor as a framework for organising research data that reflect the practitioner researcher's originality. Angela created five "Metaphor Phases" (three are presented here) relating to the craft of knitting a jumper which are informed by moments from interviews with two former teachers (Andy and Steve), two work colleagues (Pauline and Jane) and her reflective diaries, including her experience of mentoring a colleague. Angela demonstrates that you can be heartfelt and authentic to your "self" as a practitioner researcher.

Introducing Angela

I am an Early Years' teacher and manager working in a rural childcare setting with a team of ten staff. I have worked in Early Years for 28 years and see it as a privilege. I left school with few qualifications, not knowing what I wanted to do with my life. I married and had five children whilst living in a beautiful but isolated rural location. When my first son started pre-school, I was a shy young mother but took my turn on the parent rota. I would never have imagined the career and the learning journey that developed as a result. I can still remember the first time I went to Pen Green full of nervous anticipation, worrying that my working-class roots and London accent would not be accepted in the academic world. I couldn't have been more wrong.

Assignment extract

How to knit the most awesome of jumpers, and wear it

The gradual process of knitting, unpicking and re-knitting represents my learning journey and is inextricably connected to relationships. Metaphors can provide "in-depth understanding of a person's inner symbolic world" (Tosey et al, 2014:642). The concept of knitting links to my earliest childhood memories of my mother who taught me to knit and used her knitted items as a metaphorical handshake, reaching out to neighbours and sometimes strangers, with a shawl for a new baby, a hat for a toddler or a blanket for an elderly person. Relationships with others have contributed to my jumper, people have handed me new colours of wool or taught new stitch patterns. Metaphors often follow a pattern (Schmitt, 2005:360), a pattern of thinking where imaginations are aroused (Berman & Brown, 2000:5). When our brains recognise these patterns, associations between one idea and another are natural and lasting.

My five metaphorical phases represent my learning journey from early childhood to the present day with themes or threads arising from my conversations and reflective diary to create the jumper I have today. (Phases 1, 2 and 4 are excerpted below.)

Metaphor phase 1: Casting on and learning to knit

How to cast on and learning to do basic knit stitch is the beginning of learning to knit. It is the basic template underpinning all further designs. I can still hear my mother saying, "in, round, through, off, in, round, through, off. . . ."

Reflective diary entry

> My earliest learning memories are those exclusive times with Mum when my sisters were at school and it would be just us, a pot of tea and a sugar topped bun loaf. We would draw together, and I would listen to her stories and rhymes, "Once I found a fairy in my cup of tea, she was drowned, as wet as wet could be." She would always encourage me to try things, whether it be food or a new experience, "You won't know unless you try it." Those sayings gave me the dispositions I have today. "There's no such word as can't" and "You can do anything if you put your mind to it" were two of her favourites. They were made powerful because she had achieved so much herself with no support at all.

Upon reflection I am in no doubt that I learnt a lot from my mother, but some of this learning is not practical skill and knowledge, it is about the person I am and the personal attributes that I bring to a learning situation. Katz (1993:10) calls these "learning dispositions" and describes them as a different type of learning from skills and knowledge. Arnold (2015:82) explains that dispositions are concepts "concerned with *how* we approach learning rather than what subject knowledge we gain." They can be thought of as "habits of mind" (Katz, 1993:10). When you take this more holistic view of learning, a whole person view, it clarifies the ingredients for foundations of future learning habits. My dispositional attitudes have developed over years and have done so because I have had the comfort of a secure base, namely my mother (Ainsworth et al, 1979:22). I propose that these dispositions set the foundations for my future learning.

Reflective diary entry

> For a long time, I felt that I had two jumpers. One to wear in my personal life and one to wear in my study life, whichever one I wore it made me an imposter!

In Reay's (2001:337) study of working-class mature women, she found that they were "trying to negotiate a difficult balance between investing in a new improved identity and holding on to a cohesive self that retained an anchor in what had gone before." I grew up thinking that professional middle-class people were somehow "better" than me, that my London accent would create a perception of reduced intelligence. This makes me question what I am trying to achieve, am I looking for a "new, shiny, acceptable, middle-class persona?" (Reay, 2001:341). Or am I trying to hold on to my authentic self. Reay's (2001:338) study showed that "authenticity meant being able to hold on to a self-rooted in a working-class past." A sense of belonging is something people seek in social existence. The difficulty for me has been feeling this sense of belonging and maintaining my authenticity.

I spoke to my primary school teacher, Andy, about working-class academics and feelings of not being good enough.

Andy

> Ah, but that's it you see, that's the limiting factor. Everybody fears getting found out. Everybody feels that they are living the life that is just beyond their own expectations. It takes a long time in your life to realise that they're all pretending too and everybody's working at a level just beyond their own perceived competence.

Andy reinforced realisations that I am not alone in my feelings of self-doubt and in normalising these emotions. He helped remove some of the negativity that I have held for so long. It is difficult to completely escape feelings of class discrimination when living in a culture that normalises it. Once I understood my experience was not uncommon and that I *was* capable and worthy, I stopped trying to "be" – I just "was." My imposter phenomenon (Clance & Imes, 1978) will continue to make an occasional appearance but I shall be resolute in my transformational journey.

Metaphor phase 2: Learning how to follow a pattern – or not

It would be difficult for a novice to knit a jumper without a pattern. It gives you a basic template to work from. A knitting pattern tells you, methodically, what can be done with newly learnt skills. You trust the pattern completely and believe it will shape your garment. But do we all want to wear the same jumper? A talented knitter would put the pattern to one side, bearing in mind what they have learnt from it and then use their skill to make their own bespoke garment containing the excellence of all their prior learning and experience.

Reflective diary entry

> When we moved from London, I was eight and hadn't liked school so far. I remember feeling anxious about going to a new junior school. Friendships were already established, and everything was new and frightening. A newly appointed teacher, Andy, showed me that the most important elements of teaching come from positive relationships and that laughter goes a long way to building these. My feelings of security and validation were instrumental to my learning at this stage. I recall a piece of writing I did, "the cat ran, skidded, and then pounced, eager to get his hungry jaws into the pounding heart of the terrified mouse." Andy read this out to the class as an example of good creative writing – there was no shallow praise, a sticker or "well done." This was heartfelt and meaningful praise that made me feel fantastically good at writing. I have recalled this memory many times when I have been writing assignments because it puts me in a positive place to work from. Andy put a flash of colour in my grey jumper, I still love writing.

I spoke to Andy about this, I was interested to learn whether he knew he was making a difference.

Andy

> That's what I went to work every day to do. Different things work for different children. I know the child, know what makes them tick, I make them laugh in the morning, they feel happy, they don't care about education because they are little. It's like going to a lecture and knowing the lecturer is talking to you, making you feel like you matter.

My conversation with Andy confirmed my thoughts around the importance of learning dispositions in education. This was further supported when I met with Steve, my secondary school teacher. We discussed what he felt made a difference to pupils:

Steve

> The biggest one is confidence; you've got to try and make pupils feel
> confident in themselves and in their own ability. That doesn't happen
> all the time, but I have always tried to be positive about their abilities.

I remember confidence being important to me. I felt surprised at the time
when Steve suggested I think about being a doctor. Going to university
was not on my radar but I held on to this comment and took strength
from it years later when I returned to study. Steve and Andy planted
dispositional seeds that grew into self-belief and courage to try.

Metaphor phase 4: Dropping stitches, unpicking and re-knitting

It is easy to drop stitches, especially when learning. Dropping a stitch
will create a hole in your jumper but showing it to someone and discussing how to pick it up will lead you to repairing the hole and to an
understanding that mistakes happen. If you are not happy with your
jumper, you can unpick it and knit it again, incorporating all the new
stitches you have learnt and adding all the colours that have become
available to you. Before you know it, you will have the most amazing
of jumpers!

My relationship with Jane has evolved over the years, and the fact that
we are good friends but quite different people has been challenging for
both of us at times. Challenge is good. We have grown together and
without a doubt Jane has helped me find an authentic version of myself.

Me

> The metaphor is like my space in between. It was you that said to
> me, maybe it's where I find common ground between me and oth-
> ers. It's been a bit of a turning point this week; I feel different. Do
> you remember when I read the imposter phenomenon and how
> I felt I'd accepted myself, now I don't know if I had because it feels
> like that again.

Jane

> It sounds like this week has been one of those weeks. You have gone,
> "Ooh look, actually I'm not even there any more I'm over here and
> I like it, it's good." What's so lovely about it is that it always catches
> you out. That's why I was asking if you had a childhood where

you could just go off and lose yourself in whatever you were doing because that's what you still do isn't it?

It's your safe place, a place where you can just be you. Of course, the flip side is that the secondary education system didn't work for you, you hit a system where people try to put the knowledge in rather than you discovering it for yourself. You're very much about being creative, teaching isn't about filling an empty container, you're more holistic. You take what's there and nourish it and that's kind of the way it should be.

The above conversation has all the features of a helping relationship (Rogers, 1958:1). Jane was responsible for drawing out my learning dispositions and for giving me the courage to own them and use them. She showed me how to pick up dropped stitches and repair some of the holes in my jumper. Some holes remain, but that shows my *"courage* to be imperfect" (John, 2011:1). I now know that "learning where things do not go right is as valuable as when they do" (McNiff with Whitehead, 2002:90).

Implications for life

There is a golden thread running through my data, it knits together my passion for dispositional learning. I have learnt "the behaviour that most explicitly demonstrates that a teacher really cares about a student and respects his contribution is the act of really listening to what the student says" (Knowles, 1983:58). A personal implication for me is to value listening more to facilitate an adult's control in discovering their own authenticity.

Angela's reflections on the assignment

Looking back now, I am proud that my dissertation was written by my authentic self and not by a representative self I had created to conform to more traditional ideologies of academia. This was especially important to me and validated my work in a way that was not about scores or grades but about becoming self-aware and self-confident. My approach was fully supported by my tutors, and I was encouraged to explore different research methodologies that fitted and complimented my unique style.

Being able to use my learning experience and newfound acceptance remains an important part of my practice and my personal life. I have faith and high expectations of every child and every single member of my team regardless of historical, economical or educational background.

Tutor's comments on Angela's work

Angela demonstrates the value of reflecting on her learning journey from childhood to identify relationships and experiences, that inform the learner and leader she is today. She substantiates her view through a dialogic methodology, discussing her ideas with past teachers, friends, and colleagues. Angela is confident to move away from traditional ways of "writing-up" her studies and chooses to use the metaphor of knitting to explain her lived experiences alongside pertinent theory.

Conclusion

It has been my intention through the presentation of these four student assignments to demonstrate the validity of the statement that starts this chapter, "*Why practitioner research has value.*" The QAA (2022) requires that students studying Early Childhood have a highly developed ability to pose, operationalise and critique research questions, and demonstrate competence in research through practical and theoretical activities. I believe the four students represented here have achieved just that.

Laura F shows how observing a young child, Ben, closely through a schema lens (Arnold et al, 2022) informed her in terms of how to ensure she was doing her best to support his learning and developmental needs whilst in the setting. Having a more confident view of underpinning theory has enriched Laura's practice wisdom (Klein & Bloom, 1995). Although it could be said that her "interpretivist" approach (McNiff with Whitehead, 2002) could be perceived as limited by her bias, Laura has shared her observations with Ben's parents, her colleagues, and her tutor to check that her ideas are justified.

Lisa, through her engagement in degree level study, had the confidence to create a workplace focus group to explore notions of play in the home environment within a diverse community. Her work sits within action research methodology (McNiff with Whitehead, 2002). As McNiff explains to name it "action research" something must change. There is a sense of emancipation on Lisa's behalf as she questions practices and how assumptions could be made concerning a family's culture and the impact of culture on children's play in the home environment. Thus, Lisa has changed her practice to create time at the beginning of her engagement with families to find out more about their views and perceptions of play.

Laura S's autoethnographic (Adams & Ellis, 2013) study illustrates the power of practitioner researcher confidence in creating the time and space for her co-researcher, Rachel, to tell her story without limits. Together they have co-constructed their interpretation of themes extracted from this powerful narrative. It is a testament to all Early Years educators who continued to work tirelessly throughout the national lockdowns resulting for the Covid-19 pandemic. There is a flow to chapter moving onto Angela's Master's dissertation where she seeks to analyse her own learning journey through the metaphor of a knitting pattern. For me, as someone who has engaged in practitioner research over decades, the idea of unpicking stiches to illustrate how I have been back and forth, back and forth, digging deeper to make sense of work/ life experiences is powerful and one I shall use in the future. O'Reilly and Kiyimba (2015:174) come to mind when they explain that, "Reflexivity is an iterative process, and in its basic form means that researchers make visible their impact on the research process and the impact of the research process on them."

Further reading ideas

Table 5.1 Further reading ideas

Practitioner research	Research methodology	Ethics	Action research	Pen Green paradigm
Arnold	Clough & Nutbrown	BERA	Marshall, Coleman & Reason	Fletcher
McKinnon	Cohen, Manion & Morrison	Bertram et al	McNiff with Whitehead	Gallagher
O'Reilly & Kiyimba	Denzin & Lincoln	Connelly	Elliott	Prodger
Robson	Corbin & Strauss Mukherji & Albon	McKinnon		McKinnon

Endnote

1 Patrick Whitaker was an education consultant who developed and taught on all Pen Green Master's Degree courses and Leadership Training Programmes.

References

Adams, T. & Ellis, C. (eds.) (2013) (1st edition) *Handbook of autoethnography*. New York: Routledge.

Ainsworth, M., Blehar, M., Waters, E. & Wall, S. (1979) *Patterns of attachment: a psychological study of the strange situation*. London: Routledge.

Akhtar, N., Dunham, F. & Dunham, P. (1991) Directive interactions and early vocabulary development: The role of joint attentional focus. *Journal of Child Language, 18 (1)*, 41–49.

Arnold, C. (1997) *Understanding young children and their contexts for learning and development: building on early experience*. University of Leicester: Unpublished study. Cited in Arnold, C.

(2015) *Doing your child observation case study: A Step- by-step*. Maidenhead: McGraw-Hill, pp. 17–105.

Arnold, C. (ed.) (2012) *Improving your reflective practice through stories of practitioner research*. London: Routledge.

Arnold, C. (2015) *Doing your child observation case study: a step-by-step guide*. Maidenhead: Open University Press.

Arnold, C. & The Pen Green Schema Group (2022) *Schemas in the early years: exploring beneath the surface through observation and dialogue*. London: Routledge.

Athey, C. (1990) *Extending thought in young children: A parent-teacher partnership*. (1st Ed.) London: Paul Chapman Press.

Athey, C. (2003) *Personal Communications*. In Arnold, C. (2013) *Young children learning through schemas deepening the dialogue about learning in the home and in the nursery*. Oxon: Routledge, p. 2.

Athey, C. (2007) *Extending thought in young children: A parent-teacher partnership*. (2nd edition). London: Sage Publications.

Ball, C. (1994) *Start right: the importance of early learning*. London: Royal Society for the Encouragement of the Arts (RSA)

Barnes, J.A. (1979) *Who should know what?* London: Penguin.

BERA (British Educational Research Association) (2018) https://www.bera.ac.uk/publication/ethical-guidelines-for-educational-research-2018.

Bercow (2018) *Bercow – ten years on*. https://www.bercow10yearson.com/wp-content/uploads/2018/04/Bercow-Ten-Years-On-Summary-Report-.pdf.

Berman, M. & Brown, D. (2000) *The power of metaphor: story telling and guided journeys for teachers, trainers and therapists*. Carmarthen: Crown House.

Bertram, T., Formosinho, J., Gray, C., Pascal, C. & Whalley, M. (2015) *EECERA Ethical Code for Early Childhood Researchers*. European Early Childhood Education Research Association (EECERA). EECERA-Ethical Code.pdf

Bowlby, J. (1988) *A secure base. parent-child attachment and heathy human development*. London: Routledge.

Brodie, K. (2013) *Observation, assessment and planning in the early years-bringing it all together*. Maidenhead: McGraw-Hill Education.

Bruce, T. (2015) *Early childhood education* (5th edition) London: Hodder Education Group.

Cannella, G. S. & Viruru, R. (1997) *Privileging child-centred, play-based instruction. deconstructing early childhood education*. New York: Peter Long.

Carr, M. (2001) *Assessment in Early Childhood Settings: Learning Stories*. London: Sage Publications.

Clance, P. & Imes, S. (1978) The imposter phenomenon in high achieving women: dynamics and therapeutic intervention. *Psychotherapy, Theory and Research, 15 (3)*, 1–8.

Clough, P. & Nutbrown, C. (2012) *A student's guide to methodology* (3rd edition). London: Sage Publications.

Cohen, L., Manion, L. & Morrison, K. (2011) *Research methods in education* (7th edition). London and New York: Routledge.

Connelly, L. M. (2014) *Ethical considerations in research studies. MedSurgNursing, 23 (1)*, 54.

Corbin, J & Strauss, A. (1990) Grounded theory research: procedures, canons and evaluative criteria. *Zeitschrift fur Sociology, 19 (6)*, 418–472.

Denzin, N. & Lincoln, Y. (Eds) (1994) *Handbook of Qualitative Research*. London: Sage Publications.

Department for Education (2021a) Statutory framework for the early years foundation stage. Department for Education. Early years foundation stage (EYFS) statutory framework - GOV.UK (www.gov.uk)

Department for Education (2021b) *Development Matters Non-statutory curriculum guidance for the early years foundation stage.* Department for Education. Development Matters - Non-statutory curriculum guidance for the early years foundation stage (publishing.service.gov.uk)

Department for Education (2021c) *Help for early years providers: understanding the world: diversity.* https://help-for-early-years-providers.education.gov.uk/understanding-the-world/diverse-world.

Dewsbery, F. (2020) How psychoanalytic observation could support Early Years Practitioners to understand children's spontaneous play, and how this might contribute to learning within their development and support practitioners to reflect on their interactions with the children? MA Dissertation, University of Essex.

Draper, L. & Duffy, B. (2010) *Working with parents.* In Cable, C., Miller, L. & Goodliff, G. (eds) *Working with children in the early years.* Oxon: Routledge, pp. 268–278.

Easen, P., Kendall, P. & Shaw, J. (1992) Parents and educators: Dialogue and developing partnership. *Children and Society, 6 (4),* 282–296.

Elfer, P., Goldschmied, E. & Selleck, D.Y. (2011) *Key persons in the early years: building relationships for quality provision in early years settings and primary schools.* Florence: Taylor & Francis Group.

Feinstein, L., Duckworth, K. & Sabates, R. (2004) *A model of the inter-generational transmission of educational success (Research Report 10).* London: Centre for Research on the Wider Benefits of Learning.

File, N., Mueller, J. J., Basler Wisneski, D. & Stremmel, A. J. (2017) *Understanding research in early childhood education.* New York & London: Routledge.

Fletcher, C. (2014) Preface: A review of the pen green research paradigm. In McKinnon, E. (ed.) *Using evidence for advocacy and resistance in early years services.* London: Routledge.

Gallagher, T., & the Pen Green Team (2017) *Working with children aged 0–3 and their families: The Pen Green Approach.* London: Routledge.

Gelman & Gallistel (1978) *The child's understanding of number.* Cambridge, MA: Harvard University Press.

Girolametto, L., & Weitzman, E. (2002) Responsiveness of child care providers in interactions with toddlers and preschoolers, *33 (4),* 268–281.

Goldstein, M. (2005) *Parent-child play interactions in immigrant South Asian families.* Doctoral dissertation. University of British Columbia. Open Library: UBC Theses.

Goode, J., Callender, C., Lister, R. & Policy Studies Institute (1998) *Purse or wallet: gender inequalities and income distribution within families on benefits.* London: Policy Studies Institute.

Goodfellow, J. (2003) Practical Wisdom in Professional Practice: the person in the process. *Contemporary Issues in Early Childhood, 4, (1).*

Harris, A & Goodall, J. (2008) Do parents know they matter? *Engaging All Parents in Learning, 50 (30),* 277–289.

I CAN (2022) https://ican.org.uk/training-licensing/i-can-programmes/

John, K. (2011) *Belonging and significance.* Bath: The Adlerian Society and Institute for Individual Psychology Conference, 29–30 April 2011. http://www.adleriansociety.co.uk/phdi/p3.nsf/imgpages/0939_KarenJohn-ASIIPConf-April2011.pdf/$file/KarenJohn-ASIIPConf-April2011.pdf

Katz, L. (1993) Dispositions: Definitions and Implications for Early Childhood Practices. Perspectives from ERIC/EECE: A Monograph Series, No. 4. http://files.eric.ed.gov/fulltext/ED360104.pdf

Klein, W. & Bloom, M. (1995) Practice wisdom. *Social Work,* pp. 799–807.

Knowles, M. (1983) Andragogy: An emerging technology for adult learning. In Tight, M. (ed.), *Education for adults,* Volume 1: Adult Learning and Education. London: Croom Helm.

Laevers, F. (2011). Childcare - Early childhood education and care. *Experiential Education: Making Care and Education More Effective Through Well-being and Involvement, 1 (1)*, 52–55.

Lather, P. (1991) *Getting smart: feminist research and pedagogy within/in the postmodern*. London: Routledge.

McInerney, L. (2020). Education was never schools' sole focus. The coronavirus pandemic has proved it. *The Guardian*. https://www.theguardian.com/education/2020/apr/14/educa tion-was-never-the-sole-focus-of-schools-the-coronavirus-pandemic-has-proved-it

McKinnon, E. (ed.) (2014) *Using evidence for advocacy and resistance in early years services*. London: Routledge.

McKnight A., Loureiro P. M., Vizard P., Prats A., Claver A. & Kumar C. (2017) *Multidimensional inequality framework*. London School of Economics. http://sticerd.lse.ac.uk/inequality/the-framework/media/mif-framework.pdf

McNiff, J. with Whitehead, J. (2002) *Action research: principles and practice*. (2nd edition) London: Routledge.

Makaton (2022) https://makaton.org/TMC/Learn_Makaton/TMC/LearnMakaton.aspx? gclid=CjwKCAjwh-CVBhB8EiwAjFEPGW9GB-J5fcnoRSQeVEh0L3Xg5vLG-GhQYA8iQ58y-A56pVSsxeCArehoC5mwQAvD_BwE.

Marshall, J., Coleman, G. & Reason, P. (Eds) (2011) *Leadership for sustainability. an action research approach*. Sheffield: Greenleaf Publishing.

Masten, A. S. & Sesma, A. (1999) Risk and resilience among children homeless in Minneapolis. *CURA Reporter, 29*, 1–6. http://www.cura.umn.edu/reporter/99-Jan/article1.pdf Google Scholar.

Middleton, S., Ashworth, K. & Braithwaite, I. (1997) *Small fortunes: spending on children, childhood poverty and parental sacrifice*. York: Joseph Rowntree Foundation.

Morgan, D. L. (1998) *The focus group guidebook*. London: Sage Publications.

Moss, P. (2019) *Alternative narratives in early childhood: an introduction for students and practitioners*. London: Routledge.

National Quality Improvement Network (NQIN), (2010) *Principles for engaging families: A framework for local authorities and national organisations to evaluate and improve engagement with families*. London: NCB. http://www.socialserviceworkforce.org/system/files/resource/files/engaging_with_families_0.pdf

Nutbrown, C. (2011) *Threads of thinking: schemas and young children's learning*. (4th edition) London: Sage Publications.

O'Reilly, M. & Kiyimba, N. (2015) *Advanced Qualitative Research; A Guide to Using Theory*. London: Sage Publications.

PHE (Public Health England) (2020) Covid 19: Guidance on social distancing for everyone in the UK. London. https://www.gov.uk/government/publications/phe-strate gy-2020-to-2025.

Piaget, J. (1953) *The origins of intelligence in the child*. London: Routledge and Kegan Paul.

Prodger, A. (2013) A case study about Jack. In Arnold, C. *Young children learning through schemas deepening the dialogue about learning in the home and in the nursery*. Oxon: Routledge.

QAA (2022) Subject benchmark statement: early childhood studies. https://www.qaa.ac.uk/quality-code/subject-benchmark-statements/early-childhood-studies.

Reay, D. (2001) Finding or losing yourself? Working-class relationships to education. *Journal of Education Policy, 16 (4)*, 333–346. https://doi-org.ezproxy.herts.ac.uk/10.1080/026809 30110054335.

Richards, L. (2015) *Handling qualitative data*. Los Angeles: Sage Publications.

Ridge, T. (2009) *Living with poverty: a review of the literature on children's and families' experiences of poverty*. Leeds: Corporate Document Services.

Robson, C. (2011) *Real world research.* (3rd edition). Chichester, West Sussex: John Wiley & Sons Ltd.

Rogers, C. (1958) The characteristics of a helping relationship. *Journal of Counselling and Development, 37 (1),* 1–16.

Schmitt, R. (2005) Systematic metaphor analysis as a method of qualitative research. *The Qualitative Report, 10 (2),* 358–394.

Smith, A. & Barron, R. (2020) *The state of child poverty 2020. The impact of COVID-19 on families and young people living in poverty. Chances for children.* Buttle UK.

Stern, D. N. (1998) *The interpersonal world of the infant.* London: Karnac.

Sylva, K., Melhuish, E., Sammons, P., Siraj-Blatchford, I. & Taggart, B. (2004) *The effective provision of pre-school education (EPPE) Project: Findings from the preschool to the end of Key Stage 1.* London: DfES.

Teijlingen, E., & Hundley, V. (2001) *The importance of pilot studies. Social Research Update.* Surrey: Department of Sociology.

Tomasello, M. & Farrar, M. J. (1986) *Joint attention and early language. Child Development,* pp. 1454–1463.

Tosey, P., Lawley, J. & Meese, R. (2014) Eliciting metaphor through clean language: an innovation in qualitative research. *British Journal of Management, 25,* 629–646.

Vygotsky, L. (1978) *Mind in society. the development of higher psychological processes.* Cambridge, MA: Harvard University Press.

Walker, R. & Solvason, C. (2014) *Success in your early years' research project.* London: Sage Publications.

Walliman, N. (2018) *Research Methods: The Basics.* (2nd edition). New York: Routledge.

Whalley, M. & Arnold, C. (1997). *Parental involvement in education: Summary of research findings.* London: Teacher Training Agency.

Whalley, M. & the Pen Green Centre Team (2017) *Involving parents in their learning: a knowledge-sharing approach.* London: Sage Publications.

Wheeler, H. & Connor, J. (2009) *Parents, early years and learning: parents as partners in the foundation stage: principles into practice.* London: Jessica Kingsley Publishers.

Whitaker, P. (1993) *Managing change in schools.* Buckingham: Open University Press.

Whitehead, J. & McNiff, J. (2006) *Action research: living theory.* London: Sage Publications.

6 Leadership

Dr Christine Parker

[In collaboration with Anam Khan, Laura Knowles, Jade Dumbell and Mandy Richardson]

In this chapter you will find:

- A consideration of leadership in early childhood and what it means to be leaderful
- Theories that have influenced leadership in early childhood
- Extracts from assignments that demonstrate leaderful practice, how to lead change within a setting and the challenges of leading a large organisation.

When do you feel leaderful?

A common theme experienced at Pen Green, when discussing leadership in the context of early childhood, is for Early Years educators to struggle with the word itself, "leadership." It can be assumed that either leadership or showing that one is leaderful is only for those with designated leadership roles. However, when the dialogue deepens and the notion of being leaderful is better understood, the conversation can turn to thinking about both adults and children showing that they are leaderful. So, defining what is meant by being "leaderful" and what "leadership" can look like in an Early Years' context is important.

During the first two decades of the 21st century, leadership has become increasingly to the forefront of Early Years discourse. In 1994, Jillian Rodd (1994) published her important text that placed the notion of leadership into the world of Early Years. Rapid changes in the Early Years sector since 1997 with, e.gs., the Sure Start, Early Excellence, Neighbourhood Nursery and Children's Centre programmes (Whalley, 2019), created the need for designated Early Years leaders to reflect on leadership and plan for meaningful change, at the same time as holding onto the Early Years heritage of past pioneers. Leadership in the Early Years became a government priority (Whalley, 2019).

Developments at Pen Green and the professional development programmes for Early Years leaders led to the creation of the National Professional Qualification for Integrated Centre Leadership (NPQICL) (Whalley, 2019:102). This work has influenced the Leadership modules on the undergraduate and postgraduate courses accessed at Pen Green. There is a significant emphasis

DOI: 10.4324/9781003271727-6

on self-reflection and applying journaling as a tool to unpick daily happenings, which when analysed reveal vignettes of unexpected leadership. When a student recognises their leaderful practice (Raelin, 2011), this can be disequilibrating. The assignments selected for this chapter illustrate this point very well indeed. To investigate further, some students who do not hold designated leadership roles have shown courage and formed focus groups with colleagues to find out whether they show leaderful practice.

Exploration of leadership theories further enriches the adult learners' ideas about leadership within the Early Years' context. The Pen Green text "Democratising Leadership" (Whalley et al, 2019) offers several perspectives on leadership in the Early Years. Patrick Whitaker (Whitaker, 2019) explains, historical perspectives of where systems theory has influenced leadership in the 21st century. In his explanation, he embraces the notion of educators acknowledging their practice wisdom (Goodfellow, 2003) through meaningful research to inform practice, the recognition of organisational learning and the messiness experienced therein. Karen John firmly establishes the relational aspects of organisational life and presents a range of psychotherapeutic theories to support all educators within the sector (John, 2019). Bettner and Lew (1990) and their theory of the Crucial Cs to develop a sense of belonging was originally constructed for parents and educators when working with children who were struggling with relationships within a setting. However, their work, which has been further interpreted by John (2008; 2019) to be meaningfully applied to adult relationships, has proved to influence and support many working and tutoring in the Early Years (John et al, 2021).

Learners and tutors alike have been intrigued by O'Connell's Leadership "Webs of Belief" (2014:192). O'Connell has done us a great favour by thoroughly reviewing leadership literature and provided a paper that signposts its readers in many multidisciplinary directions. She then expertly creates her own theoretical framework within several principal aspects of leadership she describes as "webs of belief." They are "Learning, reverence, purpose, authenticity and flaneur."

To restate, reluctance to consider oneself as either a leader or of being leaderful can be unpicked when several leadership theories are explored and understood, to the point where I could say there are favourite writers and theorists who seem to particularly appeal to adult learners working in the Early Years field. Theoretical frameworks such as Whitaker's Leadership Development Web (2019:29). Bettner and Lew's Crucial Cs (Bettner & Lew, 1990; John, 2019:51) and O'Connell's Webs of Belief (2014:192) I would propose support the examination of notions of leadership more closely and help you to develop your leadership lens.

I have defined leadership to mean "finding a way through" (Parker, 2019:151), whether the person is a child or an adult, a parent or an educator, a nursery practitioner or a senior leader, taking responsibility for one's own actions and seeking ways of making lives better belongs to everyone. The quotation "everyone has the potential to lead because we all have responsibilities" were the words of an 11-year-old chair of a primary school council

(Parker, 2019:152). In my mind this quotation encapsulates the notion that being leaderful sits within relationships, communication, having a social conscious and acting for the good of all. This could be exemplified by the gentle action of one child supporting another to engage in their play, similarly it could be shown by Early Years educators meeting together to create a pedagogical space to think about sharing their knowledge of children, in contrast being leaderful could be sharing academic knowledge and understanding within the context of adult learning to support adult learners to become increasingly confident in their practice wisdom (Goodfellow, 2003). In my mind these vignettes are all illustrative of leadership.

Journaling to discover leaderful processes

Adult learners, at all levels, can journal to analyse their knowledge and understanding of leadership and being leaderful. Journaling is a creative method of developing and strengthening leadership in that it is a process for deep reflection akin to action research methodology (Marshall et al, 2011). In the role of reflective practitioner (Schön, 1983), the process of journaling creates the documentation of what has happened at work and during a research process. Journaling has a chronological element; recording actions, thoughts, emotional responses and outcomes. Thoughts can be unravelled, connected and viewed alongside theory. Sharp (2001:90) describes the value of reflection and developing the ability "to evaluate your own emotional literacy."

> If we accept the challenge that promoting our own emotional literacy makes us fit for the purpose of helping others to promote their emotional literacy, then the really hard choice is about whether or not we commit to action . . . to work on our self. (:90)

Leaders in the Early Years, including those who are designated, have a story to tell about how they have applied practitioner research as a vehicle for sustainable change within their workplace. The Pen Green leadership modules follow the practitioner research modules, which is a pathway that lends itself to all students recognising how leaderful they are, whatever their professional role may be within a setting and service provision.

Interestingly, leadership was a theme reflected upon by students in some of the assignments presented in Chapter 2, when considering self as learner. This is a recognition of how important reflections on and research into leaderful practice and leadership are in the Early Years. In this chapter, Anam reflects in her Level 4 assignment on the impact of colleagues on herself. Laura forms a focus group to discuss whether she shows leaderful practice in her role as a teaching assistant. Jade presents her journey of understanding the relevance of leadership and change within her work context for her Level 6 work. For her MA dissertation, Mandy explored her values and beliefs that inform her leadership as an owner of a nursery chain in the west country.

Foundation Degree (Level 4) student and assignment extract

Anam Khan

Assignment brief

On the Foundation Degree Course, learners engage in a module where they consider their leaderful behaviour at work and explore their values and beliefs about leadership. Here Anam considered how one incident at work impacted her confidence and self-esteem, initially in a negative way. On reflection she thought about how she could have approached the incident differently, applying her theoretical knowledge to help her understand what had happened.

Introducing Anam

Hello, my name is Anam. I am 23 years old working as a learning support assistant in West Yorkshire. I come from a very big family being the eldest of five other siblings. Being the eldest has required a lot of baby-sitting and helping with their homework, which had evoked my passion for working with young children, supporting their needs and seeing them succeed. I am a confident and bubbly individual who enjoys socialising and forming new friendships. I came out of education at the age of 18 to work in a primary school in order to get some experience working with children. Three years later I am proud to say I am now completing my foundation degree and moving on to my BA year hoping to become a classroom teacher.

Assignment extract

Reflection

From a young age I have been a shy person who lacked confidence. I would accept fault in many situations knowing well I was not responsible. This was due to not speaking up, and this led me to be a lonely person who believed that keeping to myself was safe. However, during my teenage years, I started to come out of my shell and make new friends. This had a positive impact on me as I noticed the positivity that surrounded me. I became a more confident individual who can now socialise and build relationships. This made me believe that communication is required to maintain good relationships. Carrying out this attribute throughout my adolescence has made me the successful practitioner I am today. Within my setting I have made many professional relationships to ensure I feel secure. I believe that maintaining good relationships allows me to communicate effectively with those I work with. An example of this is when I deliver interventions, I know that I will need to communicate back to the class teacher as to where the child is at and how we can support and plan for their needs further.

As a practitioner, I strongly believe in practice wisdom (Goodfellow, 2003) and how it shapes decision making. Practice wisdom is when you are faced with a dilemma and use your experience and knowledge to make a professional choice. I keep testing out new ways until I find a way that works for me (Dewey, 1933).

Description

In my role as a practitioner came the responsibility to cover for class teachers during their Planning, Preparation and Assessment (PPA) time in the afternoon. During my time covering, one incident evoked many emotions that I am going to reflect on using Gibbs (1988) theory.

While I was covering one lesson, the children started to show restless behaviour. Stepping up, I immediately stopped the children and revisited our rules to ensure we are all following them. One child continued to show unpleasant behaviour, therefore I referred to the school's behaviour policy. As a result, I took the child out of the room for some time out. Shortly afterwards, the child returned to his desk, however, his attitude still did not improve.

I then decided to call the behaviour mentor, who unfortunately was not available at the time. So, I sent the child to the class next door where the absent teacher was working. Soon after, the teacher returned to the classroom and took a few children, at this point I was not aware what was happening.

Later, while I was walking to the library with my class, I noticed the absent teacher and another member of staff writing something down with the children. They then took a few more children out and I heard from the ones that had returned that "Miss Khan is in trouble." I assumed that an allegation was made against me.

At the end of the day, I asked the teacher about this matter. She told me this had been forwarded to the head of year. Leaving work, I then spoke to a member of staff about my situation and was advised to write everything down for my own reference.

The following day, the head of year discussed the matter with me and said the child had mentioned I used foul language. She then let me explain what had happened and understood the actions I had taken during the lesson. She heard my version and re-assured me about the situation.

I explained how I felt about the lack of communication as well as no confidentiality adhered to when the teacher was talking to the children.

Feelings

This experience made me feel very distressed as well as question my practice. Leaving work not knowing what had happened left me feeling anxious. When the teacher started to take children out of the classroom, it made me feel uncomfortable because it had never happened before. Along with this my instincts told me that something is not right due to the lack of communication. This caused a great amount of pressure, which led me to overthink every approach I had taken with the child regarding his behaviour. Not only this I also felt alienated as there were many discussions that I was not involved in. I felt very upset knowing that my relationship with the child and the teacher was affected by this situation. This would then affect my practice within the classroom due to the awkward atmosphere around us.

Evaluation

I have always struggled to stand up for myself, knowing that I did do this on this occasion was a huge positive. Although there was a lack of communication between my colleagues and me, this situation led us to a stronger working relationship. Having a positive attitude and remaining composed in a difficult situation was also a great achievement for me. Confiding in a friend, also benefited me as I struggled to share experience in the past. This was a significant step for me.

This situation did affect my self-esteem which had a negative impact on my work. I questioned my working abilities and my role in the school overall. I was left with a loss of ambition, which affected my mental and physical health. There was a phase of awkwardness between my colleagues and I that caused a difficult working environment.

Analysis

This experience shows that, negative emotions were evoked due to the lack of communication between myself, the child and the teacher. There was no time given during the situation where we could have listened and spoken to each other to understand what was happening. I believe the reason this experience had a negative impact on my self-esteem was because of the way the teacher had handled the situation, by not maintaining confidentiality and putting me in an uncomfortable position. The reason it influenced our relationship is because there was a lot of misunderstanding between us which caused tension. This experience suggests that my ability to maintain relationships is very good as I continued to positively support both the teacher and the child throughout the academic year without feeling awkward. This is because I was able to understand that the teacher also had to fulfil her role as well as understanding that the child was having a bad day as other factors were bothering him. Being able to maintain composure and carry out my duties to the end of the day shows how resilient I am. I could do this because I followed through with my beliefs with the importance of being a positive role model.

Conclusion

From this experience I have learnt that maintaining good communication from the beginning is very important. I need to understand that it is okay to take time out for myself and call for support if situations get challenging. I have learnt that it is essential for me to speak to others about my feelings and enquire about the situation regarding myself to ensure I feel secure rather than walking away feeling worried. I believe that this could have gone differently if I had also taken time out with the child to ask him if there was anything bothering him so I could support his needs. I believe I need to develop my confidence as an individual and know that it is okay to question others about something I am unsure about.

Action plan

If this arose again, I would ensure I speak to the child first so that I can understand what they are feeling and why. This will allow me to support their needs and maintain good communication between us. I will make sure to call for support so that I have time to speak to the child or alert the class teacher so that she is aware of the situation. I will ensure that I understand further action regarding the situation so that I am not overthinking a potentially negative impact on my mental health. I will continue to share my feelings and understand that it is okay to do so as I will get further advice which I can benefit from.

Anam's reflections on the assignment

Reflecting upon my assignment I learnt a lot about my personal insecurities, and how it impacted on my interactions with individuals. I now have a different outlook on how I communicate with individuals, which has had a positive impact on my mental health. From this assignment I saw the importance of communication as it boosts my self-esteem to be confident in what I believe. I am now able to make my own decisions and can accomplish challenges I face through having a positive outlook. Reflecting on my assignment I can see how far I have come as an individual. I feel I can be a strong independent woman and express my feelings and thoughts. While journaling at the time of writing this assignment I clearly remember the emotions that were evoked within me as I was able to understand why I was upset during the challenging situation I explained. It was an emotional journey while writing the assignment, however, it allowed me to learn and make some personal changes as an individual to become the confident women I am now.

Tutor's comments on Anam's work

Anam has grasped the opportunity to reflect authentically on her learning journey and in doing so is able to make the connection between her childhood experiences and how she feels and responds as an educator. Anam acknowledges that she does have practice wisdom (Goodfellow, 2003), which is valid and a resource for her to reference in the workplace. Taking time to reflect and learn from her work experience (Gibbs, 1988), Anam approaches her work with greater confidence and a stronger sense of self-belief.

Foundation Degree (Level 5) student and assignment extract

Laura Knowles

Assignment brief

To further develop the learners' knowledge and understanding of leaderful behaviour, they are expected to form a focus group amongst their work colleagues to respond to colleague feedback in terms of the leaderful practice they demonstrate. In addition, the adult learners apply their theoretical knowledge to add depth to their reflections.

Introducing Laura

I currently work as a Learning Support Assistant at a primary school but started this degree whilst I was only volunteering. This meant I was always nervous that I did not have the experience to support myself throughout, particularly in comparison to other people in my group who have worked in education for longer. Luckily the course has been really accommodating and I feel like I have been able to manage well.

Assignment extract

I will be discussing the different aspects of leadership in practice and using this to consider how I am personally as a leader. I will draw upon theories to expand on my knowledge of leadership and management, defining what both are and then using this to reflect on my own leadership. In this paper I will be exploring the works of Raelin (2004), Southworth (1998; 2004), Tuckman (1965) and Belbin (2015) to describe my leadership style and the development of the group I belong to. Moreover, I will be analysing how my use of language supports my way of leading and so will consider Ives and Rana (2018) and Fairclough's (2013) research.

Contextually, I will be reflecting on my leadership style and ability based on the evaluation of a focus group that I carried out, which involved five members of staff at the school I work in. I have taken into consideration other times when I have taken on a leadership role. By doing this, I am able to reflect on and analyse whether my way of leading changes depends on the context. This therefore links to the notion that "effective leaders 'read' and comprehend their contexts like texts: they are contextually literate" (Southworth, 2004:1).

I am currently working as a Learning Support Assistant at a Primary school in the North of England. I am based in the Year Two class, where my responsibilities include leading small groups of children for various tasks, listening to readers and undertaking phonics intervention. In addition, I have also led several after-school sports clubs that undoubtedly helped to develop my practice wisdom, which is defined as "comprising self-knowledge, action capacity, deep understanding of practice and an appreciation of other, that imbues and guides insightful and quality practice" (Higgs & Trede, 2016:65).

Leadership and management

As this study predominantly focuses on leadership, it is important that I gained an in-depth understanding of what leadership and management are and how these correlate to my practice. On the one hand, leadership is defined as "not only the process and activity of the person who is in a leadership position, but also encompasses the environment this leader creates" (Horner, 2003:32). On the other hand, management is considered to be an accumulation of practice and theory that is meant to ensure that "the work of an organisation is developed, supported and guided by an individual or team so as to effectively meet the organisation's purposes" (O'Sullivan, 2003:5).

Over the years there have been multiple theories that explain the different approaches to leadership. Raelin (2004), for example, categorised leadership into the "Four Cs": Collective leadership means how each member of the group can be a leader and is not dependent on one person, much like concurrent leadership which refers to how there can be simultaneous leaders without the need for anyone to stand down. Collaborative leadership identifies a mutual dialogue of what needs doing and that everyone is in control. Finally compassionate leadership commits to the preservation of each individual's dignity when a discussion takes place. However, a limitation of this theory is how people might challenge their position by naturally referring back to their old roles, or others may "seek or compete for social status within the group" (Raelin, 2004:69). Prior to this, Southworth (1998) highlighted the concept of instrumental and expressive leadership where a leader will prioritise goal achievement but will remain considerate of the voice of their staff.

Several theorists have also given recognition to how leadership and management vary, especially as "education contexts differ at every level; they differ between individual children, families, local communities defined by socio-economic class, ethnicity" (Siraj-Blatchford & Manni, 2007:10). This correlates with the model of situational leadership, which was first developed by Hersey and Blanchard (1969). It indicates how a leader will consider the environment and team they are working with and will adopt the most relevant leadership style based on the following: delegating, participating, selling and directing. Additionally, this notion describes how a leader will subconsciously lean towards either task centric or relationship centric behaviours. This model was expanded by Southworth (1998) who discussed the challenges of situational leadership, for example, that changes may occur over time and how each member of the team will have different perspectives on how they want to be led. It is also theorised that leadership is "less a specific set of behaviours than it is creating an environment in which people are motivated to produce and move in the direction of the leader" (Horner, 2003:30). This differs from management as Rodd (2015) states that the core focus of a manager is to guarantee productivity by preserving the systems and the people working within them each day. Further evidence of these differences can be seen in recent studies where it is expressed how "both leadership and management involve influence, but leadership is about seeking constructive change, and management is about establishing order" (Northouse, 2018:4).

Nevertheless, how an individual leads or manages a team can be dependent on external factors such as the dynamics of the group. Tuckman

(1965) devised an early model on the various stages of group development which are labelled forming, storming, norming and performing. This, in summary, explains how a team goes through periods of orientation, conflict and resolution to hopefully reach a point of all members working together effectively. Another factor to consider is the differing personalities of the group's members, therefore linking to Belbin's (2015) nine team roles that are categorised as either being action-oriented, people-oriented or thinking-oriented.

Based on prior reflection, I have had limited experiences of being a leader or manager due to a lack of opportunities and the confidence to take charge of a group. Despite this, the setting works cohesively, particularly because of effective communication between the school's management and staff; this is advantageous since children make better progress in schools where there is strong leadership amongst other qualities (Siraj-Blatchford & Manni, 2007).

Methodology

When considering what leadership and management are, I am using theoretical knowledge to assess my own approaches to leadership for a focus group that I conducted. Focus groups are referred to as an organised discussion with chosen individuals to get various views on a selected topic (Arthur et al, 2012). Before carrying out the focus group, I journaled how I felt, what I have planned, along with any potential concerns, to which Fulwiler (1980) stipulates how the use of journaling allows for a more close and careful way of observation. After this, I led a focus group involving five colleagues at the school I work in which was then transcribed. The purpose was to gauge different perspectives and get a shared Image of the Child (Malaguzzi, 1994). Additionally, after this discussion I provided each participant with a feedback form so I could gain opinions on their experience and also how they viewed my leadership. Following the focus group, I once again journaled my own thoughts on the experience so that I can effectively critique what I have done well and what could be improved should I conduct another. By looking at a range of literature, I am then able to analyse my findings in order to reflect on myself as a leader, and ultimately reflect on my own personal learning and consider how this experience will impact on my future practice.

Findings and analysis

When reviewing my leadership approach in accordance with the Four Cs (Raelin, 2004), I believe that I connect more with the concurrent leadership phase. Although I was leading the focus group, the colleagues that were in a more leaderful position had no need to step down in order to participate. This was important to me, as from my journaling I expressed doubts about how I would be since a member of the Senior Leadership Team (SLT) took part. Consequently, I did not want to take that position of power from someone more authoritative even if only temporarily.

Linking to my own personal values and findings, I can support the notion that "leadership all depends on where you are and with whom you are working" (Southworth, 1998:37). When looking at my language, I fit in with the participating stage of the situational leadership model (Hersey & Blanchard, 1969) as it focuses more on collaborating with those under my leadership and is less task driven than it is relationship driven. In the transcript I am seen to say declaratives like "You're right, but let's think of it in a different way" so that I provide positive encouragement but also guide the participants to make more accurate responses.

One aspect of feedback that was mentioned to me was that I seemed to lack confidence particularly when having to take control and make sure that the conversation stayed on topic. In the transcript I am seen to only interrupt participants on two separate occasions, which could indicate that I did not want to talk over people, although it did guarantee that we did not stray far from the point of the focus group, as relevant interruptions also help to "control the contributions" (Fairclough, 2013:38).

I noticed how I often took pauses in my speaking, for instance in the declarative "Exactly (2) but we need to put some qualities or traits to our image," which further highlights my apprehension despite being in the leaderful position. This is not to say though that pauses in my speech resulted in weak leadership but could demonstrate how by taking time to choose my wording it helped the participants' understanding and guaranteed more insightful responses.

Reflection

According to varying literature, my leadership amongst adults currently is concurrent (Raelin, 2004) and expressive (Southworth, 1998); this indicates that given my role, I am content to remain as a team worker (Belbin, 2015) rather than a leader although with more experience I hope to build on this so that I can undertake a more authoritative role.

Implications for practice

It is important that I consider how my learning from this study will impact my future practice. I intend to take advantage of more opportunities to lead not only groups of children but also adults so that I gain experience and, therefore, should not be as apprehensive. When comparing the thoughts in my journal from before and after the focus group, it is apparent that the experience gave me more self-belief of taking on a leadership role, which supports the idea that through practice I will become more proficient. This will inevitably increase my confidence which is crucial for managers of child-centred settings who need the ability to be "proactive in their setting and to develop and shape the way things are done, and enough confidence in their role to be able to explain to others" (Isles-Buck & Newstead, 2011:2).

By leading the focus group with colleagues from my setting, it has improved my working relationships with those involved. This will mean that I can work more effectively with my colleagues and will ultimately improve group cohesion within our school. In summary, within my current practice I am more comfortable as a leader with groups of children and as a team worker (Belbin, 2015), although I am certain that with experience I will be capable of taking on more permanent leadership elements.

Laura's reflections on the assignment

Personally, I really enjoyed the Leaderful Learning module as I found the literature and topics interesting which I believed to have helped when writing the assignment. For my feedback, it was mentioned that I included a good range of literature and made relevant links to my practice, particularly in the Leadership and Management section. I was advised for future assignments to proofread since I had a few errors in my writing, and to also explore a range of literature to deepen my understanding.

Tutor's comments on Laura's work

Laura shows how she grasps a range of leadership and management definitions and demonstrates her developing critical writing by considering a range of viewpoints. She clearly defines her focus group research method and describes the research process with clarity. Laura responds to colleague feedback concerning her leaderful practice to support her leadership learning. She applies several relevant leadership theories to reflect on her own leadership, for example, Raelin's (2004) four Cs of leadership.

Bachelor's Top-up Degree (Level 6) assignment extract

Jade Dumbell

Assignment brief

In this assignment adult learners are expected to draw on knowledge of leadership in Early Years to support critical reflection on their own leadership. They are required to articulate the vision, values and principles that underpin their own practice and the practice in their setting. Learners need to consider how they will develop their capacity to lead, coach and supervise professional practice. For many learners, critically analysing change processes for their settings comes to the fore as illustrated by Jade in this assignment extract. Jade adopts critical reflection, planning and implementing change to improve the workplace culture.

Introducing Jade

My work within my local community has spanned over the past 20 years. As a teenager I started out navigating a world of community and youth work, and quickly found that I had a natural ability to connect with people. My urge to want advocacy and justice for people started to develop. For the past 13 years, I have been involved in the local children's centre. I attended sessions and activities with my first and second child. I was supported by the Special Educational Needs and/or Disabilities (SEND) worker and through this support I found my voice. I started to support other parents through a community parents' programme. The head of centre had noticed my interactions with my own children and asked if I had considered working with the younger children. I had plenty of experience with teenagers and children with additional needs but my only experience at that point of younger children was with my own children. I worked as supervisory assistant at lunch time, spent time supporting in the nursery and supporting the SEND Co-ordinator. I grew and developed as a practitioner. I spent time in the children's centre initially as a community engagement worker and then on to early intervention family support. Whilst in this role I heard that Pen Green was offering an upcoming degree course. Returning to study was something I had always wanted to do as I loved learning and absorbing new information to support my growth. On the first day the tutors arrived,

I had a conversation with my line manager, and she encouraged me to participate. It was a whirlwind of decision making. Thankfully the tutors were incredibly supportive and worked with me to ensure everything was in place for me to be able to attend. It was one of the best decisions I have made for myself personally and professionally.

Assignment extract

Change

Change moves us from something known and predictable to the unknown and unpredictable. Leaders need to be aware of how they themselves respond to change as well as how the team responds to change (John, 2008). Change which occurs that is out of an individual's control or has a negative consequence, such as the Covid-19 pandemic (Save the Children, 2021) can threaten a person's well-being. Leaders need to be aware of how significant changes can impact individuals. To survive the challenges to our well-being, being able to adapt to change is crucial according to Day et al (1998), who argue that organisations should have an emphasis on personal welfare and well-being alongside professional development. Peck (2006) would say that we can find life difficult because it is difficult. Often, we struggle to keep up appearances in our professional work to conceal negative emotions that we are experiencing (Peck, 2006).

As social beings, we want to feel that we belong in this world, and we want connection to others (Adler, 1931/1992). Adler (1931/1992) further believed that feeling equal to, connected and respected by others was fundamental to empathy, communication, contribution, co-operation and mental health. Bettner and Lew's (1990) work on "Crucial Cs" extended Adler's (1931/1992) work to describe how our fundamental psychological needs to feel connected, to feel capable, to feel we count and to have courage are all part of our self-esteem needs for life. Moyles (2006) acknowledges that ultimately if people have their voices heard and they feel knowledgeable, informed and involved then they will feel empowered and connected to others. This led me to consider reflection. Dewey (1933) advocated a view of reflection that not only contemplated the descriptive but included a consideration of beliefs and underpinning knowledge.

Change in setting

I am the deputy co-ordinator within a small team, and together we have good professional and personal relationships with each other. During the early stages of living and working in the pandemic, I noticed there were struggles and tensions amongst the team. There was an authoritarian approach to changes being made to our service delivery and there was no democracy. The team were facing challenges personally and professionally, and there were emerging challenges arising due to breakdowns in communication within the team. Whitaker (2001) says that the mood of a group is expressed in what is said, how things are said and how people behave non-verbally. On the surface the team was plodding along and there was communication between team members, however, I noticed how it made me feel at times being in the work environment. There was nothing anyone had said, it was simply a feeling. I recognised that as a team we needed time to connect and to truly listen to each other. If we were not having open, honest conversations and truly taking time to connect and listen to each other, then how could we possibly offer support for those children and families that relied on us? Work would be unsustainable. Food is always a common enjoyment for the team. Therefore, I arranged a shared lunch at a time in the week when we were all available without distraction. We had our favourite foods, and I was conscious of truly listening during that lunch. I was aware that I did not interrupt or listen with the intention of responding. Over the next week I modelled this at every opportunity. I took time to consider when I felt negative towards a member of the team to understand the reason for this and referred back to the "Crucial Cs" (Bettner & Lew, 1990). I tried to empathise and understand rather than become annoyed. This change in me was a catalyst for the change amongst the team. There was a shift in the mood over the following weeks and where there had been judgement, this shifted to empathy. Previously where there was disconnect, there were connections which felt more authentic. I did not verbally state that I was making a change, however, by changing my own behaviours and challenging my own thoughts, a discernible change was made within the team and team members individually.

Analysis

Authority to me represented a power over others, and this has led me to being reluctant to be seen as a leader. This meant that when I needed to consider a change which I had instigated, I found this challenging. I felt the change had to be something "major" and anything less than that felt inadequate –I felt inadequate. After thinking hard and struggling to come up with anything I felt was worthy, I decided to send a message out to my team whom I trusted would give me some genuine feedback. One of the responses was how I have "brought awareness to our own mental health and the importance of looking after ourselves in order to look after others." Dudley (2010) says how often we do not see ourselves as others see us and how people can be inspired by "lollipop moments" (Dudley, 2010).

Whitaker (2001) discusses how in groups we may try to distract from serious feelings by behaving in a joking manner or other silliness. As a team I felt that we were using distractions through humour to avoid discussing genuine feelings. I find it incredibly uncomfortable sitting with an atmosphere or mood and can often use humour as a distraction. As a team we started to share our vulnerabilities and there was a visible change in the attitude and morale of the team. When instigating the change to truly listen and to connect as a team, I did not anticipate a change to occur so promptly. This was further confirmation that this was a change which needed to occur. It was like a domino effect between each team member.

In a journal entry, I reflect on how the mood had changed following a supportive, empathetic conversation amongst the team when a team member acknowledged their own struggle with a particular issue. I wrote: "I felt bad for her today as she doesn't open up usually so when she does, I think she must really be struggling." As a team if we can allow ourselves to be vulnerable with each other, then we will be able to be better able to support families as our own feelings will be contained in a safe way. A great friend of mine, Reverend Henry Corbett, has been influential in my life. I respect and admire him. In Corbett's (2020) writing, he discusses the importance of leaders taking time to listen with the intention to understand. Corbett (2020:13) says: "Leaders who do not take time to listen, to understand the various back stories, to appreciate the tensions, hopes and fears, is a leader who is likely to quickly antagonize." Collectively as a team we were able to offer a listening ear with no judgement, no offer of a solution, just listening in this instance and this helped to connect the team whilst supporting the team member to feel valued.

A major part of what I bring to my role is to speak up if something does not sit comfortably. Ajayi (2017) says: "Being yourself is a revolutionary act" and speaking what she calls "thoughtful truths" not only when things are difficult but especially when things are difficult. When the change occurred, conversation felt more authentic and in one journal entry I notice how a colleague came to me and put her hand on my shoulder and thanked me for speaking up and being assertive. She felt more confident to speak up after hearing me speak my truth. Ajayi (2017) argues that people can be afraid to speak their truth for fear of consequences and by listening and speaking with the intention to feel connected as a team, I had given permission for somebody else to do the same. This further led me to consider what Dudley (2010) argues, that we have made leadership into something that is beyond us by de-valuing our everyday actions. The most significant impact we may have on someone's life may be something we may not even remember.

I know how I felt when I had no voice, no say and no control over things happening to me or decisions that affected me. Therefore, I strongly advocate for my children, my community and the families I work with. The drive behind this comes from when I have not felt my Crucial Cs (Bettner & Lew, 1990) and not felt counted. There have been many experiences in my life where I was unable to speak my truth and I value people having the opportunity to share their truth. People need to feel human by affirming that they are there, that they are seen and they matter. The change was about appreciating that each person has their own individual needs, however fundamentally we all need to feel the Crucial Cs to provide support for children and families.

If as a team we used Formosinho's (2004) "Pedagogical Isomorphism" as a framework for supervision, it would help to foster "emotional intelligence" (Goleman, 1998) for individuals and as a team. Empathy and compassion rely on our ability to notice and connect with people (Goleman, 2013). My emotional intelligence (Goleman, 1998) allowed me to distinguish between individual's tensions and pressures and then emotionally pitch my response accordingly.

Concluding thoughts

Reflecting on what leadership now means to me, I have been able to re-evaluate the importance of showing compassion, care and connection to people. Being able to truly listen and strengthen connections has reinforced my understanding of what values I cannot let go off and which values I have that are negotiable. Having both a managerial and leadership responsibility, I am aware that my strengths may also be my weaknesses. The skills, knowledge and competencies I have can both support me in my role and undermine or limit my ability to make changes. There are different dynamics within the organisation, and sometimes the political or emotional drive can mean that even when I feel capable, I may be incapable to assert change. To overcome these challenging situations, I need to take responsibility for my own behaviour if I want to remain resilient and have my Crucial Cs met to show courage.

As a leader I value the importance of making decisions collectively where possible. The process has shown me that individuals can take responsibility for meeting their own needs, and this must be respected to create a supportive working environment. My desire to encourage people to use their voice, to speak up and advocate for themselves and their communities is part of who I am. My biggest challenge is that sometimes I am unable to do the thing I am asking of others, therefore for my own integrity and respect for myself I need to continue to find the courage to speak my truth even when it is uncomfortable.

Jade's reflections on the assignment

Writing my leaderful practice assignment was quite a challenge for me, as my experiences of leadership and management left me with negative connotations of what a leader looked like. I struggled to see the leaderful qualities in myself and as a result I was not sure how I was going to approach the assignment brief. My understanding of leadership developed, and I began to see how as a practitioner I was being leaderful with my colleagues and families I worked with through working together. It was what Dudley (2010) described as "lollipop moments" that supported my shift in how I saw leaderful practice. I had a lightbulb moment when I understood leaderful as an idea that was not just about me and my practice but about the collective and how aspects such as making decisions, being heard and listening to others were important. I relied on my journals to unpick some of the challenges that came up during my writing. I tried to not be so harsh on myself as I am my own biggest critic. I enjoyed the exploration that came with the writing of this particular assignment.

Tutor's comments on Jade's work

Jade has been courageous in considering change within her team as a shift in how they communicate and relate to each other. Initially Jade thought that considering "change" within the context of leadership meant a change in practice with children or as a response to an external demand. Through her process of consideration, including journaling as a tool for reflection, Jade came to understand that she needed to identify a way of changing the mood or atmosphere as experienced by herself and which she recognised amongst her work colleagues. Jade has interwoven skilfully the theoretical underpinning that has supported her decision making in becoming more active in her listening which she terms as "truly listening." It had to be a conscious effort from Jade to make this change and she is surprised at how rapidly this idea impacts on team relationships and the work climate.

Master's Degree (Level 7) extract from research dissertation

Assignment brief

Mandy Richardson

For the MA dissertation, learners demonstrate their ability to critically evaluate, synthesise and apply the knowledge they have gained throughout the course through undertaking a substantial independent study into a significant area of theory and practice in the Early Years. Their learning from the independent study should generate creative and innovative solutions to practice issues. Learners must develop critical understanding of the application of their chosen research methodology and the reasoning for identifying this from a range of approaches.

Mandy journaled her reflections during a period of turmoil in her settings and yet at the same time she was striving for outstanding Ofsted (2019) judgments. As well as journaling, Mandy had formed an "Owners' Group" to discuss the dilemmas they experienced and to seek support from each other. In these extracts the focus is on Mandy discussing her views on leadership, including her underpinning principles and beliefs, the impact of devastating news on her ability to lead and how reflecting on containment influenced Mandy's leadership learning.

Introducing Mandy

I am the owner and sole director of a small group of five day nurseries. The business employs over 90 people, all of whom look to me for leadership and guidance. I am confident in my knowledge of Early Years pedagogy, but my confidence in the leadership of people is where, I believe, the origin of this study derives. My earlier career, whilst always in the Early Years sectors as a teacher and consultant, placed me at the centre of a team. I was supported and offered support, I contained and was contained (Bion, 1968). Now I find myself in a slightly lonelier position, often required to remain measured and controlled when facing adversity and hardship. Occasionally, I'm hesitant to admit, I have been unaware of impending difficulties, unsure of my position. More recently I embarked on a transformational mission, to educate myself in the business acumen that were profoundly lacking. I sought the support of an adviser who profoundly altered my perspective. He gave me the confidence to trust my "business owner" persona and much as I trusted the "teacher." My knowledge was not lacking, just not recognised. His support gave me conviction in my values and allowed me to question my practice more deeply, thus leading inadvertently to this research.

Assignment extract

My leadership journey

"One might, if one had to be outdoors and struggle with a turned-inside-out umbrella and cold rain trickling down the back of a neck, be inclined to say that this was not a Friendly Day" (Allen, 1997).

I consider that I hold a leadership approach that focuses on relationships (Raelin, 2011). I fundamentally practice a moral and emotional perspective within my approach to leadership. However, there are instances where I am compelled to take a very different stance. Convincing leadership is intermittently required to subdue the apprehension of those who are followers (Grint, 2008). I acknowledge that as a leader I have a perceived position of power and privilege which consequently carries the weight of responsibility. This has been prevalent in this research journey, especially on those "(un)friendly days" (Allen 1997).

Authenticity is deeply imbedded in my core values, and consequently I frequently choose an authentic leadership approach (O'Connell, 2014). In definition this style requires recognising myself and my beliefs to express myself and behave according to my convictions. Throughout this study and the challenges I encountered, it was essential that I maintained my principles even when faced with situations that confronted my integrity. This leadership style has developed and continues to develop over time, moulded by past professional and personal experiences. I believe that the conflicts, contradictions and inconsistencies of earlier experiences, influence and shape a more mature, effective and authentic leader (Denison et al, 1995). Authentic leadership (O'Connell, 2014, Gardner et al, 2005) derives from a value-based approach that reaffirms my beliefs and parallels my philosophy of a continuous reflective style of living life as inquiry (Marshall, 1999). I strive for understanding of self and others, appreciating their stories and retracing my own. I appreciate how our narratives intertwine. Consequently, I turned to an authentic leadership style as I built on relationships within my team throughout my research. Relationships based on authenticity and care with all members of the team are essential, even with those who can be the most difficult to engage with.

Whilst reflecting on my leadership journey, I referred back to a "life map" activity I completed at a study week in Pen Green. It depicted life events and people that had in some part created the person I am today. What presented itself unmistakably were recurring themes of team, values, authenticity, belief and frustration. These themes remain with me, and I consider the "human" nature of them and the link to the ancient Greek term "praxeology." I contemplate how both my life, and career journeys have joined to develop me as a person, a practitioner and a leader. I borrow the question from Parker (2019:151): "Can I call myself a Praxeologist?" My leadership values surround people and our community and the complexities they bring, yet I become entangled with the extreme pressures of current social policy (Parker, 2019).

My leadership has developed to connect action and reflection, theory and practice in the pursuit of practical solutions to issues of pressing concern to people, specifically my team (Reason & Bradbury, 2001). This is reminiscent of "a theory of action" designed by Argyris (1999) and further developed into the single and double-loop learning-concepts (Argyris et al, 1985). In single loop action people and organisations modify their actions according to the difference between expected and reached outcomes. In single loop learning, the participant observes and reflects on the situation in which they face problems, errors or inconsistencies and adapt their own behaviour and actions to alleviate and improve the situation accordingly (Smith, 2001). Single loop learning uses accepted values to maximise performance and considers cycles of action and reflection. Smith (2001) questions that when acting in this way, only the symptoms are removed whilst the root causes are still remaining, leading to repeated future problems. However, double loop learning challenges accepted values and opens conversation up (Argyris et al, 1985). In double-loop learning the underlying causes behind the problematic action are addressed. Double-loop learning leads to deepened understanding of conventions and better decision-making in everyday processes; additionally, it leads to organisational learning (Smith, 2001). I identify with this process in my leadership role. I have begun to develop my self-awareness to identify what is often unconscious or habitual and to be conscious of the honesty and openness needed to recognise mistakes. I take responsibility for the need to change our action or methods and how we can learn from difficulties.

Containment in groups

Journal extract

My research was proposed as an exploration of my journey to an "Outstanding" Ofsted judgement. I wanted to understand whether I was alone on the journey or if other nursery owners shared the same desire. I needed to determine whether this could be achieved without paying a high cost, both financially and emotionally, for myself and my team.

Drath et al, (2008) support a view of leadership that embodies the purpose of bringing members of a working collective together towards the "achievement of their mutual long-term goals." This collective leadership was tested whilst conducting my research. Unexpectedly one of my nurseries experienced an unannounced Ofsted inspection. The previous judgement was "Outstanding" and the team were eager to retain this judgement. It transpired that this was not to be and the judgement from the inspection was "Good." The details of the inspector's judgement were not in question, the outcome was fair, but I experienced deflation in the team. I felt a sense of contradicting pressures. I had steered them on a journey to outstanding and allowed them to deem that we had fallen short. My leadership skills were called upon to contain my team (Bion, 1968) and to be authentic to my felt and espoused leadership values (Gardner et al, 2005). It was somewhat unsettling to realise the extent to which my own values and beliefs had shaped the team and that in the role of leader I was responsible for both creating this shared vision and then needing to "contain" the team (Bion, 1968).

The primary task dichotomy

The primary task of my nurseries is undoubtedly to provide highest quality care and education for Early Years children (Rice, 1963). The monetary concerns provide an additional burden, yet Rice (1963) defines the purpose of a business as that of making a profit. The debate that continues to be a problem for me is that as a nursery, we are providing a service befitting of my primary task, yet because of government policy and funding I am constantly limited by the constraints of money. The more clearly defined a primary task is, the more difficult it becomes to make a profit; with core values constraining the decisions that must be made.

Compelled by Marshall (1999), I effortlessly turned to my own reflections to consider the problem. Political, economic, legal and social constraints, predominantly out of my control have a vast impact on my nursery business ensuring that my primary task (Rice, 1963) is not performed in isolation. I discovered that alignment between my espoused values and my practice is not always evident, and I feared might be getting confused (Argyris & Schön, 1974). I reflected on past studies of my leadership to question how I had maintained equilibrium.

Gardner et al (2005) advise that authentic leadership must be consistent with felt, and espoused end values, accordingly I sought counsel from a colleague, Craig. Craig tasked me with considering the various personas

I assumed in my daily life and reflect on how I spoke, acted and even dressed as each one.

Journal extract

> I considered Craig's brief and have decided on a few personas. . . . Mother, daughter, wife, nanny, teacher, business owner, book club member, friend, to name a few.

When we next met, we discussed the characteristics of these personas at length, including how I was perceived by others when I assumed each one. He concluded that I must carefully choose which persona to embrace to confront the diverse challenges I encounter. I considered his advice as valuable learning and carried it forward with me.

A place for containment

During the course of my study I faced a devastating setback. A lease at my most profitable, "Outstanding" nursery was being withdrawn. Financially, reputationally and emotionally this was devastating. It was essential that I find an alternative property. The alternative was intolerable not only to me but to the staff, children and families.

My first thoughts were for the families and the staff, therefore honesty and authentic leadership (O'Connell, 2014; Gardner et al, 2005) guided my actions.

Denison et al (1995) uphold that it is the conflicts, contradictions and inconsistencies of experiences and environments that create more mature, effective and authentic managers. This could never have felt more poignant. My philosophical approach and continuous reflective style, of living life as inquiry (Marshall, 1999) permitted me to seek genuine understanding and afford genuine respect for others. My approach was to offer honest, clear communication and open dialogue with all stakeholders, thus containing them but nevertheless detoxifying the information before returning it to them (Bion, 1968).

The epic journey that followed soon revealed that the quest for another home for the nursery would be neither stress-free nor inexpensive. The journey is not over yet, but the end is imminent. However, the personal cost, emotionally and financially has been enormous. Throughout the expedition, as that is what it has been, I have found comfort in the owners' group. Their emotional proximity helped me to think through situations and consequences allowing me to take positive actions and competently function (Bion, 1968). Being contained by the group gave a sense of safety, where feeling informed thinking and thinking informed feeling, assimilating body and mind (John, 2019). I identified a fundamental psychological need in myself in the Crucial

Cs (Bettner & Lew, 1990). In the group, I needed to "connect," to feel "capable," to "count" and assume responsibility, and to seek "courage" to have good judgement.

This unforeseen change of circumstances struck hard; my reflective journal records the desolation I felt.

> Today's news has come as a devastating blow. The roller coaster of emotions I have gone through today have left me exhausted. I am angry with the landlord, annoyed with myself for not seeing it coming and fearful of the future and devastated about what I would have to share with the staff and parents.
>
> This evening Pippa, a close colleague (employee), arrived at my home unexpectedly. She brought flowers and chocolate as she had been so saddened for me. Hesitantly she also handed me a small book. "I hope you're not offended." She said, "My mother gave me this when I was young, it gives me strength when I'm in need of it, I think you need strength now." It was a Christian book of "Promises."

The content of the book, whether it aligned with my beliefs or faith, mattered little. What affected me was the act of giving something so meaningful. She had parted with something of significant, personal value to comfort me. The book has remained by my side as a symbol of comfort, a reminder of the containment that the gesture brought. I recognised that I inadvertently belonged to two groups; both groups performed a fundamental function inversely, guiding and seeking guidance, containing and being contained.

My journey to understand and achieve outstanding, whilst partially achieved, has essentially initiated a more pertinent journey of understanding. I have established a shared and respected understanding with my team concerning our approach to high quality, outstanding provision. I have recognised that I do still pursue the accolade of achieving an "Outstanding" Ofsted judgement but not at all costs.

This research has demonstrated that there is a requirement for social policy change in order to support small independent nursery owners to deliver the high-quality care and education that they evidently aspire to. Additionally, it has proven that being an independent nursery owner is a lonely and often challenging role, and that members of the owners' group concur. I have recognised that the need for containment does not only apply to my team. I have realised that I need this, too, to have the courage that the role necessitates (Bettner & Lew, 1990).

Whilst my research was very small scale, my further reading around current social policy and recent sector disquiets offers it further gravitas.

Consequently, I am conscious that my findings have exposed unexpected material that with retrospection I would have enjoyed the opportunity to explore further.

What became evident from my research is the aspiration of my team to accomplish the best care and education for the children in the nurseries. Their dedication and commitment are like my own. They too strive for the accolade of the "Outstanding" judgement from Ofsted. Whether this is intrinsic within them or whether it is a product of my influential leadership is unclear. However, it does highlight the requirement for me to continue to support and contain them in this journey (Bion, 1968).

This will require two aspects of development in our practice. Firstly, it is necessary for me to practice my collective perspective of leadership (O'Connell, 2014) and to remain authentic to my felt, and espoused leadership values (Gardner et al, 2005). Practically this will involve me remaining central to the team, being present and facilitating necessary changes to practice. I consider that I am strengthened to take on this role, as my findings have offered validation. I will further explore the Education Inspection Framework (Ofsted, 2019) and collectively with the team will begin the journey of further improving practice.

Secondly, I have discovered from my reflective research that the team frequently look to me for support and confirmation. My journal reflections confirmed my sentiments: "I had led them on a journey to outstanding but had allowed them to deem that we had fallen short."

My leadership will be needed to contain my team during the next part of our journey. Their well-being will be central to future success. I will explore ways of consistently offering high levels of support for well-being issues (Ofsted 2019).

Mandy's reflections on the assignment

Reflecting on the research and writing process, I realise what a cathartic route I have travelled. Reading back my own words filled me with emotion and pride. My journey has been long and at times arduous, but it has been mine, and this has compelled me to respect and accept the journey and enjoy the leader I have become. Furthermore, I reflect that the "expotition" (A. A. Milne), to discover the leader in me is not over. From my early encounters of Winnie the Pooh with my English teacher Mr Healing at 11 years old, I have discovered and learned and I continue to absorb and acquire understanding and perception. Soon after completion of this assignment, I was faced, like many, with the most challenging obstacle to traverse on my leadership path, a global pandemic. Over one hundred of my team and their families relied on me to safely navigate a route previously untrodden. I found myself relying heavily on my previous learning to cope with my fear and uncertainty, whilst once again needing to "contain" the group and to seek containment via my newly found love of Zoom.

Tutor's comments on Mandy's work

Mandy has shown the courage to be authentic in her thoughts and reflections about leadership and specifically within her context as a nursery owner. She has deliberately considered aspects of leadership she found particularly challenging, and her leadership learning has been strengthened through this process. Through these processes of deep reflection and learning, Mandy is able to consider aspects of her role that have previously remained hidden to her. By then considering a range of theories to substantiate her thinking is she is able to establish new ways of working and accept that she herself can be contained (Bion, 1968) by her colleagues.

Conclusion

Reflecting on the students' assignments presented here, it is evident that the relational aspects of organisational life have come to the fore. Without properly supported and funded supervision (John, 2019), it is my belief that, the Early Years' workforce suffers. Opportunities to feel and be leaderful are diminished. This is exemplified by Mandy who recognises in her role as "lead leader" (Parker, 2019) that she still has a need for containment (Bion, 1968). Supervision provides those dialogic moments where educators can analyse critical incidents as, for example, experienced by Anam, and identify supported ways forward. As explained in my introduction, defining leadership and being leaderful as "finding a way through" for me, defines the purpose of supervision.

Further reading ideas

Table 6.1 Further reading ideas

Leadership in early childhood	Leadership theories	Practice wisdom	Change in organisations	The emotional aspect of leadership
Rodd	O'Connell	Klein & Bloom	Fullan	John
Whalley	Whitaker	Goodfellow	Lewin	Bettner & Lew
Klavins	Hargreaves	Marshall	Whalley	Sharp
Vaggers	Senge	Formosinho & Formosinho		Goleman
Tamati et al	Raelin			
	Tuckman			

References

Adler, A. (1931/1992) *What life could mean to you: on the psychology of personal development.* Oxford: Oneworld Publications.

Ajayi, L. (2017) Get comfortable with being uncomfortable.TED Conferences. https://www.ted.com/talks/luvvie_ajayi_jones_get_comfortable_with_being_uncomfortable.

Allen, E. R. (1997) *Winnie the Pooh on management.* Reading: Cox and Wyman Ltd.

Argyris, C. 1999. *On organizational learning.* Cambridge: Blackwell.

Argyris, C., Putnam, R. & Smith D. M. 1985. *Action science: concepts, methods, and skills for research and intervention.* San Francisco: Jossey-Bass.

Argyris, C. & Schön, D. (1974) *Theory in practice: Increasing professional effectiveness.* San Francisco: Jossey Bass.

Arthur, J., Coe, R., Hedges, L. & Waring, M. (2012) *Research methods and methodologies in education.* London: SAGE Publications.

Belbin, M. (2015) Team roles in a nutshell. https://www.belbin.com/media/1336/belbin-for-students.pdf

Bettner, B. L. & Lew, A. (1990) *Raising kids who can.* Newton Ctr, MA: Connexions Press.

Bion, W. (1968) *Experiences in groups.* London: Routledge.

Corbett, H. (2020) *Leadership for the long term: affirming the value of staying.* Cambridge: Grove Books Limited.

Day, C., Hall, C. & Whitaker, P. (1998) *Developing leadership in primary schools.* London: Paul Chapman Publishing.

Denison, D. (1995) *Toward a theory of organizational culture and effectiveness,* Vol. *6.* Organization Science.

Dewey, J. (1933) *How we think.* New York: DC Heath and Co.

Drath, W. H., McCauley, C. D., Palus, C. J., Van-Velsor, E., O'Connor, P. M. G. & McGuire, J. B. (2008). Direction, alignment, commitment: Toward a more integrative ontology of leadership. *The Leadership Quarterly, 19,* 635–653. Center for Creative Leadership.

Dudley, D. (2010) Drew Dudley-Leading with lollipops. TED Conferences. https://www.ted.com/talks/drew_dudley_everyday_leadership.

Fairclough, N. (2013) *Language and Power.* Oxon: Routledge.

Formosinho, J. (2004) *Transformational leadership in early childhood centres as integration.* European Early Childhood Education Research Association (EECERA), 14th Annual Conference. Malta. September, 2004.

Fulwiler, T. (1980) Journals across the disciplines. *The English Journal, 69 (9),* 14–19.

Gardner, W. L., Avolio, B. J. & Wernsing, T. (2005) *Authentic leadership development: Getting to the root of positive forms of leadership.* United States: Gallup Leadership Institute, College of Business Administration, University of Nebraska-Lincoln.

Gibbs, G. (1988) *Learning by doing.* Oxford: Further Education Unit (FEU).

Goleman, D. (1998) *Working with emotional intelligence.* New York: Bantam.

Goleman, D. (2013) Daniel Goleman – leadership and compassion – empathy and compassion in society 2013. https://www.youtube.com/watch?v=TnTuDDbrkCQ.

Goodfellow, J. (2003) Practical wisdom in professional practice: the person in the process. *Contemporary Issues in Early Childhood, 4, (1).*

Grint, K. (2008) Wicked problems and clumsy solutions: The role of leadership. *Clinical Leader, 1, (11),* December 2008, ISSN 1757–3424, BAMM Publications.

Hersey, P. & Blanchard, K. (1969) Management of organizational behaviour: Utilising human resources. *Academy of Management Journal, 12 (4).*

Higgs, J. & Trede, F. (2016) Professional practice discourse marginalia. The Netherlands: Sense Publisher.

Horner, M. (2003) Leadership theory reviewed. In Bennett, N., Crawford, M. & Cartwright, M. (ed) *Effective educational leadership*. London: SAGE, pp. 27–44.

Isles-Buck, E. & Newstead, S. (2011) *Essential skills for managers of child-centred settings*. Oxon: Routledge.

Ives, G. & Rana, R. (2018) *Language and power*. Cambridge: Cambridge University Press.

John, K. (2008) *Leadership mentoring and staff supervision in children's centres*. Corby: Pen Green Research.

John, K. (2019) Holding the baby: leadership that inspires and contains ambition and anxiety. In Whalley, M., John, K., Whitaker, P., Klavins, E., Parker, C. & Vaggers, J. *Democratising leadership in the early years*. London: Routledge, pp. 38–86.

John, K., Austin, Z., Benford, J., Clark, K., Hewitt, E., Parker, C. & Tait, C. (2021) Understanding basic psychological needs across the life span: The role of Crucial Cs. *The Journal of Individual Psychology*, 77 (*2 Summer*).

Malaguzzi, L. (1994) Your image of the child: where teaching begins. https://www.reggioalliance.org/downloads/malaguzzi:ccie:1994.pdf.

Marshall, J. (1999) Living life as inquiry. *Systemic Practice and Action Research, 12*, (*2*), 155–171.

Marshall, J., Coleman, G. & Reason, P. (Eds) (2011) *Leadership for sustainability. An action research approach*. Sheffield: Greenleaf Publishing.

Moyles, J. (2006) *Effective leadership and management in the early years*. England: Open University Press.

Northouse, P. (2018) *Introduction to leadership: concepts and practice*. London: SAGE Publications.

O'Connell, P.K. (2014) A simplified framework for 21st century leader development. *The Leadership Quarterly, 25*, 183–203.

Ofsted (2019) Early years inspection handbook for Ofsted registered provision. https://assets.publishing.service.gov.uk/government/uploads/system/uploads/attachment_data/file/828465/Early_years_inspection_handbook.pdf.

O'Sullivan, J. (2003) *Manager's handbook*. Leamington Spa: Scholastic Publications.

Parker, C. (2019) We all have the potential to lead because we all have responsibilities. In Whalley, M., John, K., Whitaker, P., Klavins, E., Parker, C. and Vaggers, J. (2019) *Democratising leadership in the early years*. London: Routledge, pp. 139–170.

Peck, S. M. (2006) *The road less travelled*. London: Arrow Books.

Raelin, J. (2004) *Preparing for leaderful practice*. TD March. pp. 65–70.

Raelin, J. (2011) From leadership-as-practice to leaderful practice. *Leadership*, 7 (*2*), pp. 195–211.

Reason, P. & Bradbury, H. (2001) *The SAGE handbook of action research. Participative inquiry and practice*. Los Angeles: SAGE Publications.

Rice, A. K. (1963) *The enterprise and the environment*. London: Tavistock Publications.

Rodd, J. (1994) *Leadership in early childhood: the pathway to professionalism* (1st edition). Bucks. Open University Press.

Rodd, J. (2015) *Leading change in the early years: Principles and practice*. Berkshire: McGraw-Hill Education.

Save the Children (2021) https://www.savethechildren.org.uk/how-you-can-help/emergencies/coronavirus-uk-outbreak-facts?ppc=true&matchtype=&s_keyword=&adposition=&s_kwcid=AL!9048!3!458052851960!!!g!!&gclid=Cj0KCQjwnNyUBhCZARIsAI9AYlGzBFwTsetAUxvSI5k14vEY-RoX7UFDN3tKghQk4gScrQnP3_mH38caArQCEALw_wcB&gclsrc=aw.ds

Schön, D. (1983) *The reflective practitioner: How professionals think in action*. Farnham: Ashgate Publishing.

Sharp, P. (2001) *Nurturing emotional literacy: a practical guide for teachers, parents and those in the caring professions*. Abingdon: David Fulton Publishers.

Siraj-Blatchford, I. & Manni, L. (2007) *Effective leadership in the early years sector: the ELEYS study*. London: Institute of Education.

Smith, M. K. (2001, 2011). Chris Argyris: theories of action, double-loop learning and organizational learning. *The Encyclopedia of Informal Education*. http://infed.org/mobi/chris-argyris-theories-of-action-double-loop-learning-and-organizational-learning/

Southworth, G. (1998) *Leading improving primary schools: the work of head teachers and deputy heads*. London: Taylor & Francis.

Southworth, G. (2004) *Primary school leadership in context: Leading small, medium and large sized schools*. London: Routledge Falmer.

Tuckman, B. (1965) Developmental sequence in small groups. *Psychological Bulletin, 63 (6)*, pp. 384–399.

Whalley, M. (2019) Leadership as activism. In Whalley, M., John, K., Whitaker, P., Klavins, E., Parker, C. & Vaggers, J. *Democratising leadership in the early years*. London: Routledge, pp. 87–114.

Whalley, M., Whitaker, P., John, K., Klavins, L., Parker, C., & Vaggers, J. (2019) *Democratising leadership in the early years*. London: Routledge.

Whitaker, D. (2001) *Using groups to help people* (2nd edition). Hove: Brunner-Routledge.

Whitaker, P. (2019) Applying systems theory to early years leadership. In Whalley, M., John, K., Whitaker, P., Klavins, E., Parker, C. & Vaggers, J. *Democratising leadership in the early years*. London: Routledge, pp. 14–37.

7   Conclusion

Sandra Clare, Dr Christine Parker and Joanne Benford

[In collaboration with Caroline Griffiths, Antonio Griffiths-Murru and Katherine Clark]

In this chapter you will find:

- Conclusions about what adult learners need
- Themes are drawn together about how learning from each of the topics has impacted on students' practice, their ability and confidence to challenge orthodoxy, and what difference that makes to children and their families
- How students have created original work and gained confidence to explore the potential of returning to education
- The chapter adds weight to the notion that the youngest children are best supported by the highest qualified practitioners. Thoughts from past students offer authentic illustrations about the power of deeply reflective, practice related, studies.

Decades of studies have consistently shown early childhood has the most profound impact on life chances and that it is the adults around those children who have the greatest influence on outcomes. The educational attainment of those caring for children in their early years makes the most significant difference – knowledgeable parents and a graduate workforce really do matter.

Despite their importance, the Early Years workforce in the UK has long faced a range of challenges including high workloads, low pay, emotionally charged labour and limited opportunities for training or career progression. The Covid-19 pandemic has exacerbated many of these issues, as thousands of settings are closing, there is a national recruitment crisis and those remaining in the sector feel confused and angry, hungry and overwhelmed. Students repeatedly share a desire to have their professionalism properly acknowledged, with both recognition and recompense.

Throughout this book we have illustrated ways in which Early Years education has endured, redesigned and changed, but to some extent *stayed the same*. The ideas of McMillan (1919) to "educate every child as if he were your own" ensuring access to the outdoors, encouraging imaginative play, providing nutritious meals, working with parents and formal training for the very important job of educating the next generation are as relevant today as 100 years ago.

DOI: 10.4324/9781003271727-7

Student reflections throughout the book highlight the learning journeys adult learners have embarked at Pen Green, without diminishing the impact of prior learning and knowledge and experience acquired since childhood. How adults come to "claim" their education is varied, many come from practice, an emerging number are coming straight from school, while others will have experienced being a parent at Pen Green and want to further or formalise their learning. As our colleague Eddie McKinnon (2014) noted, routes into and through Pen Green are very varied. We highlight how students have been mindful of making a difference either directly with children or with adults to then develop their practice wisdom to the benefit of children.

Reflections from students

Caroline's reflections

I made the decision to commence studying at the age of 37 alongside my role as a family worker and raising my family. Prior to this I fostered for the local authority. My goal was to improve my practice and to get down on paper the knowledge I knew I had, yet often struggled to relay. I have always been passionate about working with families and having the opportunity to specifically think about my work felt rewarding. The journey through the degree was one of self-discovery and personal achievement. I found school difficult and received no support, teachers in the late 80s would tell me I was stupid and this gave me self-doubt for many years. I learnt how to get by and "blag," I never put my hand up in class for fear of being embarrassed and left school with limited qualifications, going straight into work at 15.

When I started the degree, it became clear to me this was going to be one of my biggest challenges. I had underestimated the volume of reading required but utilised the skills I had to pretend I had read the academic papers.

During my second year, I was diagnosed with dyslexia and had mixed emotions, a sense of anger and frustration because I had struggled for years together with sheer determination to progress academically despite the challenges. I remained focussed on achieving my degree and found ways to read key areas of interest without having to sit and look at the pile of books I had taken out of the library under the pretence that I would read them, this was never going to happen! Instead, I found TED talks, YouTube clips, and journal papers more manageable. I began to realise I could work in a different way to other students.

I found tutorials extremely stressful and avoided going to them, while drafting my dissertation I felt able to verbalise this to tutors. I would encourage all students to consider their own personal needs as a student and talk to the tutors. I realise now I should never have struggled.

Studying reignited my passion for fostering, and I made the bold decision to resign from my role as a family worker and pursue my passion to become a foster carer once again. It feels a privilege to be able to consider *one* child and invest all my knowledge and experience to provide him with opportunities in life. I am a professional who is *his* advocate, *his* educator, *his* secure base, available to offer him endless love. I am the person who will challenge decisions made by professionals about him and keep everyone focussed on their role in raising him.

Antonio's reflections

I became a teacher because I adopted two children with my husband and did not have any knowledge of children or how to bring children up. I had been told I needed to do the volunteer course at Pen Green if I wanted to adopt children and then did voluntary work at a primary school my children were going to attend. I studied more deeply when our children arrived as I still did not understand their needs or enough about pedagogy. I needed to know how I could support them with life and the traumas they brought with them.

The positivity and support at Pen Green throughout all my studies allowed me to graduate with a decent result and find a job in an outstanding school where I still learn every day. I am not the expert; I am learning every day from my colleagues. Every theory and strategy I learn and practice in school also supports life at home with my children.

I come from Italy where from their first year in primary school, a child sits in their chair learning different subjects of the curriculum. The very different approach, and relevance of theory to your whole life, in the UK has been difficult for me for to understand.

Learning at Pen Green has not been without challenges. I could not work in groups because we do not do this in Italy. I thought it was crazy. Especially the "check-in" and "check-out." I felt very uncomfortable at first, but tutors allowed me to explore ways of working without forcing me, supporting me to become part of the group slowly. Education is not only about the content, how we learn is so important.

Schema theory blew my mind but to start with I hated it. It was when we focused on it in a research project that I really understood the value for working with children with complex needs. Engagement in the project gave me the space and time to try out a range of approaches to meet the specific needs of children in my class, to think in a different way. I would have liked more opportunities to do this during my studies.

Schema theory also helped me understand myself. I noticed a pattern of behaviour when I am under stress. I realise I am under stress because I am not very tidy, I fall down everywhere and trip over obstacles. I walk in a rotation doing nothing in an aimless way. I know when that happens I need a 5-minute break. My learning journey has been about understanding my behaviour as well.

Children in my class struggle with the pronunciation of words, however, this is something I struggle with too, being an Italian speaker. I can share my strategies and it becomes a fun task, in that moment I am not the teacher and we help each other.

I have serious difficulties with my vision and am using this weakness with the children to show them a weakness can be overcome. I want them to understand having a disability is an okay thing and together we can overcome it. Sometimes we can do this independently or we can do this together.

Finally, as a male practitioner I believe children need a male figure from an early age, however, the way some schools are structured and expectations in terms of male and female figures, or salaries, male workers with the youngest children are not always supported or even encouraged. Pen Green supported me to fulfil all the duties of an Early Years educator. It would be useful for there to be a national protocol to support male practitioners working with the youngest children.

Katherine's reflections

I became a mother before I was a woman. I was asked to leave school when I was pregnant with my first child, possibly to the delight of anyone who had the misfortune to try and educate me. As I fell in love with my children, I fell into a career in Early Years. I began volunteering at my local children's centre, studied childcare and joined their nursery team. Twelve years into my career I transitioned from being a nursery practitioner and group leader to co-leading a nurture service for families living with complexity. At times I felt overwhelmed with the rawness of this intimate work. I nervously enrolled in a degree course to seek some deeper understanding of how I could better serve families. Through this process I came to notice education as a gift, one that passed me by in my youth. My previous immature jokes about "spending most of secondary school in the woods," brought about the painful realisation that I had spent my teenage years feeling disconnected, unheard and demoralised through education. My struggles to value or engage in learning had been met with teachers who did not care if I was in school or in the woods. A lack of engagement in secondary school has been rivalled with a passionate drive to learn as an adult, however, maturity has taught me that passion is a privilege. As an adult studying at Pen Green, I fell into learning with dedicated educators, a key element in my engagement was the investment that tutors made in me. Experience taught me that feeling engaged in learning is about the connections made with others and the learning journey, it is more than the formalities of studying.

Froebel (1968) illuminated the importance of bringing together the internal and external world, in order to fully educate individuals. He considered the development of thought and education as a route to becoming "free." His ideology of freedom through education stemmed from the unity of internal drives and external lives, this spoke to my experiences. Adult education freed me from a disconnected youth, engaged me in a wonderful career and enabled me to recognise myself. I am a woman who has "reclaimed education." The interplay between learner, tutor and learning environment holds a significant role in my reclaiming. When I was asked to leave school, I believed my educational journey had ended and I was delighted it was over. I never imagined

I would become compelled to learn again, I certainly never thought I would be excited by education itself. Shortly after I graduated, Joanne Benford called and asked me to join the teaching team, I vividly recall asking her if she had called the right person! Initially I observed practice and shadowed others. I learnt the craft of teaching adults much as I learnt childcare, by being fully emersed and alongside dedicated others. I believe those committed to the Early Years sector, must address the education of adults working in the field, with the same conviction used when addressing children's education. This is evident every day within Pen Green Research Base. I currently research and teach on a range of Early Years courses at Pen Green; being part of the alumni gives me innate understanding of the ethos of education within the organisation. Ultimately, how I educate others has been deeply influenced by my own learning experiences. I view my role as a commitment, geared towards creating robust learning opportunities, inciting social justice and developing a strong, well-informed Early Years workforce.

Tutor reflections

Sandra, Joanne and Christine

As tutors and alumni ourselves, we are all keen to create relationships within which adult learners feel cared for and able to take risks. Making friends, "checking-in and -out" and eating good food are often reported as being the key ingredients of study with Pen Green and to some extent this is the reality. However, these practices represent the beginnings of a process of relationship building between adult learner and tutor. A trusting relationship is the aim, where both student and tutor can be confident to be authentic and show their true selves. In the same way the expectation is students will take this way of learning alongside each other to their Early Years' setting, described by Clare and Clark (2021) and Formosinho & Oliveira-Formosinho (2012) as isomorphic, values and principles advocated at Pen Green are transferable to working with children, colleagues and families in settings. This relational aspect of the learning process is challenging, it is not a "soft" option, it require emotional labour and deeply reflective practice.

How do we know we have made a difference to children and their lives?

Part of the assignment process requires adult learners to consider what they have learnt and how that will impact their practice. It is an expectation that early childhood students identify areas for development and how they intend to implement these. The notion of practitioner research implies that the adult learner will engage in a research project to make a difference for possibly one child, a group of children or a community of children and their families. As Cath Arnold (2015) reminds us, it is important to think about *how* we research more so than what we *do*. Alternatively, the adult learner could be supporting other adult learners as a team leader, or owner of a setting or within a higher education context. In these situations, the Pen Green student will consider aspects of leadership and andragogy to identify how best to support colleagues and possibly plan for change and responses to new initiatives imposed externally. Identifying "Implications for Practice" at the end of each assignment invites the adult learner to stop, pause and reflect, and identify the aspects of their learning that are relevant to a wider context and therefore potentially make a difference to more lives. Dissemination is an important part of life at Pen Green, and over decades Pen Green educators have presented papers at national and international conferences, as well as developing a book series with Routledge and Sage publishers. It is our hope that wherever you are studying for an Early Years degree that you will take something of value from this book and join us in our work to create a better world for all children.

References

Arnold, C. (2015) *Doing your child observation case study. A step-by-step guide.* Maidenhead: Open University Press.

Clare, S. & Clark, K. (2021) 'Virtually Pen Green': Developing a synchronous teaching response for adult learners studying early childhood degree programmes during COVID-19, *European Early Childhood Education Research Journal*, DOI:10.1080/135029 3X.2021.2016882.

Formosinho, J. & Oliveira-Formosinho, J. (2012) *Pedagogy-in-participation: Childhood Association Education Perspective.* Braga, Portugal: Sponsored by the Research Centre on Child Studies of the University of Minho.

Froebel, F. (1968). *The education of man.* Bath: Chivers.

McKinnon, E. (ed.) (2014) *Using evidence for advocacy and resistance in early years services.* London: Routledge.

McMillan, M. (1919). *The nursery school.* London: Dent and Sons.

Glossary

Dr Christine Parker, Joanne Benford and Sandra Clare

In this glossary you will find:

• The terms that are used in this text as well as on Early Childhood courses.

Adult pedagogic Strategies (revised)

(This version is derived from observations of adults interacting with 0–3-year-old children).

1. Subtle intervention – The adult watches and listens to what the child is doing before intervening.
2. Linking experiences – The adults are aware of the child's experience with other adults at home and in the setting.
3. Acknowledging – The adult acknowledges the child's presence, emotions and capability by:

   a. being physically close to them including using touch if appropriate to make contact (see also strategy 8).
   b. tuning into the child's facial expressions and vocal intonation, including playfulness and teasing.

4. Working with the child's initiative and agency – The adult considers what the child is bringing to each interaction, checks out the child's meaning and gives the child time to respond or to question. The adult encourages the child's curiosity and ability to make choices including taking appropriate risks.
5. Adult learning – The adult is committed to his/her own learning. S/he is open to play and learn alongside the child, encouraging new learning for both child and adult.
6. Adult attitudes – The adult is aware of the impact of his or her own attitudes and beliefs and how these might affect the child's learning.
7. Using language – The adult knows about the child's home vocabulary, offers new information to the child, including preparation for what is

about to happen and describing what has just happened, and language to support the child's actions.

8. Using the body – The adult affords learning experiences using the body ranging from using slight touch to whole body experiences if appropriate. The adult knows how individual babies and children like to be held, rocked and comforted (Gallagher et al., 2017).

Andragogy The appreciation of adult learners as individuals and the understanding that each brings a unique experience to the learning environment. Andragogic strategies embrace tutors to:

1. Always do what you say you will, and if you are not able to do this say so
2. Be sensitive to individual students' needs and circumstances
3. Be available for students as they experience challenge, dis-equilibration and success
4. Provide an environment where students feel valued and respected
5. Provide opportunities for equal dialogue
6. Understand and appreciate each student's context
7. See the potential in students
8. Be flexible during teaching and be prepared to change direction or depth depending on the discussions and responses from the students. (See Chapter 1.)

Attachment Attachment theory was identified and defined by Bowlby. It is the process by which an adult carer, usually the mother, creates an emotional bond with her infant (Bowlby, 1988).

Attunement The act of understanding another person's emotional well-being and being actively aligned to their ways of thinking (Stern, 1985: 207–11).

Co-construct A learning theory that builds on the theory of constructivism where there is a belief that people learn best in the company of others (Stern, 1998).

Constructivism A learning theory that defines the act of learning as an internal cognitive process which Athey describes as the process of "coming to know" (Athey, 1990:30).

Containment As defined by Bion, this is the act of supporting another person, child or adult, either consciously or sub-consciously to enable the individual to feel safe and secure (Bion, 1962).

Critical reflection The skill of articulating your work and study experiences in a way that has been thought out; identifying dilemmas that need to be addressed as well as aspects of work to be celebrated.

Data The "stuff" of research. All the narrative and numerical information that is generated through the research process.

Dialogue   The process of active communication with at least one other with the intention of being authentic, respectful and honouring similarities and differences in opinions, ideas and experiences.

Epistemology   The theory of how knowledge is constructed.

Ethical stance   To develop your ethical stance, you need to be deeply respectful of everyone who is engaged alongside you any research process as well as mindful of how you protect yourself. The consideration of confidentiality and anonymity are important here. You need to demonstrate that you adhere to accepted ethical guidance, such as BERA (British Education Research Association) (2018) and EECERA (European Early Childhood Education Research Association) (Bertram et al., 2018).

Experiential learning   The learning process an individual will go through when they identify their experiences and learn from them (Kolb, 1984).

Interpretivism   In the process of analysing data, the qualitative researcher is open to "interpreting" what they find according to their research paradigm and praxis (understanding of the relationship between theory and practice). Frequently this research process generates the identification of themes and supports a thematic approach to data presentation and analysis.

Leaderful practice   Leaderful practice is the acknowledgement that anyone, child or adult, has the potential to be "leaderful" whether they are in a designated leadership role or not. Being leaderful and allowing that to inform practice means that you can reflect purposefully and consider changes that will improve practice but that you never consider you are acting alone, you are a member of a learning community. There is a fundamental understanding that to be leaderful, relationships are at the forefront of your concerns and how to communicate effectively with all you engage with.

Leadership   The term leadership has endless definitions, but for the purposes of this text it is described to mean when and how an individual or group "finds a way through" (Parker, 2019).

Ontology   The act of articulating notions of truth and how they are evidenced.

Paradigm   The notion of where you stand in terms of your worldview, beliefs, values and principles. Your paradigm could be either child-centred, or deeply religious, or ecological, or political, or economic or a cluster of ideas. Your beliefs and values will inform your research paradigm.

Pedagogical isomorphism   The recognition of conditions that encourage growth and change in an individual. These conditions include opportunities for dialogue, challenge, containment and reflection (Formosinho & Formosinho, 2005).

Pedagogy   The process by which adults support children to be successful in their learning within development (Dewsbery, 2020). Pedagogical strategies are evident when an adult is sensitively attuned to each child's context, needs and interests. "Pedagogy is for the teacher what medical knowledge is for the doctor" (Athey, 2007:27).

Pen Green Paradigm   Identifies the notions of "Involvement" and "Insights" as the key ideas that are embraced and developed at the Pen Green Centre.

Positivism   A scientific approach to research where it is believed that we cannot make assumptions in research but that all findings must be observed, scrutinised and proven (Moss, 2019).

Praxeology   A way of thinking about how theory and practice are inter-linked and thus inform an Early Years' educator's practice wisdom.

Praxis   How the practitioner's knowledge and understanding of theory informs their embedded practice and capacity to self-reflect (Freire, 1970).

Qualitative research   Research where data is generally gathered in the form of words, narratives, visual techniques and/or film. It is considered that qualitative research is limited because of its subjective nature. However, more recently, with qualitative research being presented rigorously and extensively peer reviewed, it is increasingly acknowledged in terms of validity by academics.

Quantitative research   Research where most data generated is numerical. Quantitative research, in contrast to qualitative research, is commonly perceived to be objective. However, it is recognised that statistical data can be manipulated and is equally subject to researcher bias in the same way that qualitative data is.

Reflective practice   Reflective practice enables more precise and detailed explanations. Reflective practice is likely to raise challenges, tackling contentious areas, both personal and from practice. An insight into your own preferred ways of learning, hang ups and preferences can be the most helpful tool to guide and shape you as both a learner and educator (Schön, 1983).

Reflexive practice   Engagement in reflexive practice implies that you repeatedly reflect on practice and this process strengthens your pedagogical stance. You make your learning visible and understand the impact you are having, whether that is either on children or adults.

Research   The process by which you investigate an identified and evidenced concern.

Researcher bias   Every researcher has bias which they can define through the consideration of their belief systems and worldview.

Research limitations   The identification of the limiting factors around your research project. These factors can include limitations of time, location, a limited number of research participants and the impact of personal circumstances including illness.

Research methodology   Research methodology is the overarching means by which you intend to carry out your research project and find some solutions to what is troubling you.

Research methods   Research methods are the "how" of research. In this text we show examples of observation, focus conversations, questionnaires and autoethnographic methods including journaling.

Research paradigm   Ideas that are specific to recognised research processes, such as being either interpretivist or positivist (McNiff with Whitehead, 2002).

Research techniques   Research techniques are the more detailed aspects of your research methods, such as, the type of observation you implement, including the application of technology to conduct interviews or focus groups.

Social constructivism   The belief that people learn best in the company of others, all with a common purpose, a desire to seek shared understandings and knowledge, and actively seek solutions to dilemmas (Vygotsky, 1978).

Theory   A particular way of thinking about an idea that has been rigorously researched, peer reviewed and applied by others in the field.

References

Athey, C. (1990) *Extending thought in young children: a parent-teacher partnership* (1st edition). London: Paul Chapman Publishing.

Athey, C. (2007) *Extending thought in young children: a parent-teacher partnership* (2nd edition). London: Paul Chapman Publishing.

BERA (British Educational Research Association) (2018) *Online resource.* https://www.bera.ac.uk/publication/ethical-guidelines-for-educational-research-2018.

Bertram, T., Formosinho, J., Gray, C., Pascal, C. & Whalley, M. (2015) *EECERA Ethical Code for Early Childhood Researchers.* European Early Childhood Education Research Association (EECERA). EECERA-Ethical Code.pdf

Bion, W. (1962) *Learning from experience.* London: Karnac.

Bowlby, J. (1988) *A secure base. Parent-child attachment and heathy human development.* London: Routledge.

Dewsbery, F. (2020) How psychoanalytic observation could support Early Years Practitioners to understand children's spontaneous play, and how this might contribute to learning within their development and support practitioners to reflect on their interactions with the children? MA Dissertation, University of Essex.

Formosinho, J. & Oliveira-Formosinho, J. (2005) *National Professional Qualification for Integrated Centre Leadership (NPQICL) Pilot Programme, An Evaluative Research Study.* Corby, UK: Pen Green Research.

Freire, P. (1970: 1996 Edition) *Pedagogy of the oppressed.* London: Penguin Books.

Gallagher, T. & the Pen Green Team (2017) *Working with children aged 0–3 and their families: The Pen Green approach.* London: Routledge.

Kolb, D. A. (1984) *Experiential learning theory: experience as the source of learning and development.* Englewood Fields, NJ: Prentice-Hall.

McNiff, J. with Whitehead, J. (2002) *Action research: principles and practice* (2nd edition) London: Routledge Falmer.

Moss, P. (2019) *Alternative Narratives in Early Childhood: An Introduction for Students and Practitioners.* London: Routledge.

Parker, C. (2019) *We all have the potential to lead because we all have responsibilities.* In Whalley, M., John, K., Whitaker, P., Klavins, E., Parker, C. & Vaggers, J. *Democratising leadership in the early years.* London: Routledge, pp. 139–170.

Schön, D. (1983) *The Reflective Practitioner: How professionals think in action.* Farnham: Ashgate Publishing Ltd.

Stern, D. N. (1998) *The interpersonal world of the infant.* London: Karnac.

Vygotsky, L. (1978) *Mind in society, the development of higher psychological processes.* Cambridge, MA: Harvard University Press.

Index

Milton Keynes UK
Ingram Content Group UK Ltd.
UKHW031712310124
437006UK00016BA/230